THE HOUR OF TESTING

FATHER DONALD HAGGERTY

The Hour
of Testing

*Spiritual Depth and Insight in
a Time of Ecclesial Uncertainty*

IGNATIUS PRESS   SAN FRANCISCO

Cover image:
Christ Mocked by Soldiers. 1932.
Oil on canvas, 36¼ × 28½" (92.1 × 72.4 cm).
Georges Rouault (1871–1958)
© 2025 Artists Rights Society (ARS), New York /ADAGP, Paris
Location: The Museum of Modern Art/New York, NY/U.S.A.
Given anonymously.
PHOTO CREDIT: Digital Image ©
The Museum of Modern Art/Licensed by SCALA /Art Resource, NY

Cover design by Roxanne Mei Lum

© 2025 by Ignatius Press, San Francisco
All rights reserved
ISBN 978-1-62164-768-3 (PB)
ISBN 978-1-64229-339-5 (eBook)
Library of Congress Control Number 2024950903
Printed in the United States of America ∞

To Father Paul Mankowski, S.J.
(1953–2020)

CONTENTS

INTRODUCTION

Joseph Ratzinger famously began his 1968 classic *Introduction to Christianity* recalling Søren Kierkegaard's story of the traveling circus clown and the burning village. The circus grounds have been struck by a fire, and the manager of the circus, in desperation, sends the clown, already dressed-up and ready for a performance, into the village to plead for help to halt the fire. The villagers see him in his clown's outfit and his painted face and thereby take his demonstrative shouts to be a deliberate act of amusement aimed at drawing the crowd to the circus. They laugh at him, enjoying the gesticulations and weeping cries of the man in the clown's suit as though watching a pantomime performance. His pleas are not taken seriously; in fact, they provoke an opposite reaction of hilarity. The result is that the clown is ignored, and the fire eventually burns down the circus and the nearby village.

The picture of the circus clown crying out his urgent plea and meeting only amused stares and laughter can be invoked in a fresh manner today. The general sense of uncertainty in the Church, even of advancing crisis, is evident to many Catholics. Bolder spirits in our day may put forward warnings and predictions, but these remain acts of speculation about an unknown future. Perhaps they elicit a reaction much like that of the crowd in the village who did not take seriously the cries of the clown. Nevertheless, a question in every age of the Church is to penetrate more deeply the impact of the current era in the Church upon the serious pursuit of spirituality. Every historical period in the Church, in a sense, has a distinct tone in the clarion call that summons souls to give themselves generously to the pursuit of God. Each era in the Church makes unique demands for a recognition of God that cannot be separated from the real history of that time.

The driving impulse of this book is to deepen our spiritual lives with insights that arise from this necessary merging of spirituality with a sense of our own historical time in the Church. We are led to give ourselves more fully to God when we look up, as it were, and perceive a certain urgency facing us in the spiritual dangers and needs of the day. Setting our minds on divine things, as Jesus exhorted Saint Peter, is to seek the eyes of God's vision on our time. We cannot penetrate all the vicissitudes of time or place ourselves accurately on a predictable timeline. Yet we can be affected spiritually by a deep awareness in faith that God is at work providentially in all realities of ecclesial and earthly life to invite souls to the greater gift of themselves and to salvation. Matthew Levering refers to this importantly as the sacramental principle: "Behind earthly realities stands the presence and causality of God: real history is never separated from God's presence and action."[1] History moves forward, including the history of the Church, under the providential hand of God; within that broader providential context must advance the history of the personal gift of ourselves into the hands of God. The gift of self can be intensified when we sense perhaps a greater significance in our day as God may see it.

The book is divided into three parts. The first part is an effort to engage the question of the current historical era as a preliminary meditation before seeking related insights

---

[1] Matthew Levering, *Newman on Doctrinal Corruption* (Park Ridge, Ill.: Word on Fire Academic, 2022), 19.

for spirituality in the latter two parts. The reflections on spirituality in the latter two sections do not stand apart, detached and separated, from what is written in the first part, any more than we can live a spiritual life unaffected by the spiritual forces and influences operative in our day. The great task of serious spirituality today may be precisely to recognize the cultural darkness and ecclesial uncertainties of the present hour as a catalyst to a more fervent commitment to God and his Church in all faithfulness and love.

A word about this first part of the book might be helpful. In these initial five chapters, we give some space to contemporary spiritual trends and proclivities that can be read as signs of the times calling for discernment. These chapters comment on the disappearance of God and the loss of faith in our day; the rise of prophetic speculation about the Second Coming of Christ; the current ambiance of ecclesial confusion and doctrinal ambiguity; the breakdown of morality and metaphysical common sense; and some thoughts on the Church in a future last era and the figure of the Antichrist. The endeavor in this first part is not to add burning coals to the fires of speculation about the era in the Church that we are living. It is rather to place these reflections before the mind and spirit in a sober manner for the sake of invigorating spiritual pursuit in our day. While there is considerable somber commentary of a "darker" nature in these early chapters, the view is that these truths must be confronted for serious spiritual living today. As an introductory remark, it must also be said that the question of what is yet to come in God's plan, and when it might come—in future decades or after distant centuries—remains locked behind a door of divine silence. Spiritual sobriety and a humble acceptance of our incomprehension of God's designs are necessary dispositions of soul in our day.

The latter two sections of the book can be said to draw

the gravity of their challenge from the initial five chapters. Indeed, the relations we pursue with our Lord in the current day demand a deeper intensity of awareness, which is a wonderful truth for the concentration of our spiritual lives. The Passion of Christ, for example, as we will see in the second and third parts of the book, takes on a central importance in our spiritual life after these earlier reflections. The theological idea, for instance, that at some point in history the Church herself will live out the last week of Jesus' Passion, repeating in a mysterious manner the afflictions Jesus suffered in his last days, is a provocative thought for spiritual life. Any serious soul of prayer and self-giving to God will participate in a personal way in this mystery. It is an example of a gain in spiritual vision by an engagement with possible scenarios beginning perhaps to show their first signs. The divine invitation to suffer with Christ in his Church, remaining committed in our love for the Church, follows from embracing this insight. Fidelity to the Church, no matter what struggles may ensue, is a commitment in love to Christ himself.

The second and third parts of the book, then, probe deeper questions of spiritual life, again with the background awareness that we may be living at present the early preliminary phase of a momentous time in history. These reflections commence with the mystery of a vulnerability in God wounded in love and the repercussions of that awareness. The Passion of Jesus hovers as a silent presence here and, indeed, throughout the subsequent chapters. The focus of these following chapters is on all topics related to a greater offering of our lives to God: the gift of self to God intensified by a desire for union with Christ crucified; receptivity of soul to the God who asks for all; the challenge and opportunity of suffering for love of Christ; the afflictions of

Christ in particular details of his Passion and their meaning for our time; the great mystery and gift of the Eucharist. These topics are followed in the third part by reflections that again summon an essential insight for us today in a love for the Passion of Christ: the humility of God and our embrace of this virtue; the internal wounds of Jesus animating deeper dispositions of prayer; trials and discoveries in the pursuit of deeper interior prayer; the divine desire for victims of his love in our day; the awakening of a providential sense of God's near presence and the desire for sacrificial living; and, finally, reflections on a necessary contemplative spirit in the current day of ecclesial testing.

These chapters in the second and third parts could be read without the opening section. But it is my sense that they would not have been written without their link to what is presented earlier and so should not be received without the thought of perhaps living in a period of history of significant magnitude. Joseph Ratzinger included as well in the opening pages of *Introduction to Christianity* a story told by Martin Buber in which a certain learned Rabbi Levi Jizchak was visited in his room by an unbelieving Jew of Enlightenment sympathies who wanted to argue religion with the Rabbi. The Rabbi simply paced about in his room with a book in hand, ignoring his visitor, until he suddenly looked up and said—"But perhaps it is true after all"[2]—thereby shattering the skeptical man's resistance to faith. "Perhaps" may be a serious word for our own time, not regarding the truth of our faith, as in that encounter between the Rabbi and his visitor, but concerning the era in which we live. The essential truth to recall is that spirituality and history do not exist apart from each other. In a last era of the Church, if

---

[2] Joseph Ratzinger, *Introduction to Christianity*, trans. J. R. Foster (New York: Herder and Herder, 1970), 20.

such a time does approach in the decades ahead, or in distant centuries, this truth acquires great importance. It may be that "perhaps" must claim the final word in any speculation about our contemporary period of history. But spirituality cannot wait for absolute historical clarity, nor can it flourish with a "perhaps" at the center of a soul. Deeper spirituality must plunge forward always in a passion of love toward the mystery of God and his providence. Let us see how the gift of souls to God and his Church expands and deepens in our time in the face of the unknown events yet to come even in our lifetime.

PART ONE

LEANING OVER THE PRECIPICE: THE MOUNTING LOSS OF FAITH

The face of God is noticeably disappearing. "The death of God" is a very real process, which today extends deep into the interior of the Church. God is dying in Christendom, so it seems.[1]

—Joseph Ratzinger

One can say that the ultimate origin of "modernity" is the refusal of all faith, which follows the refusal of mystery. Modernity refuses mystery. It will always know more, explain more. But it will not really understand anything anymore, because it has refused mystery.[2]

—Henri de Lubac, S.J.

Relativism, that terribly effective bleach, has wiped out everything in its path. Doctrinal and moral confusion is reaching its height. Evil is good, good is evil. Man no longer feels any need to be saved. The loss of the sense of salvation is the consequence of the loss of the transcendence of God.[3]

—Robert Cardinal Sarah

---

[1] Joseph Ratzinger, "Why I Am Still in the Church Today", *Fundamental Speeches from Five Decades*, trans. Michael Miller (San Francisco: Ignatius Press, 2012), 138.

[2] Henri de Lubac, S.J., *A Theologian Speaks*, trans. Stephen Maddux (Los Angeles: Twin Circle, 1985), 25.

[3] Robert Cardinal Sarah, *The Day Is Now Far Spent*, trans. Michael J. Miller (San Francisco: Ignatius Press, 2019), 47.

The strong insistence by Jesus to be *watchful* in the period before his Second Coming must have a definite reason. The likely explanation is that the most significant sign of his return will be largely ignored. Perhaps very few will recognize what is taking place. If we read the Gospels carefully, however, the crucial sign of his Second Coming is revealed in the simple question of Jesus: "When the Son of man comes, will he find faith on earth?" (Lk 18:8). Although it may be difficult to envision, a near total collapse of faith in God, perhaps in a generation or two, or by the end of century, is historically possible. This would suggest a spiritual crisis hard to miss. Yet the disappearance of God from lives may draw little notice because the vast majority in that time may be indifferent to God and religious faith. The sign will be evident, but the very absence of faith will make a recognition of it impossible, except in those who still have faith. For people with no concern for God, the loss of God will mean nothing. For them the question of faith will be unimportant and inconsequential. We are surely not at this moment in history, and there are many fervent souls of faith in the Church, but who would deny that the extinction of religious faith has already begun to show itself on a grand scale, especially in Western Europe? I was told recently by a French monastic Sister that only four percent of Catholics in France currently attend Sunday Mass. We might watch as the years continue for a less observable sign inseparable from the loss of faith. When faith collapses, prayer disappears. In a variation of his question, Jesus could have asked whether, at his return, he will find souls who pray? Surely there will always be souls who pray, but in a last era of the Church, this may be a small remnant who pray in a committed and devout manner. Prayer may become in time like a foreign language hardly spoken or understood, forgotten except by the few.

We can observe signs already of this loss of prayer in many lives, although souls of serious prayer among the young are quietly arising as well. Perhaps they are the holy remnant who with a fierce fire in their souls will carry the faith in their older age into a last era of the Church. They will surely be intensely prayerful souls, another sign of that time.

~

The loss of God today in lives is not typically an explicit conversion to atheism. Rejection of God by a clear decision seems not so common. For many people, faith in God simply fades away undramatically because he is given little thought or attention. For many people, God exercises no traction on the mind, no need to settle the truth of whether he exists or can be known, as if the question were not worth the trouble of examination. No spiritual pause takes place to consider God as a real possibility. The loss of God does not seem to trouble people, perhaps because there is no sense of losing anything. Formal religious commitments cease, not by people slamming doors in a loud rejection of God, but by slipping out unseen and never looking back. Many lives today from early youth have no religious experience at all. I heard a homeless older man on a street of New York say recently that the name of God is like the letters on an outdoor sign of a country church too long battered by wind and rain. The letters faded away over time, and nothing clear can be read; the name of God is simply gone. This disinterest in God is tragically not understood for its gravity, especially for the young. Today there is in fact a strange form of godlessness, an absence of inquisitiveness about God, even in young children. There are a great many families in which even a small prayer to God has vanished as a lesson learned in

the innocence of childhood. Before too long a large portion
of a generation may come of age without ever attempting
in childhood to pray to God. Prayer will be an unknown
experience as they become adults. In their incomprehension
of ever turning to God in a prayer, they will be like children
who never learned to play a sport or a musical instrument.
But in this case, the neglected experience may become a
lifelong disregard for God.

~

If the coming decades witness no halt in the decline of faith,
we may arrive at a point in which a kind of religious am-
nesia will have swept across the West. The climactic event
of history—God in the flesh of Jesus of Nazareth suffering a Roman crucifixion in ancient Jerusalem—will seem as
though erased from memory. His death at Calvary will draw
a reaction of love only in a small remnant of still believing
souls. The death of our God on a Roman Cross two thousand years ago will in effect die as a truth in history. The ultimate testimony of divine love in history will be buried in a
tomb of indifference enclosed by a massive stone of general
unbelief. The God who took upon himself the poverty of
human flesh many centuries ago will become poor again,
more destitute than in the years he lived on this earth. His
poverty will be like a second sojourn in the barren desert,
this time in the desert of human hearts without a thought
of him. His marred face of suffering at Calvary will hide
in the forgetfulness of human neglect. If we do love him,
let us anticipate a need to love him ever more deeply in the
face of the world's indifference. In our prayer, if we desire this greater love, we might note as well a change in the
hiddenness of God from previous centuries. God's conceal-

ment will no longer be a sacred tactic of divine love to provoke the intense searching of hungry souls for himself. His concealment will describe the divine condition in a world of disinterest toward him. He will hide, not by his choice to draw souls to a greater love, but because the world will be indifferent to him and satisfied to leave him unknown. Even the possibility of this happening urges us to gaze at his divine face in the Passion, transported to the hour of his sweating agony on that Roman Cross. Let us be wounded anew with the thought of our God still offering us salvation on a cross at Calvary.

$\sim$

The "death of God" is no longer a Nietzschean poetic proposal of an earlier century to shock the innocent ears of religious believers. It is rather becoming an accurate description of the collective soul of a Western society in its denial of the divine. God dies in a society, not because men commit sins, but when a desire for God dies in souls on a vast scale. The loss of God in lives can seem a dark stain on individual souls and a society in general until we arrive at a point in history when the unbelief of atheism will perhaps become the common human condition. The banality of unbelief, an unbelief without passion, will take over the spiritual tenor of such an era. It will be a kind of grey atheism, not stark in its black and white contours, but nonetheless sinister in its effects. The time of angry rebellion against God or defiant rejection of religion will have passed. Atheism will no longer be the mark of the rebellious outsider; unbelief will require no fiery revolt or aggressive attack against religion. Rather, unbelief will breathe like an undetected poison in the shadowy air, communicated through media and education, soaking into souls in the most unobtrusive way. Indifference to God will be an ordinary state of mind and draw no attention to itself. It will give no hint of abnormality, because it will be the shared condition of a great portion of the population. It will be the typical life of an average person to give no thought at all to God. What will exist societally at such a point in history is not evidence of a concerted rejection of God in any hostile fashion, but simply massive apathy and indifference toward him. God will disappear, removed from human concern, as though an expiration date passed in history, and his name at some unknown date became no longer useful or serviceable.

~

In a sense, we are witnessing today in the spiritual realm a quiet rejection of God that has a certain correlation in contemporary human relations. Often today unmarried people in a relationship of intimacy simply tire of the relations, at times quickly, and cast a person away as no longer important or desirable in their lives. It happens coldly, uneventfully, without much drama. Cutting off contact suffices to terminate relations. This same pattern of cold dismissal and easy forgetfulness seems to be rapidly taking place toward God. A generation beset with fatigue toward the pursuit of committed, lifelong love in marriage has also tired of God. There should be little surprise in the fact. If people can be coldhearted in human relations of love, and end them easily, it is just a logical extension of the same spiritual emptiness to sever relations with God as though nothing significant happens in that act. But, of course, that is quite untrue. The relationship with God does not conclude peremptorily. God continues to suffer wounds when he is rejected, and he continues, sometimes in stunning ways, to seek after souls that seem to care little for him.

～

God dishonored inside his own house, that is, within Catholic churches, where the tabernacle continues to hide the Divine Presence of Jesus Christ in the Holy Eucharist, reflects the diminishment of faith in our time. Summertime in a Catholic cathedral in a large city of Europe or the United States can be a telling test case of the lack of faith in people of Catholic identity. Crowds milling about, standing in aisles taking photos, loud voices, coarse laughter, even at times during Masses: the signs of disrespect are more than a forgetfulness of decorum or reverence during the time spent within the walls of a church. With the widespread loss of faith, the sense of the sacred has also disappeared. In many cases the external bearing may reflect an unacknowledged absence of faith. Many people may enter and depart a cathedral of great beauty without a single phrase of a personal prayer whispered within those walls. And yet at the same time, always, amidst the noise and commotion, there are people in the vast space kneeling with their heads bowed in prayer. In that sense, an urban cathedral may be a vivid picture of a future in which people without faith and people still fervent in faith will mingle together under the same roof. Older beautiful churches will attract visitors who come to admire architectural structures and stained glass windows, ornate carvings and the stone of statues. Perhaps some will recall vague spiritual longings no longer felt. But there will always be the uncommon soul resting a pair of tired knees in prayer before God. These souls will always be there, in the corners, in the shadows, turned in the direction of the tabernacle.

~

The ease with which unconcern for God has overtaken lives has a telling factor in our day: the incapacity of souls to resonate with transcendent realities of truth. Knowledge beyond the factual, the verifiable, the informational, is rarely sought. This narrowness of soul is a byproduct of the technological modern age. The obsessive use of technological devices seems to coincide with the mind's disinclination to give a thought to God. It is clear enough if we examine our own experience. Technological devices answer a need for companionship. In an earlier period, the radio or television accompanied many people's private hours. Today the cell phone or cellular device is a reliable companion, carried everywhere, available for use anywhere; it provides immediate relief from loneliness. Few people seem to perceive a connection between the impulsive turning to a cellular device, the checking of text messages or internet sites, and a deeper loneliness of soul that is being ignored. In former days, before the ubiquity of technological gadgets within immediate reach, feeling empty or alone, without an easy access to distraction, left the soul open to spiritual hunger. A thirst for God was possible that in many lives has now disappeared. And in that greater possibility of interior hunger and greater silence, God was never so far away, at least in some lives. Today people can be indifferent to God without taking the trouble to reject him in any decisive manner. The only requirement to ignore God is to keep the electricity turned on and the technology plugged in at full throttle. The ability to forsake God in this manner without a conscious rejection of him is already perhaps an early preparation for the disappearance of faith that Jesus warned would come before his return at the end of time.

∼

In this dependency on technological distraction, the Gospels are for many people never opened, an unread text collecting dust on the back shelf of the contemporary world. The extent to which Jesus Christ is ignored is not adequately realized by those who remain faithful to him and still pray. Yet if God is pushed far from the mind and soul by many, he does not abandon us. In an era of growing neglect toward God, it would seem he concentrates himself more intensely upon those who do still desire him. The more God is cast off and forgotten, the more those who still live their faith will receive a gaze of tender love from God. But these souls must deepen their personal offering to God. The spiritual adventure of living in a time of indifference to God, of an increasing apathy to God, is that he will turn his love strongly toward those who desire him and offer themselves to him. These souls may become ever fewer in number, but they will receive a notable grace of courage to bear witness in faith, most of all through committed prayer and their spirit of self-offering to others. And God always, in every century, loves those who long for him as the one thing needful in life, with no other rival for their love. The years to come may see a contagious ground swell of love for him centered first in a deep love for his presence in the Holy Eucharist.

∼

Apathy toward God is not the same as agnostic uncertainty about God. Agnosticism suggests that at least a thought about God intrudes on occasion and demands some attention, that a decision about God is still unresolved. The question of God continues to agitate an agnostic mind, because the question does not go away. We are witnessing something more spiritually destructive today. The apathy becoming more pronounced today is a terrible indifference to God. The problem of indifference is that it does not cause distress at all; it is untroubling, ordinary, a simple fact of life. Yet this absence of God in lives cannot be without repercussions. The loss of God is perhaps like an unnoticed page missing in a book. The meaning of a text disappears when a passage in a book is torn out or a page is removed; yet if that missing page goes unobserved and a person continues reading, a reader's mind darkens while reading and it suffers at a loss to overcome the incomprehension. There is no sense of a reason or explanation for the incomprehension. In a similar way, when God disappears from the mind and soul through sheer indifference to him, incomprehension invades the soul. Yet this absence may go unrecognized, leaving behind only the emptiness of soul and mind. There is no awareness of the missing hunger of soul that can be fed only by God's love. This cloud of indifference to God is perhaps the great spiritual evil of our own time. The evil of it is not primarily in a conscious attitude, but in the vulnerability to evil influences that is bound to ensue from indifference to God. Spiritual vacuums are like natural vacuums; they do not remain empty permanently. Darker hungers arise and soon replace the natural desire for God.

∼

The prevalence of the demonic presence hiding in concealed shadows, intent on the destruction of souls, is a truth of our day. No one should be foolishly naïve about this, for it is increasing. We live today in an era of satanic ascendancy that parallels the deterioration in religious faith. The phenomena of esoteric occult activity, of dependency on spiritualist healers and guides, on paganistic rituals and incantations, and indeed of participation in explicit satanic practice are unprecedented in history. The loss of traditional religious faith is partly to blame. But there is something inexplicable, and quite shocking, in the ease with which in recent years a door has been opened to the demonic. The entry point for many people has been to explore by some form or another of spiritualist practice the untapped resources of psychic energy and power. For some people, the desire to possess psychic power and insights, to be strong and formidable in mind, to gain advantages of manipulation over others, is seductive. These are often people who have not known any sense of superiority in their lives, and when it is offered and tasted through new age practices, the experience has an enticing appeal. The seduction often requires nothing but a first favor, and their inhibition is set aside. Quite soon a conviction of possessing an inner sanctum within selfhood known only to the spiritually elite becomes tantalizing to the psyche. The experience of energy and power emanating from there is the great seduction that can steal a soul for the devil like a professional thief taking a prized possession in the quiet darkness of the night. If faith continues to decline, we can expect greater activity from demonic entities to agitate societies and the Church herself in the decades to come.

～

The comparison of far greater barbaric evils perpetrated in different periods of history than our own time would naturally lead to the thought that present day evils are relatively tempered. We are not living in the time of the Nazi depredations or the Soviet gulags. The massive destruction and death attending the twentieth-century world wars are not our trials. There is no modern city today reveling grotesquely in the godless mob violence of the guillotines of Paris in the French Revolution. The one exception, however, never seen in history with such concealed magnitude and numbers, is the rabid blood thirst in modern societies to kill babies in their mothers' wombs. And perhaps the coldhearted killing of children and the ideological support it draws from the ordinary public do speak of an evil more sinister than anything in the past. It is the evil of indifference in its starkest expression, the absence of a thought for what may inflict the greatest wound on the heart of God in the current era. Unconcern for the children killed is disdain for the God who brought these children into existence. The insensibility to this grave evil taking place within the vicinity, as it were, of our residence and doorstep is a strong symptom of a loss of God that may only accelerate. The indifference to abortion is like a heavy stone thrown into a pool of blood at Calvary that splashes up into the face of Jesus on the Cross. The wound to the heart of God may be ignored, but it does not cease to pierce his heart. Souls of prayer need to be aware of this wound.

~

Christianity submerged in an Antichristian culture cannot but tend to a dangerous and unstable condition. It can plummet into crisis without much warning if it does not remain strong in the bedrock of traditional faith. More than is acknowledged, the survival of religious faith can become precarious and uncertain, subject to the shock of public events and personal struggles. Public scandals like the report of clerical depravities, for instance, derailed religious commitments in a short time when Catholic lives were not deeply rooted in the mystery of faith. Superficial faith can fade quickly if faith is primarily a cultural or familial attachment rather than a personal conviction of love for the truth of Jesus of Nazareth as our Lord and God. Yet these uncertainties about the staying power of faith in individual lives seem to some extent true throughout the history of Christianity. The faith is learned and lived within a cultural context. In those times and places where religious commitment is respected, and religious faith is expected among respectable people, the living out of some form of Catholic faith becomes an ordinary fact of life. In these circumstances, faith plants its roots within the soil of a cultural ambiance. Regular practice of the Catholic faith is inseparable from a cultural context of loyalty, as it was so strongly in Ireland until recent decades. But what happens when a culture becomes hostile to religious commitment? Can religious faith survive except among those of unusual interiority in their convictions? What happens when the surrounding culture becomes aggressively irreligious and godless, replacing God with an idol of unrestrained lawlessness cut off from moral limits? What happens when the principles of morality taught by religion are viewed as intolerant prejudices incompatible with modern life and its values? Religious truth in those times, as seen in recent decades, can disappear fast under clouds of suspicion and cynical skepticism. A society that loses God often turns to attack formal religion as the hiding place of a God who is no longer welcome. It will tolerate no trace of God hiding surreptitiously in a corner of its own culture in the strange, contrarian souls who still cling to religious notions. Their faith is viewed as an unnatural quality, a sign of unfitness cutting them off from normal relations with reasonable, sensible people.

~

It happens sometimes that people walk into a trap unaware of the harm about to occur. A glance ahead would alert them to the danger, but they seem incapable of looking up and seeing. This truth is not just observable in personal lives. History itself marches forward at times into destructive periods while the general population is for the most part blind toward what is soon to happen. We do not have natural talents of perspicuity for the historical unfolding of events. I remember asking my parents on a few occasions in their later years whether, as teenagers growing up in the 1930s, they had premonitions of the coming disaster of a world war that was to shake their lives so violently. Did they perceive in the rise to power of Hitler in Germany a menace that would bring terrible suffering to lives and serious disruption to their own? They answered naturally that no one really thought of this at all. They were young and taken up with the concerns of the young. No one sat in a high school classroom in those days thinking that some of the desks around them held young men who would go to their deaths in a few short years. Who would think such a thing? Yet history moves fast, without waiting to see if we are paying attention. At certain times in history, we may be edging toward momentous events and will suddenly plunge into them before we have a chance to realize their magnitude. And this is not because these events are entirely disguised.

If we have eyes to see and discern, we can have some sense spiritually what is perhaps coming. The hints and signs of anticipation may be present. The Lord's admonition to be alert and watchful is addressed precisely to the capacity we possess to open our eyes and see.

∽

The risk of a more serious collapse of Christianity is quite real. The key warning sign is the displacement of Jesus Christ at the center of Christian faith, most notably in the Catholic Church. Jesus of Nazareth as depicted in the Gospels is the revelation in the flesh of God himself; yet a cloud of unknowing increasingly covers this supreme truth of Christianity. I heard an older Irish woman remark with a bit of a smile, after bringing Holy Communion to her in a New York apartment, that Jesus was kidnapped years ago and taken to an untraceable location. He lives now, she said, like a king in exile, waiting to come back to his country, once the revolution is over. This is exaggerated language, yes, but perhaps not beyond our sympathy. The disinterest in Christ that permeates the contemporary world has entered the doors of the Church also. Yet the Church does not seem for the most part to confront the truth that his voice is silent and unheard, his words and actions unknown. If Jesus of Nazareth is not proclaimed with insistent clarity as the exclusive Lord of all history, and necessary for salvation, the consequence is grave in the long run. As the divinity of Christ vanishes from view, perhaps simply by neglect and silence, his truth as God is forced to compete with ideologies and foreign beliefs presented as alternative sources of salvation. It is not uncommon now in Western countries to encounter a quasi-Hindu mentality that expresses no explicit rejection of Christ but sees him as only one figure among many who may offer a path to enlightenment and salvation. This diminishment of Christ accompanies the demand for an acknowledgment of equality among all religions. Respect for human persons ignorant of the truth of Christianity is one thing; obeisance and honor accorded to false beliefs incompatible with Christian revelation is quite another. The effect is predictable: increasing disbelief in the truth of God becoming a unique man in history. Is the time approaching when the truth of traditional Catholic faith will largely disappear and only a remnant of genuine believers will remain?

∼

"We must transmit as we have received. We did not make the Church, we may not unmake it" (Saint John Henry Newman).[4] These words need to be honored today. The difficulty of Catholic faith in the coming years is the risk of a fragmentation of core beliefs, a breaking apart of doctrinal commitment, so that for many Catholics only a portion of Catholic faith will be retained. Doctrinal ambiguity in our day has unfortunately become an intellectual ambiance in the Church. Even now contradictory positions on matters of doctrine seem to coexist publicly within the hierarchy of the Church. If the Church over time shows increasing signs of doctrinal disunity, it is likely that a kind of Catholic agnosticism will spread. Truths of faith, especially in the realm of morality and sacramental practice, will seem to be unresolved and, therefore, open to question or private interpretation. In the days ahead, periodic tremors of doctrinal uncertainty may possibly shake the ground beneath the

---

[4] John Henry Newman, "Submission to Church Authority", *Parochial and Plain Sermons* (San Francisco: Ignatius Press, 1987), 605.

feet of the common believer. The mind of the Church may increasingly adopt a spirit of irresolution on settled matters, much like the mind of the agnostic refusing to surrender to belief. This will cause harm naturally. Catholic faith thrives when a quiet communal strength within the Church is experienced as a communion of shared belief. When, by contrast, doctrinal uncertainty becomes a general condition, a vast insecurity is bound to permeate the Church. It may not take decades to see this phenomenon arrive at a dangerous condition. If moral doctrines taught for centuries, for instance, are revised in a manner incompatible with the Catholic moral tradition, it will be a sign of entering an unprecedented era in which serious wounds are taking place within the Church. If that happens, Jesus' question whether he will find faith on the day when he returns would seem to come alive and pose an immediate challenge to the Church. The beginning of the birth pangs—"all this is but the beginning of the sufferings" (Mt 24:8)—will be an evocative phrase to recall from the Gospel.

～

The upsurge of disinterest in God so prevalent today naturally does not signify his withdrawal from the world. But perhaps while remaining close to us, the gaze of God on his creation is stifled in pain. His presence at this time of history may be the wounded presence of a God looking at the theft of his own creation. His children suffer injury, and it is as though he must stand back and allow a promise to complete its course—the promise granted to the freedom of intelligent creatures. We cannot know whether a tragic denouement awaits the world when life without God persists for a lengthy period of historical time on a vast scale.

A forsaken God can seem to be a powerless God unable to rescue his children. Yet that is not so. The fact that worse disasters have not ensued can only be due to the souls who remain close to the heart of God and draw his mercy by their prayer and sacrifice. For God has certainly not disappeared from some hearts and souls; just the opposite, for there is now an intense desire among a portion of fervent people, often hidden from others, to offer their lives in love for him and for the world.

2

RUMINATIONS ON A LAST ERA IN THE CHURCH

The whole of Christianity is contained in a sign of the cross; no theory of Redemption expresses half as much as a simple crucifix hung on a wall, erected as a wayside shrine or put on a tomb or altar. . . . This is why mere believers can transmit the whole of Tradition, even when they are quite ignorant of the terminology and subtleties of dogma.[1]

—Yves Congar, O.P.

Newman himself once remarked that the Church's mind was like a schoolboy's; both knew very little when relaxed but recovered their memory when threatened.[2]

—Aaron Pidel, S.J.

But prophecy is not prescience. It is spiritual anticipation.[3]

—Henri de Lubac, S.J.

One expression of intense religiosity in the present day is the conviction by some people of a fulfillment of scriptural

[1] Yves Congar, O.P., *The Meaning of Tradition*, trans. A. N. Woodrow (New York: Hawthorn Books, 1964), 72.

[2] Aaron Pidel, S.J., *Church of the Ever Greater God: The Ecclesiology of Erich Przywara* (Notre Dame: University of Notre Dame Press, 2020), 52.

[3] Henri de Lubac, *The Drama of Atheist Humanism*, trans. Edith M. Riley and Anne Englund Nash (San Francisco: Ignatius Press, 1995), 329.

prophecy in our time. The talk of "end times" is not unusual even in Catholic circles. Typically, it is posed, not as a
speculative idea to be pondered, a possibility that might be
tentatively considered, but as a real prospect in our lifetime.
But is this assurance not without dangers? Expectations of
the Second Coming of Christ have provoked spells of en-
thusiasm at various times in history. They are not reducible
to a single pattern. They are embedded in a particular era
and a reaction at times to the religious and cultural malaise
of a time. A despair about the current hour in history seems
to be a common passion accompanying them. It may be no
different today. Those now convinced of Christ's imminent
return usually express a parallel conviction of the unprecedented rise of evil in the world—abortions, child trafficking, murder, drug abuse, satanism. Possibly they are right,
and we are on the edge in the years or decades ahead of
a further triumph of evil and the emergence even of the
figure of the Antichrist. At the same time, a serious caution
must be urged. Saint Paul must have realized in his later
years that the time for our Lord's return was not in fact so
imminent. A readiness to persevere down the long path of
lifetime faithfulness in the Church and prayerful commitment is always imperative.

~

Anxious spiritual prognostication in a time of historical
uncertainty is foolhardy; it simply agitates the soul. The
impulse to speculate whether a final period of history is already underway confronts God's refusal to answer impetu-
ous questions. If there are notable signs of a grave hour in the
present day, in the Church and outside her, they nonetheless
do not by any means indicate a definitive time of reckoning

in the near future. History has shown repeatedly that it can survive the catastrophes of the current day and extend its life longer. There is much that may be permitted in the designs of God, much even of shocking evil, and events we cannot yet imagine. Yet while allowing God to keep from us these secrets and the unknown turns of future history, perhaps it is still necessary that we treat our own time in history as significant and even as moving at its own pace to what may be some climactic moment. The question what to expect, what to anticipate, what to prepare for as possible sufferings in our time need not preoccupy our thoughts or deflect us from the essential demand of seeking deeper relations with our God. But being alert to significant displays of contradiction or confusion within the Church, for example, would seem a requirement if we are to suffer for the Church we love. "Let the day's own trouble be sufficient for the day" (Mt 6:34). These words of Jesus from the Sermon on the Mount confront the uncertainties of the present day; at the very least, they demand our serious daily effort of prayer and sacrifice for the Church and for souls. It is not to be thought, even in the most difficult historical circumstances, that these words can ever be excised from the Gospel or forgotten.

～

Those who seek a clear, unhindered view across the horizon of time desire an impossible knowledge. This truism is appropriate as well for the unknown developments that may await us in the Church herself. No reliable predictions can be undertaken with confident certainty. Speculations about the future state of the world and the Church are for that reason ill-advised. Perhaps God does not allow us to know what is coming next in history precisely because he wants from us a serious approach to prayer. The real uncertainty about the current time urges us to commit to a deep prayerfulness and to make prayer of intercession a key component in our prayer. The recourse to prayer in turn reminds us by the very nature of prayer that future events are matters held secretly within the providence of God. Nothing is fixed and determined in accord with a timeline, because God allows prayer to affect both personal lives and history itself. This is a constant reminder in the messages contained in the approved apparitions of Mary. The history of a last era of the Church, once we have entered it, will be no different. It will have an unknown timeline subject to the impact of prayer upon the heart of God. The horizon of time offers us only the vantage of a distant gaze with clouds often blocking our view. It is not proper to expect the comforting clarity of a timeline. Who can say how a last era in the Church will play out over time? It may be a long period, even many decades, of a cumulative and converging series of unknown shocks. In all this we will be asked to deepen our faith in our Lord's firm grip holding close to him those who remain united in their souls to him and to his Church.

~

"He who no longer has the Church for his mother cannot have God as his Father" (Saint Cyprian).[4] The capacity of a soul to give itself fully to God cannot be detached from a need to do so within the Church. In a time when the Cath-

---

[4] Saint Cyprian, *De Ecclesiae Catholicae Unitate*, 6, quoted in Andrew Louth, *Discerning the Mystery: An Essay on the Nature of Theology* (Oxford: Clarendon, 1983), 64.

olic doctrinal tradition seems unsteady, facing uncertainty or opposition, spirituality may find itself tone-deaf to an essential task in our spiritual life to give all to God within the Church. No one can become holy except within the current state of the Church, even in times of serious ecclesial crisis. This truth was evident in the saints of the Reformation period. And yet how challenging this demand can be when the Church is in a time of grave difficulty. Indifference to doctrine as a general atmosphere in the Church is a noxious air to breathe. It is clearly not conducive to fostering the ideal of committed faithfulness, which is an essential component in holiness. If our soul desires to pursue the path of holiness, it must confront the current state of crisis and uncertainty within the Church. We cannot live without the Church, even when the Church is unstable and agitated. Always a soul seeking holiness must find a setting for a radical commitment within the Church. Only within the Church can we offer our life entirely to God. In the current circumstances of the Church, we may need to ignore somewhat the confusions inflicting the Church, lest we deflect ourselves from an ultimate pursuit of Jesus Christ himself. The Church and her turmoil must be in a certain manner released from a fixated view, held in abeyance, as it were, in order that we may give ourselves fully to the real presence of Christ within the Church. Jesus can never separate himself from his Church, even in times of serious turmoil and confusion. The clearest sign of this truth is that he always remains ever present in his Eucharistic reality, even if very few respect his extraordinary gift in the Mass and his humble presence in a tabernacle.

∼

Discretion toward what is still unknown in history, not yet clarified, only implied in events as a possibility, is an important disposition in a time of speculation about the era in which we live. The ascetical refusal to grasp at interpretations of what cannot be known so clearly, of what still awaits us, is a need today. Perseverance through uncertainty, when there is no clear idea what may be taking place in the Church or in the world, is becoming a crucial discipline of mind and soul. This does not mean simply to wait passively for events in the Church to unfold or to wade into the deeper waters of ecclesial confusion without caution. It signifies rather to avoid the propensity for premature conclusions. Remaining still blind, not knowing entirely what our Lord is doing or permitting, is a condition of faith in every age. The difficulty of our own era in the Church may be precisely this uncertainty. For a time at least, until a clear vision is granted in the years ahead, we must accept that no definitive signs exist that we are in anything more decisive than early birth pangs before a greater time of upheaval comes upon us. Even that initial possibility we cannot know with clear certainty.

∽

It is not extraordinary to hear today that we are on the edge of a historical threshold of serious import in the Church. It would be unfair to dismiss this thought as merely anxious speculation induced by strife and disorder within the Church. Nor is it sufficient to repeat the truism that the history of the Church displays a neverending rhythm of crisis and recovery throughout the centuries. In fact, a collective spiritual intuition seems to be growing that we should be preparing for Christ's Second Coming. Such a comment, not long ago, would have been dismissed as unbalanced and delusional, an idea confined to the piety of Bible Belt Protestant circles. Today the possibility of Christ's Second Coming is a question also among many Catholics. This collective intuition deserves some sober consideration. It may reflect a variation on the notion of the *sensus fidelium*. The idea of the *sensus fidelium* is that faithful Catholic souls at certain times in history are filled with a conviction of a truth that only later is confirmed doctrinally in a formal manner by the Magisterium of the Church. Viewed in retrospect, it becomes clear that the certainty felt by the faithful, with a source in the light of the Holy Spirit, helped to prepare the way for the subsequent doctrinal confirmation. This would have been true in the declared dogmas of the Immaculate Conception in 1854 and of the Assumption of the Virgin Mary in 1950. But can this idea of a collective intuition among faithful Catholics also be operative in the increasing thought that the return of our Lord is showing signs on the horizon? Many would discount such a possibility as irrational and highly unlikely, a form of science fiction with a religious twist. And it is true that more than a few eras in the Church's history have indulged the thought of the end times in ways that proved illusory. But this observation does not preclude the fact that at some point we will enter a final period of the Church. History does not simply turn on an endless reel that never comes to a stop. Time is not ceaseless, and history has a terminating point that concludes with our Lord's return. We affirm this doctrinal truth in every creedal recitation at Mass and in the Rosary. Perhaps it is true that our era is simply a troubled period in the Church's history. Or, on the other hand, perhaps we are living in a preliminary phase of grave significance, in preparation for the Lord's return. How long such a period of preparation would last is of course quite unknown. But if that is even possibly so, commitment to prayer, sacrifice, and fidelity must intensify among serious souls as a critical demand. Even if we are mistaken, the gain for souls, both for those who intensify their prayer and for those in need of prayer, is undeniable.

~

The prophecies of the Old Testament regarding the Messiah were fulfilled in Jesus Christ, a truth evident now to the Christian believer. During Jesus' lifetime, this was not recognized. It was only after the completion of his life that the messianic prophecies were properly understood. Their fulfillment involved the whole life of Jesus and could be comprehended only with the completion of his life. Only gradually, piece by piece, were these predictions fulfilled, culminating in the sufferings of his Passion and in his Resurrection on the third day. What, then, do we say of prophecy in our own time? There is talk today, yes, of the Second Coming of Christ. Yet the scriptural statements of prophecy about the end times are mysterious and for now largely indecipherable. They point to an era of crisis, of a possible grave and unprecedented persecution of the Church, before the coming of the Lord. At the same time Jesus himself proclaimed that no one, not even the Son, knows the day or hour of their fulfillment. What, then, are we to say about our time in relation to such prophecy? Perhaps the great mystery of prophecy in our own day is the manner in which the Church in a last era will display a striking identification with Jesus as he lived the hours of his last week. Just as the drama of hostility surrounding Jesus arrived at a climax in his last week, so, too, the Church may face her own climactic hour. In his inner life, Jesus knew this hour of oblation was coming, and he longed for it. A silent prayer of solitary offering filled his soul in this last week, but it was not a new prayer. All his life he was preparing for this climactic hour. So, too, is the Church over the years of history in a long preparatory state for her own passion in a last era. Jesus' desire to complete his mission was firm; no hesitation or thought of turning back obstructed his mind or heart. He was resolutely determined to make his last journey to Jerusalem, knowing what awaited him. Perhaps in the Church we must embrace more deeply this resolute determination to remain united to the heart of Jesus as he begins to relive his Passion in our own day.

$\sim$

"Dostoevsky warned that 'great events could come upon us and catch us intellectually unprepared.' That is precisely what has happened" (Aleksandr Solzhenitsyn).[5] Can this astute observation be pertinent as well to our own time in history? The swift tide of depraved moral darkness sweeping across the civilized western world may be indicative that a climactic moment in history is slowly approaching. And what would that be? History is always moving in the direction of a final destiny according to revealed Christian truth. The Second Coming of Christ may be a distant event many centuries away, or it may not be; perhaps we are at the beginning of the birth pangs of a last era. We do not know details or possible scenarios or timelines, but it would seem clear that prior to the Second Coming of Christ, a period of dark godlessness will descend upon societies. The loss of God and the collapse of morality will deepen as signs of a time

---

[5] Aleksandr Solzhenitsyn, Templeton Lecture, May 10, 1983, in *The Solzhenitsyn Reader: New and Essential Writings, 1947–2005*, ed. Edward E. Ericson and Daniel J. Mahoney (Wilmington, Del.: ISI Books, 2006), 578.

of spiritual magnitude. Both signs, at least as preliminary indications, need to be recognized in our own day, no matter what the time of history in which we currently live. Indeed, let us not be blind, for the public emergence of the Antichrist, as prophesied in Scripture, is not a fictional notion or an impossible or far-fetched possibility as the decades of this century proceed. An unreflective dismissal of this idea may be comparable to the blind unawareness toward historical figures like Hitler or Stalin, who often went unrecognized in their evil intentions during the early years of their ascendancy to power. A similar lack of understanding may happen when the figure of the Antichrist is climbing his way up the steps onto the stage of history. The great majority of people may not recognize the reality of an evil presence because they have both lost faith in God and embraced a depraved acceptance of godless immorality as a normal reality.

∽

If we look at certain societal trends of our time, we might speculate that a fine preparatory work has already been taking place for the possible arrival of an Antichrist figure in the coming decades. And how so? The more subtle developments in history are sometimes the most damaging and sinister. One example comes to mind. The elevation of the nonjudgmental attitude of tolerance to a supreme status in the hierarchy of moral virtues has evolved rapidly in our time. We have moved quickly in a single generation or two from hesitant tolerance of perverse behaviors to a general attitude of mindless indifference toward them. Moral desensitization has soaked especially into the souls of the young. The acceptance of actions reprehensible in the eyes of God as quite normal in the present day is a sign that the satanic presence has been gaining victories for some time. Many traditional norms of morality in effect no longer exist for large segments of society. What the figure of the Antichrist may do one day will be to add a brilliant touch of clarity to the societal ambiance of amorality. The attainment of a higher form of morality in a new humanity may be one of his primary spiritual ambitions. The narrow focus on individual morality understood in a traditional manner will give way under his forceful spiritual leadership to an expansive sense of universal brotherhood as the preeminent object of the new code of ethical behavior. He may insist strongly that a leveling of all lives to a single plane of human brotherhood will become possible on one condition: the acceptance of each person to live freely, to choose freely, without any external restraint or interference. No one is to object or attempt to limit the free expression of another's individual behavior or choice. The test case for this kind of freedom has already been conducted in our own time in the realm of sexual identity, sexual behavior, and sexual aberration. Tolerance toward all expressions of sexuality without exception, largely achieved in our day, has perhaps been a sinister preparation for this new understanding. Peaceful and permissive relations among men and women will be preached as eminently attainable under the sway of the new understanding of morality. The success of the figure of the Antichrist in all his efforts will be directly tied to the collapse of faith in God and a loss of sensitive moral awareness in the general population. We are unfortunately moving swiftly along on this path, and so the need in our day for serious prayerful watchfulness.

~

I met a man some years ago, a man of serious prayer and virtue, not at all eccentric, who had a strange story to relate about an experience in his earlier life. He said that in 1979 he began to study with intense curiosity the Book of Revelation. He read commentaries, and for a while one item absorbed his attention: the reference in the Book of Revelation to the mark of the beast, the figure of the Antichrist, "that is, the name of the beast or the number of its name" (Rev 13:17). The passage continues and proposes a means of identification: "let him who has understanding reckon the number of the beast, for it is a human number, its number is six hundred and sixty-six" (Rev 13:18). The passage has often been the source of overdramatized fanfare. This man told me he took it seriously and read in a commentary that ancient numerology assigned the number six to the first letter of the alphabet, the number twelve to the second letter, and so forth. The letters of every name when added up would come to a particular number. Naturally, the chance that any name might arrive by such calculations at six hundred and sixty-six is almost less than infinitesimal. Yet he played with a few names out of curiosity. It was in late November, 1979, at the time of the Iranian hostage crisis, when fifty-two Americans were being held captive in Tehran after the Islamic Revolution under the leadership of Ayatollah Khomeini. He tried the Ayatollah's name by this method of calculation, but it far exceeded six sixty-six. Then he remembered, on a Wednesday, that *The New York Times* on the previous Sunday had displayed on its front page a photo of the Ayatollah with his son. He had already discarded the Sunday paper, so he drove to his local library to ask for the paper in order to see the name of the son, which was Ahmad. Then he did his calculation there in the library: Khomeini comes to 512 and Ahmad to 154. He told me this as though it meant little now, some decades later, because in 1995 Ahmad Khomeini died in Tehran. On the other hand, he said it was impossible that this was just a co-incidence. It was a strange sign of mystery, he said, perhaps even a deception from the evil one, before the real figure of the Antichrist would emerge in history. He told me with a calm intensity that this was a secret that he had carried for years, telling very few people, but it had led him first to enter a monastery and, then, after departing, to dedicate himself even while in the world to a life of serious prayer and solitude.

~

It may indeed be that the era prior to the Lord's Second Coming will be marked in a mysterious way by a resemblance to the last week of Christ's life. It will seem as though the concealed tensions of hostility toward Jesus depicted in the Gospel accounts are being brought back mysteriously to life, repeating themselves in a subtle parallelism to the present day, but within the Church herself, both as a protagonist and as a victim of events. The Church is the Body of Christ in history, the real presence of the mystery of Jesus our Lord in history as the Church progresses through time. We should not be surprised, in that last era, if we see the Church live out her own Passion. Let us pay attention to the Passion of Jesus in our silent prayer. Our Lord's internal sufferings in his last week, pondered with love, may become a sacred prism of interpretation. What he quietly suffered in that week, even prior to his last day at Calvary, he may live again as a series of wounds within the Church. Perhaps, in a last era, the Church will suffer a kiss of betrayal like the deceptive embrace that Judas gave Jesus in Gethsemane. As one of the

Twelve, Judas lived in the inner circle of Jesus' closest con-
fidantes; he was likely ordained a priest at the Last Supper
and likely received the first Eucharist—sacrilegiously. His
betrayal was a preparatory episode that supplied a context for
Jesus' arrest and condemnation. Betrayal of doctrine within
the Church, if such a thing were to happen, may serve in a
parallel manner to bring the Church herself to an internal
condition of crucifixion. The more that any form of doctrinal dismissal takes place at higher echelons in the hierarchy,
the more we may be seeing preliminary signs of a time of
immense significance that the Church is entering.

~

Jesus Christ will likely come in the time of a last era, in his
union with his Body the Church, by a descent into vulnerability, once again humiliated and scorned, as in his Passion.
He may become an unwelcome presence within portions of
his Church, a figure of contradiction to the reigning spirit
of the time, one who is again oppressed and afflicted, a man
of sorrows within his own Church, despised and rejected
by elements of betrayal in a last era of the Church. He may
relive again the humiliation of rejection that he suffered at
the hands of the scribes and elders of his own time. As
in the past, he may remain silent and not open his mouth.
We should expect that in a mysterious way within his own
Church he will suffer without protest, without defending
himself, as he did in that last week of his life. He will hide
his deeper wounds from those who inflict these wounds and
hand him over to his enemies to be despised and rejected.
And it will take place all under the guise of loyalty and
friendship with Christ, much like the external demeanor of
Judas at the Last Supper, who never shed his mask ·in that

setting or changed his expression when he bestowed his kiss on Jesus and burned our Lord's face with his falsity. The presence of Jesus among us in that time of a last era may be the Jesus of Gethsemane, painfully aware of his abandonment by his apostles, anticipating the kiss of betrayal from Judas that would pierce his human soul.

~

The manner in which the Church, as the invisible presence of Christ in history, will repeat the pattern of our Lord's last week cannot be anticipated with exact accuracy. Yet the fact of this replication taking place in mysterious ways would seem to be certain. There will be veiled signs of his suffering within his Church. Not the whole Church as a single body, but certain elements within the Church will likely suffer in a singular union with him as a hidden sign of his Passion once more lived out in our midst. At the time of his Passion, Jesus was rejected with contempt by the scribes, chief priests, and elders of the people. His own people decided his death, justifying it for reasons of expediency. A rejection of some kind like this may occur in the Church in ways that will go largely unnoticed. There may be, for instance, a persecution of holiness within the Church, a not-so-subtle animosity for those who have pursued holiness in their lifetime. Whatever is holy and sacred to God may face demeaning opposition and disparagement within the Church herself. Those wielding ecclesial power may exercise arbitrary restrictions and prohibitions at the places of most serious prayer in the Church. This is bound to be a strange phenomenon, unrecognized for the most part. Coercive pressures exercised by ecclesial authorities against traditional religious orders who have kept their structures of life unscathed by the turn to laxity in the modern period would be a possible example of this. It would not be surprising to see the contemplative religious congregations face interference and a dismissive attitude for their uselessness and obsolescence. A fervent zeal by those in positions of power to attack what is insignificant and powerless in any worldly sense within the Church would be a striking echo of the malice that Jesus faced in his powerlessness before Caiaphas and the Sanhedrin. Few Catholics would likely perceive a parallel between Jesus' rejection and such scattered episodes of hostility toward souls desiring holiness and a complete gift of themselves to God. But these souls in their union with Jesus Christ crucified may understand this connection in due time.

∼

A trial may await Jesus as the years proceed. The trial before Caiaphas, when Jesus was led before the Sanhedrin, had a predetermined verdict of condemnation. It concluded with a display of indignation when Caiaphas the high priest tore his garments and declared his outrage at Jesus affirming himself as Son of the Most High God. Perhaps a drama resembling this will take place at a future hour in a future decade. In some unknown manner, our Lord will be placed on trial within his own Church, subject to an interrogation like the harsh questioning that Dostoevsky depicted in the brilliant chapter of "The Grand Inquisitor" of *The Brothers Karamazov*. In that chapter, in the fictional musing of the unbelieving Ivan Karamazov, Jesus has returned to earth, but in an unobtrusive, quiet manner. Nonetheless, he soon attracts notice and is recognized. The austere Cardinal Archbishop of Seville hears of his presence and goes out to meet

Jesus. The exchange is a monologue, Jesus remaining silent before the arrogant and condescending tones of the prelate. The cardinal rebukes Jesus for misreading the true needs of people. Instead of using his divine power to turn stones into bread and feeding the multitudes throughout history, taking care of material needs, and thereby becoming popular and making humanity subservient to himself, he left men free and capable of revolt. He could have been worshipped with the fidelity of a dog to the master who feeds him, and instead he found himself in history rejected and cast aside. His insensitivity to the needs of humanity cost him the loyal subjection he could have obtained with his divine power for the miraculous.

~

Perhaps Jesus before too long will face a similar interrogation and rebuke, with a variation on his failure in history to see to the physical needs of human desire. The interrogation will be conducted again with condescension and a predetermined verdict. The Church's teachings in the realm of sexual morality, truths taught for centuries, may be charged with the crime of an unacceptable intolerance, as indefensible in the light of modernity's knowledge, and undergo a needed correction. Hierarchical prestige will prevail, as Jewish leadership prevailed in Jesus' own day, as though invested with the divine will. The significance of such a development, if it were to occur, will transcend any convoluted theological discussion. Few may perceive that Jesus is being spit upon once again. If it happens, he will suffer this trial in his Church as he suffered before Caiaphas—with silence and by turning his cheek for the next blow. It may be the nature of our time in the Church, and as the decades continue, that our Lord will endure everything—humiliation, insult, and disrespect—with the same silence he lived two thousand years ago. It will be a silence in this case lived out in the purification of souls who remain faithful to him despite all events. The contemplative spirit of self-offering may rise in that time to new levels of union with our Lord's Passion.

3

ECCLESIAL TENSION: PERMANENT TRUTHS AND UNCERTAIN TREMORS

The Passion of Christ continues. We grasp a strange law in this, repugnant to our eyes; it is necessarily so. But it is a salutary law. It was necessary for Christ to suffer. And that it is still true: it is necessary for the Church to suffer. . . . Martyrdom is one of her charisms.[1]

—Cardinal Montini (Pope Paul VI)

It is nothing to suffer *for* the Church. The keenest suffering is *at Her hands.*[2]

—Père Clérissac, O.P.

The Rock of St. Peter on its summit enjoys a pure and serene atmosphere, but there is a great deal of Roman *malaria* at the foot of it.[3]

—Saint John Henry Newman

The current hour in the Church's history defies easy prognosis or prediction. It is as though we are living days of

[1] Giovanni Cardinal Montini, February 13, 1960, quoted by Henri de Lubac, S.J., *More Paradoxes*, trans. Anne Englund Nash (San Francisco: Ignatius Press, 2002), 58.

[2] Père Clérissac, O.P., killed at Verdun in 1916, quoted in Erasmo Leiva-Merikakis, *Fire of Mercy, Heart of the Word*, vol. 4 (San Francisco: Ignatius Press, 2021), 340.

[3] John Henry Newman, *A Letter Addressed to His Grace the Duke of Norfolk* (London: Longmans, Green, and Co., 1900), 71.

uncertain preparation for unknown events that nonetheless approach with quiet inevitability. The clouds of spiritual drama hover over us, yet it is not clear what might yet happen in the Church and in the world. For those who pray and strive for God, it is not possible to be relaxed in faith and at ease, blindly ignoring the turmoil affecting the Church. A cloister of the heart cut off from current ecclesial tensions would seem an unholy escape, a refusal to suffer with the Church in her hour of need. For many people who are spiritually sensitive, a climactic moment appears to draw nearer. Perhaps dramatic world events in the coming decades will converge with spiritual events inside the Church. It is not impossible that we may witness greater ecclesial tensions and even the negation of certain doctrinal truths in the Church. A crucial need in such a time will be a capacity for spiritual perception. The ability to distinguish what is coming apart in the confusion of the time and what remains solidly in place will be essential. The reality of our Lord's presence will protect those who remain faithful within the Church. What is important is to be vigilant and awake, not succumbing to panic or mindless impulse, not listening to the demonic temptation to abandon the Church when she is in need. Otherwise, we risk being swept up in ignorance, misreading the true significance of the time, which may have more troublesome things to show us in the days and decades to come. The essential demand is to remain souls of prayer faithful to the crucified Lord and his Mother, always united to the power of his Eucharist in our lives.

~

The assumption that the Church is just passing through another difficult era in history and will in time recover her

traditional moorings and proper direction may be a superficial optimism. The signs of the time point rather to the
possibility of ecclesial developments that will inflict serious
wounds on the Church. The desire for radical change in the
Church's doctrinal teaching in areas of sexual morality, particularly regarding homosexual relations, is quickly arriving
at a state of crisis. If a threshold is crossed, it will not destroy
the Church, which is impossible. But the crisis is real and
the refusal to lie to ourselves is important. The realization
that we may encounter some forms of isolated betrayal in
the Church which cross a line and break with the tradition
of the Church must be faced in truth. A kind of visceral
aversion to developments of this sort will ensure a healthy
state of soul. If, on the contrary, we accept credulously all
that occurs within the Church as simply the will of God,
this spirit of naïve passivity may forfeit the protection of our
Lord himself. The Church in her exercise of authority has
no guarantee from God that she will uphold all truth in all
her public pronouncements. There is the dark possibility of
the lie of Satan influencing high levels of authority within
the Church. Perhaps this development will take place, not in
signed documents, but in a pastoral strategy of encouraging
permissibility toward acts always forbidden as intrinsically
evil in the Catholic moral tradition. The possibility in our
time that irreformable Catholic moral truths may be altered
or refuted is not implausible, even if this occurs by subtle
methods of pastoral acquiescence. The result will be a test
for those devoutly united to Jesus Christ as Lord. Such a
moment in the Church will not be so vague or ambiguous in
its external manifestation. We will know it clearly enough
by the contradiction of moral truths honored for many centuries in the Church. A refusal on our part to accept teaching
explicitly at variance with the moral tradition of the Church

cannot be viewed as a rebellion against a sacred authority. It will be rather an immediate test of our soul to respond to our Lord's demand that we live and give witness to truth. This demand remains always, whether it involves the truth of his divinity or of unchangeable moral truths. We can pray that a great strength rises up in priests and bishops and the pope. The unknown impact of doctrinal contradictions on priests and leaders within the Church may entail in some cases a true martyrdom of souls.

$\sim$

"I tell you, you are Peter, and on this rock I will build my Church, and the gates of Hades shall not prevail against it" (Mt 16:18). Why does Jesus speak of the gates of Hades? It would seem perhaps more apt for him to say that no violent persecution, no assault or battering, no heretical attacks against the Church, will ever take down this sacred edifice of truth and her immovable solidity. But he refers instead to the gates of Hades as a supreme test to the Church. Perhaps this image of a gate is significant. A gate can be opened, a threshold can be crossed. The great danger that the Church faces throughout history is a deception from Hades, from the satanic lie, that would lead temporarily to some form of betrayal. The possibility of walking into an ambush from the powers of evil is quite real if the Church should open a gate and exceed limits that should not be passed. Once such a line has been crossed, one must expect more intense aggression from the powers of evil. Perhaps the image Jesus used here is suggestive of a test the Church will face in the decades ahead. The gates of Hades would then be a crucial metaphor. If the Church in her authority passes beyond limits she must not cross in doctrinal matters, a gate is opened from below to a destructive spirit rising up from satanic realms. There may be a period of attack in such a time toward Catholic tradition and doctrine. Nonetheless, the Church retains the Lord's promise: the Church herself will prevail. She cannot be destroyed, and yet this promise does not ensure an immunity from a testing and purification of grave magnitude. In such a time of testing, the visible institutional Church may appear unstable and swaying, with tensions and internal struggles, and with some elements of leadership open to darker influence. But the holy faithful in the Church, a deeply prayerful faithful, will live a form of purified sanctity. They may suffer a type of spiritual martyrdom within the Church that will bring the Church to an even greater holiness.

~

A crisis of doctrinal clarity in the Church inevitably spills over into spirituality. This does not require heretical pronouncements issued in official Vatican documents. Steadfast doctrinal ambiguity or even silence toward doctrine are sufficient over time to undermine healthy spirituality. The repercussions are inevitable. Religious commitment is bound to waver whenever doctrine in the wider Church seems open to question or possible revision. The link is soon noticeable. The post-Vatican II period of the 1970s and 80s is illustrative. It was a time in which inattention to doctrine fueled an abandonment of traditional spirituality. Commitment to prayer, respect for religious vows, the regular discipline of ascetical practices, obedience to a teaching authority in the Church, were treated dismissively at a time when doctrinal teaching in the Church was increasingly questioned and subject to reconsideration. The disregard for doctrine found its counterpart in a relaxation of rigor and determination in spirituality. When the habit of supernatural faith no longer provokes hunger in souls toward the revealed realities of Catholic life, the first casualty is likely a fading of love for the Eucharist. Love for the Eucharist, a need for time spent in prayer before a tabernacle, is always indicative of a Catholic soul's sense of the personal presence of God. This link of faith and spirituality, of love for the Eucharist and prayer, is inevitable: depth of spirituality has its source always in a quality of serious faith. In the immediate decades after Vatican II, doctrinal ambiguities seemed to sap the spiritual energy needed to make the greater gift of selfhood to the unseen presence of God known only in faith. Now, in a new resurgence of life in the hidden core of the Church, we are seeing an intense desire by some souls to give themselves to the fullness of Catholic spiritual practice. This is taking place precisely in a time of even greater doctrinal upheaval. The sign of contradiction in this phenomenon is perhaps a telling indication of our time. The tension between intense desire for God and an indifference to God and truth is becoming more taut, and at some point, this tension may arrive at a breaking point in the Church.

~

Any Gospel passage in which a parable portrays the refusal of an invitation has a pertinence to our own time. Those invited to the wedding feast, for instance, who make excuses for their absence and grieve the host are persons of our own time. The divine invitation expressed in these parables is not directed simply to the Jews of that period who would miss the great encounter with God in Jesus of Nazareth. The people invited today are the baptized Catholics who withdraw from committed Catholic practice under various semblances of excuse and thereby insult the host who invites them to the wedding banquet. The banquet is the Eucharist, of course. Today the invitation to come and receive the complete gift of the Lord himself in his Body and Blood is callously refused in too many Catholic lives. The falling away from a commitment to Sunday Mass among Catholics points to the immediate reality of the lesson in this parable. It should be read as a revelation of God's divine displeasure with our ingratitude toward his divine gift in the Eucharist in the falling away from Mass attendance on Sundays. The observation should lead us to a serious desire to love our Lord more in the gift of the Eucharist, choosing to spend time in prayer before a tabernacle.

$\sim$

"Take away dogma and you take away God; to touch dogma is to touch God; to sin against dogma is to sin against God" (Pierre Rousselot, S.J.).[4] Those exercising authority within the Church in these days may not realize well enough that they are not protagonists in a movement of inevitable progress by which doctrinal change advances the necessary development of Christianity. The idea that entrenched truths of morality protected and perennially taught in past centuries may be reinterpreted and declared no longer valid in this new age is not authority exercising its proper role as a servant to truth. It is, rather, a sign of decadence and collapse in a difficult period of the Church. If a formal rebellion against the moral tradition of the Church does take place by the reversal of explicit moral teachings, this action

[4] Pierre Rousselot, S.J., *Intelligence: Sense of Being, Faculty of God*, trans. Andrew Tallon (Marquette, Wis.: Marquette University Press, 1999), 182.

will not destroy the Church, which has the promise of God to remain until the end of time. But the phenomenon of rebellion in the realm of morality does require a refinement of our understanding of our Lord's presence within the body of the Church. It is possible in a historical era that the heart of Jesus will become mysteriously one with the martyred soul of the Church. The martyrdom will not be an execution resulting in a death, for the Church will not die. One might compare it, rather, to a sustained torture over many hours, like Jesus' own Passion or the sufferings undergone by the North American Jesuits in the seventeenth century. If aberrant modifications on moral issues like homosexuality are even being discussed at high levels in the Church, it is in effect a dialectic of descent into some degree of doctrinal betrayal. This ought to be understood, not simply as a trial, but perhaps as a sign of our Lord suffering within his Church in an early sign of the birth pangs before his eventual return.

~

An understanding of authority within the Church that considers nothing unchangeable in the realm of traditional morality and views every moral doctrine as open to corrective interpretations is clearly a profound danger today. An assault of this sort on perennial Catholic teaching undermines the expectation of divine protection upholding throughout the centuries the inspired truth of moral doctrine in the Church. For that reason it would seem impossible that such a thing might occur. A change in teaching that has been considered infallibly taught by the ordinary Magisterium of the Church would be to rupture a continuity in truth intrinsic to the Church's mission of truth. Yet there appears to be a serious push in this direction within the Church. This is not a sign simply of straying from sound theology by a misguided intellectual detour. Rather, a questionable ecclesiology is at work in the assumption that moral doctrine can be open to radical shifts and transformation. Acts forbidden as intrinsically evil in the tradition, allowing no exception to the prohibition, such as homosexual actions or the ban on artificial contraception, may soon be declared in some circumstances sinless or even morally advisable. Only by a grave disrespect toward the Holy Spirit as God's presence of governance and moral guidance within the history of the Church can this step be taken. The authority within the Church that would presume to alter moral doctrine upheld for centuries cannot claim a justification of new insights from a new century. It is a sign of a vacant understanding of the Divine Presence of God governing the Church and protecting the moral teaching of the Church throughout many centuries.

∼

The doctrinal ambiguity that has exploded again in recent years as a kind of intellectual ambiance in the Church has certainly touched the tenor of spirituality with its own forms of vagueness and ambivalence. The reason is not hard to recognize. By its nature, Catholic faith demands firm adherence to unchangeable doctrinal teaching, including moral doctrines taught for centuries. When Catholic teaching is not clearly presented as sacred and inviolable, but instead open to possible alteration, it is not surprising that experimentation and uncertainty begin to permeate the notion of spiritual pursuit. Innovation begins to supplant tradition in spirituality. Eclectic approaches in the use of non-Catholic

forms of prayer become acceptable. Without firm ground-
ing in dogmatic truth, claims of mystical experience grow
in number. The search for experiences of the divine begins
to dominate a privatized pursuit of God. These trends and
fashions in spirituality reflect a kind of unmoored quality
in the faith of souls, a haphazard drifting away from traditional foundations in faith. The solidity of spiritual pursuit rooted in sacraments and sober commitment to prayer
no longer elicits confidence. These effects on spirituality
are inevitably felt when doctrine itself seems unsure and
is vaguely proposed. Certainly, the sacramental life, dependent on doctrinal awareness, diminishes or even disappears
at such times when doctrine is not clearly expounded and
proposed with attractive prominence. A sense of isolation
and fragmentation takes place within many souls of a certain
religiosity, consumed with their personal quest for the private experience of God. The private quest for religious experience tends to replace the communal commitment within
the Church to serve others and seek the salvation of souls
as Catholic doctrine fades in importance.

~

A successful satanic ploy in our day is to identify the *de facto*
realities of history or of the human condition with the express will of God. The existence of a multiplicity of religions
in the world, for example, has been proclaimed at high levels of the Church to be the will of God. The thought there
is not that God permits with a certain indulgent tolerance
the existence of different religions, each claiming truth for
itself, but that the variety of religions, incompatible in their
systems of belief, is the desire and choice of God. In this
view, the collective phenomenon of religions is the divine

preference of his holy will, and not the result of ignorance or error. The idea is that he reveals himself in each religion to some degree and inspires each in a unique fashion. Underlying this thought is an assumption that what exists in the world must necessarily be the will of God. But that false notion ignores the wounded nature of humanity and of history due to sin. No sense of original sin and its repercussions tainting the experience of persons is acknowledged. This kind of thought is in truth a fine example of a tactical victory for demonic advancement within the world. It subverts the truth of a fixed, stable permanence of perception in the eternal mind of God. Instead, the developments in history can be viewed under a prism of uncertainty, monitored and chosen by the hand of God as a sign of his evolving engagement with history. This understanding of God cannot be correct if we embrace in faith the true transcendence of a God who is not subject to passing time. Another related element of truth should be considered. There is a failure here to perceive a satanic presence in history seeking to undermine the truth of God. The satanic deception is strong in its desire that historical developments are viewed as stages in the evolving plan of God. A true perspective on history, on the contrary, can only come in realizing that an invisible war is taking place for the prize of truth and for the salvation of souls. The truth must be sought and sieged, lest it be handed over to an enemy of malice who seeks to destroy both truth and souls.

～

Another grave example of the contemporary subversion of truth is to view the existence of homosexual practice, so accepted now in Western societies, as a natural condition rooted in the choice of God, and thus again the will of God. The idea that God expresses his capacity for infinite creativity in establishing the sexual differentiation of various lustful tastes in the human condition is blasphemy of a high degree. The view again is to take what is a *de facto* reality in the current day and interpret its acceptance and prevalence in society as an indication of the divine will. Only now, in the modern era, do we realize, with our more profound religious enlightenment, that God the Creator is more open-minded than we previously credited him with being. The practices of homosexuals, given that we are more accustomed to their presence among us, should determine our understanding of the truth of God's wider preferences in exercising his holy will. In this view, the homosexual action need no longer be prohibited as a grave offense against God. It is capable of being blessed when partners in lust declare their fidelity to each other before a religious witness. This development in the Church must be considered a significant sign of the times, a dangerous rupture with unchangeable moral truth.

∼

In Genesis, the serpent's initial question to Eve—"Did God say, 'You shall not eat of any tree in the garden'?" (Gen 3:1)— is an opening gambit to draw her mind under the sway of his superior intelligence. She answers properly, identifying the tree in the middle of the garden as a fruit forbidden by God, with the penalty of death if she and Adam violate the divine prohibition. The serpent, who is the father of lies, then responds in character, denying the pronouncement of God. "You will not die. For God knows that when you eat of it your eyes will be opened, and you will be like God, knowing good and evil" (Gen 3:5). The deceiver's tactic is to propose to Eve that she is being deceived by God. They will not die, but rather they will see with their own eyes, not depending on another. They will perceive openly the truth of good and evil. Indeed, they will not just know good and evil, but once they eat this fruit, it will be they who decide what is good and evil. It will be their choice, not God's, to determine what is good and evil. This primordial temptation, to which Adam and Eve succumb, is enormously significant, not just for the original sin that follows in its wake with all its dire consequences. The temptation itself—it is for you to decide what is good and evil, not God—repeats itself throughout history. The temptation is strongly seductive in some eras of moral instability. It may seem quite irresistible: your eyes will be free and finally be opened as you determine for yourself what is good and evil. You will at last grasp the truth when you have the courage to exercise your own decision. Certitude in deciding for oneself what is morally good or evil, or what is no longer forbidden, is at the heart of this temptation. The Church is perhaps facing a grave recurrence of this primordial temptation to decide for herself what is good and evil, forsaking what God has pronounced as forbidden for centuries and under the threat of death as a punishment. The idea that we can declare the correct understanding on moral issues, even by a vote in a parliamentary procedure, on matters that God has pronounced in revelation as forbidden without exception and reprehensible as behaviors in his sight, is a strong sign that we are in an era of grave significance.

∽

Saint Peter's inspired profession of faith in Jesus as the divine Son of the living God did not prevent him from rebuking our Lord when, soon after his confession of faith, he heard Jesus speak of his approaching Passion. "God forbid, Lord! This shall never happen to you" (Mt 16:22). It is one thing to get the answer right, pronouncing the dogmatic truth of the Incarnation in correct terms and with firm certainty, and quite another to face the unknown implications that are concealed in the humanity of a God who has entered our unstable historical circumstances. Peter's rebuke of Jesus is in one sense as important as his affirmation of faith. It reminds us that we can mix contradictory approaches to our Lord, one more abstract and fixed in concept, the other more personal and subject to fluctuation. In fact, they are inseparable, and when they oppose each other, they undermine any truth expressed in the one or the other. The temptation of some good souls is to pull our Lord down to a level of immediate accessibility and perhaps at times to remonstrate with him for not getting matters right, for not seeing what needs to be seen, for not acting with prompt displays of omnipotence. The temptation to instruct God, as Peter did, is a sign of arrogance, and yet it is a common impulse, as we see in Peter when he shifts from a dogmatic declaration to look at the face of the man immediately in front of him. But this man is God himself in the flesh. There is a strong lesson for our prayer: the realization that it is God himself in his majestic infinitude before whom we stand and whom we address in prayer when we are inclined to perceive nothing but an easy companion ready to respond to our own needs.

~

Often in the Gospel it can seem that Jesus is never entirely comfortable with the crowds that surround him. He will address them and at times teach profoundly before them, but it is as though he knows that crowds are an unreliable audience for the depth of his message. A classic example of this truth is when he asks "Who do men say that the Son of man is?" (Mt 16:13). followed by the direct question to the apostles—"But who do you say that I am?" (Mt 16:15). The crowds remain always an unstable reality. They move here, then there, shifting their convictions and opinions in accord with dominant voices, flowing too easily with the movement of loud voices and the illusion of accord. Jesus to this day always wants a depth of private conviction in us, which often means to stand apart and resist the opinion of the overconfident crowd around us. The primary reason, however, why Jesus was not comfortable with crowds was because he was aware already in his public life that the crowds would eventually turn on him. On the last morning of his life, a worked-up, frenzied Jewish crowd in the praetorium would cry out "Crucify him. . . . Crucify him" (Mk 15:13-14), egged on and quick to answer to the instigation of proud, malicious men. He was aware from the prophecies well before that last day that a crowd of taunting, mocking people would surround him at Calvary as he hung in torture on a cross. This crowd at Calvary would think nothing of the horrific pain he was undergoing. They would be intent to outshout each other, challenging him to come down from the Cross and show himself to be the Son of God. Crowds are in fact easily swayed in demonic ways, and we see this truth in the scene at the crucifixion. And Jesus knew this long before the crucifixion. It is why we sometimes see him hesitant before crowds, as though aware that an undertone of hostility is ready to arise when he is speaking to a larger group of people. Perhaps we should take great care in our own time to be wary of the crowds who exercise a fleeting power before our eyes.

∽

"Beware lest the obsession to save the masses tempt us into seducing them with vulgar attractions, similar to those used by their temporal masters. Saint Peter and Saint Paul, arriving in Rome, did not try to find some substitute for the amphitheater to offer the pagan masses" (Henri de Lubac, S.J.).[5] These words seem more than ever necessary to heed. The proclamation of God become man in Jesus of Nazareth is the one truth that, if neglected or set aside or taken for granted, empties the Church of her essential mission in the world throughout history. A Church preoccupied overmuch with matters extraneous to the ultimate truth of Jesus Christ as God buries the single treasure that gives value to everything else she does and teaches. Caught up instead in vain pursuits, the Church can be tempted at times in history to chase after prestige and relevance in the world and thereby to scatter herself like dust tossed into the passing political and ideological winds. Despite all her efforts, nothing the Church does to affect worldly matters is perhaps much respected, or carries significant influence, precisely because at certain times in history the impression is that the spiritual truth for which the Church stands is no longer so central a conviction. And this is a dangerous symptom of our own time, recognized even by those outside the Church. The unwillingness to give witness to the extraordinary truth of

[5] Henri de Lubac, S.J., *Paradoxes of Faith*, trans. Paule Simon and Sadie Kreilkamp (San Francisco: Ignatius Press, 1987), 66.

revelation that God became man in Jesus Christ is indicative of a diminished faith at the heart of the Church. Deep convictions of Jesus Christ as our Lord and God produce the opposite effect, leading souls in ecclesial leadership to bear witness to Christ in the strong language of genuine faith. The substitution of fashionable worldly concerns in place of fiery testimony to the truth of Christ is a prominent sign of our time. What it might be revealing already is a preference for silence about fundamental dogmatic truths in the Church in the coming years.

~

A factor in the diminishment of strong Catholic faith in our time has been the reluctance of Catholic clerics to face scorn and disrespect from the wider society. This failure coincides in recent decades with the decline of fatherly authority in society and family life and perhaps draws less notice for that reason. Unfortunately, we have witnessed for some time a loss of fatherly character in the priesthood. The sacred prototype of a priest as a father concerned for souls and their eternal destiny was replaced after Vatican II by the emergence of popular clerics shedding their Roman collar and smiling their way companionably through the crowds of Catholics losing their faith. Priests of former days may not have been saints, and some were certainly compromised by worldliness. Despite their sins and foibles, however, priests in the more distant past understood how to read a spiritual scorecard. It was clear to them that there are spiritual winners and losers by the end of the contest we call life. Without that kind of supernatural sense of an eternal destiny at stake in each life, no fight for souls is seen in priests. The consequence is evident in the preoccupations of the priest in exercising his public role. Preaching the traditional truths of Catholic morality, for instance, disappears. The willingness to be a fool for Christ and speak Catholic moral truths that may cause discomfort and resentment is not a negotiable matter in the job description of a faithful priest; today, of course, it may pay rather meagerly in spiritual currency. The priestly image of amiable inoffensiveness, by contrast, the preference to salute truth only from a distance and avoid Catholic issues of contention, reflects the loss of a fatherly spirit in the priesthood. It is an urgent time to see the scale swing back again and a new breed of priests emerge, which in fact has been happening in isolated spurts over the last forty years. But this resurgence needs a violent jolt at this critical hour in the Church. Men in history have always been ready to fight for a worthy cause, to the point of giving up their lives. The cause of Christ crucified at Calvary for the salvation of souls is the ultimate worthy cause. What has always been true is true now: Those willing to die heroically in some form or another for Jesus Christ crucified are invited to step forward without delay. They are really the only suitable candidates for the priesthood. For love of the Church in the current day and in the decades to come, we might pray for that intention daily.

4

METAPHYSICAL REBELLION AND THE RUPTURE OF MORALITY

When the Devil says in the third chapter of Genesis: "your eyes would be open and you would become like God", these words express the full range of temptation of mankind, from the intention to set man against God to the extreme form it takes today. . . . But the time has now come: this aspect of the Devil's temptation has found the historical context that suits it.[1]

—Karol Wojtyła

It is much easier to imagine ourselves in the place of God the Creator than in the place of Christ crucified.[2]

—Simone Weil

Christ also died for "barbarians", but he did not become man as a barbarian, nor did he live among them, or choose his disciples among them.[3]

—Theodor Haecker

Few people today realize the spiritual conflict taking place between a deeper contemplative desire for God and a nihilistic

---

[1] Karol Wojtyła, *Sign of Contradiction* (New York: Seabury Press, 1979), 34.

[2] Simone Weil, *Gravity and Grace*, trans. Arthur Wills (New York: G. P. Putnam's Sons, 1952), 142.

[3] Theodor Haecker, quoted in Tracey Rowland, *Beyond Kant and Nietzsche: The Munich Defense of Christian Humanism* (London: T&T Clark, 2021), 39.

indifference to God. This hidden clash is at the center of an intense struggle between faith and atheism that may be slowly approaching a climactic hour. We might say, in a figurative sense, that the contemplative and the nihilist are fighting an invisible war of influence for the life of souls. This contest does not reflect simply a struggle between religious faith and materialistic secularism. The world seems to be rapidly settling into a stark collision between God and the satanic reality, between those who long deeply for God and those embracing godlessness and idolatry. When the tension of this opposition arrives at a breaking point, perhaps a barrier will collapse, and the battle will shift to more direct confrontations. Until that time, the clash between these two essential spiritual tendencies at the core of the human spirit is bound to escalate as the decades continue. It will be almost as though two spiritual chemicals are joined incompatibly in a single vial waiting to explode. Despite what may seem disinterest in spiritual matters, an intensification of spirituality in the soul of humanity is taking place in the conflict between these diametrical opposites, the one side turning to light, the other plunging into darkness. Contemplative or nihilist aspirations, as it were, not only divide souls into two camps that exist apart, separated; the spiritual differences are colliding head-on in the realm of the invisible realities. The division can be observed, for instance, in a striking phenomenon of our time: the attraction for serious prayer drawing a sizable portion of young people of faith today and, on the other hand, the spread of very dark pursuits of demonic interest and the search for preternatural powers growing among young people as never before.

∼

I remember a French theologian in my seminary days, a visiting scholar for a semester, who spoke very keenly about a mode of interpretation by which we might discern with spiritual insight the current day as we pass through the years of history. The basic premise was simple: both goodness and evil intensify as history progresses in time. The current state of evil and corruption in the world is always greater than in any prior period in history. Evil gets worse, corruption deepens, even as societies may seem to assume greater calm and less violence for a time. The history of wars, for instance, because of technological advancements in munitions, is a history of more destructive and vicious acts over time, leading eventually to the development and use of atomic weapons. Conversely, the presence of goodness in holy souls carves more deeply into history as the years progress, even in the most hidden ways. The great saints of a later era will outshine those of an earlier time, if not publicly, then in God's concealed gaze. This is not verified in biographies so much as a reality seen by God. Holiness builds on holiness; saints become greater from the influence of previous saints in history. Naturally there are extraordinary figures like a Saint Francis of Assisi, unique and unmatched. But the intensity of self-giving increases over time in those fully given to God. An interpretive tool results from this premise: The truth of history conceals a hidden war between the power of goodness and the forces of evil; indeed, a progressive tension between good and evil is leading over time to some final climax. This understanding would raise a question for our own time. It might suggest that the violent malice so extreme and horrific in the last century, so visible and documented, has perhaps remained present in the soul of societies, slowly metastasizing as a concealed cancer, so to speak, inside the hidden regions of the human soul. The cold destructiveness evident in the twentieth century may now reside more closely to the core of the human soul. It lies somewhat dormant there, but also quite active, ready to manifest itself once again in the future. At the same time, the presence of holiness also continues to flourish within concealed depths of the human soul, lived out in the commitments of holy, prayerful souls. The grave question of the present hour is perhaps whether a spiritual battle awaits us in the coming decades that will bring this tension of opposites in history to a conclusive denouement. Are we perhaps getting closer to this day?

～

The idea of a metaphysical mutation of values occurring at rare junctures in history, as proposed, for instance, by the French writer Michel Houellebecq in *The Elementary Particles*, may be more than a poetic conceit. The idea that a radical alteration in the values embraced by a society can go hand in hand with a violent shift in the religious perspective of a generation is quite plausible. A profound change in the understanding of God can indeed be a catalyst to a radical transformation in values. But the opposite form of influence also happens: when ethical values alter radically, the perception of God is affected. As an example of the former, the advent of Christianity with the central belief that God took our flesh in Jesus Christ introduced into the pagan world of the Roman Empire a powerful impetus to self-sacrifice, martyrdom, humility, and saintly dedication to others. A different type of radical transformation happened in the Renaissance with the development of scientific method and a desire to untap the secrets of nature. The assumption of God operating mysteriously as Creator and sustaining his creation gave way gradually to an immense drive to unveil the secrets of nature. Religious faith was bruised in the aftermath. The dispensability of God as a need for our souls was first experienced. We are now living in a much later stage of this removal of a need for God from society and culture. In fact, the question of the day is how rapidly the loss of God will accelerate in this century.

~

The current era in history over the last hundred years seems to have undergone its own metaphysical mutation. The progressive abandonment of God and religion has combined with the loss of traditional moral values. In turn, the disintegration of moral values has facilitated the subtle infiltration of a nihilist spirit into the soul of modern society. The essence of nihilism is the absence of spiritual meaning. But what lies behind this loss of meaning? The removal of God from human lives, the sense of his absence, leads inexorably to an emptiness of soul and a sense of inner vacuum. The desperate measures to deny this experience of inner emptiness and boredom and replace God with alternative objects of adulation define the spiritual character of our day. Whether by self-worship in egoistic aspiration or by adoration of public entertainment figures or simply by the descent into the mindless distraction of sensual satisfaction, the great underlying effort of the soul without God is to suffocate any possible encounter with God. Religious believers who do still pray need to face the true condition of the time. The obsessive egoism and technological distractions of our time—with their absence often of intrinsic value or meaning as human activity—are symptoms of the era's godlessness. The response of the prayerful, believing soul must be to choose a life of contradiction to societal trends. For a prayerful soul who believes, reality awakens sharply in kneeling before a tabernacle with the immediate presence of Jesus Christ crucified not far from one's blind eyes.

～

A type of metaphysical rupture in society, a loss of reality, is naturally inevitable if faith dies and the thought of God disappears among people in a massive way. Belief in God affects our understanding of what it means to exist humanly in a singular way. Without God, with no reference to him as the Creator, we can easily become arrogant and foolish in a manner that touches metaphysical truth, and this can happen on a vast societal scale. The Vatican Council II was prescient in this regard: "When God is forgotten . . . , the creature itself grows unintelligible" (*Gaudium et Spes*, 36). Indeed, without God, the tendency to burrow inside the psyche and create our own reality becomes a great temptation. What is real and self-evident is denied; increasingly, people become submerged in the dark waters of pure subjectivism. The result can be a metaphysical crisis of sorts, prophetically expressed in these other words: "From now on," wrote Pope Benedict XVI, addressing the Roman Curia on December 21, 2012, "there is only the abstract human being, who chooses for himself what his nature is to be."[4] Then, at some point, when the denial and rejection of nature crosses a line of general acceptance, it is as though a

---

[4] Pope Benedict XVI, "Address of His Holiness Benedict XVI on the Occasion of Christmas Greetings to the Roman Curia," www.vatican.va/content/benedict-xvi/en/speeches/2012/december/documents/hf_ben-xvi_spe_20121221_auguri-curia.html.

tear in the metaphysical fabric of reality takes place. Reality becomes at that point an unstable notion, subject to manipulation and willfulness. In some issues of the current day, such as gender identity choice as an autonomous preference, it seems as though this line has been definitively crossed and even that a societal psychosis is at work. It cannot be that an appropriation of godlike independence from God the Creator can continue for long without some hard confrontation with truth.

~

If respect for traditional morality splinters with the disappearance of God from the thoughts of men, it is equally true that belief in God collapses with the rejection of traditional moral constraints. Moral systems that in effect require the absence of a final judgment before God urge the expulsion of God from the exercise of conscience. Our own time is indicted on both counts. The permissiveness in Western societies toward abortion, homosexuality, promiscuity, pornography, drug use, and self-centered greed cannot be separated from an underlying spirit of godlessness. The legal sanction of murderous actions against the innocent, in particular the killing of the child in the womb, demands that any thought of God be silenced. A criminal logic operates that parallels the murderer's calculation to leave no witnesses behind. In our time, killing the innocent is never enough. The action of murdering the innocent child in the womb calls necessarily for killing God as well, as a witness who might testify later against our actions and judge us condemned.

~

"The two most opposite ideas in the world are coming into collision, . . . the Man-God has met the god-man" (Fyodor Dostoevsky).[5] It is as though an underground metaphysical explosion had been ignited with the societal rejection of God, leaving in its wake fractures in the foundation of reality. The metaphysical breakdown of the present day seems to have melted down an ability of human persons to perceive truth. The capacity to see with clarity what confronts our eyes has collapsed in a large portion of the general population. Interpretations of reality rooted in unreality have replaced a simple encounter with what is real and unchangeable. Distorted perception has become a common prism of everyday vision, dependent as it often is on technological devices. This inability to engage and face what is given as real in our common experience—often with refusal and willful rebellion—is accepted as a type of new normality in society. The incapacity to confront what is real is a loss of a natural human capacity; the repercussions remain to be seen. The metaphysical darkness and confusion that result do not recreate reality; rather, a dark fiction ensues and begins to rule in displays of societal delusion. Reality has not changed, only human perception on a vast scale. This inward turn to a private world as a measure of reality has fostered a chaotic inclination to unreality in the general population. One can only wonder whether God stares with a divine dismay of sorts at what his children have done with the inheritance that he bestowed on them in their humanity.

∼

The electrified world of technology has played a significant part in this loss of God and a sense of truth. The excessive

---

[5] Henri de Lubac, *The Drama of Atheist Humanism*, trans. Edith M. Riley and Anne Englund Nash (San Francisco: Ignatius Press, 1995), 319.

reliance on technological gadgetry to occupy attention damages the capacity for quiet reflection. Introspective searching for spiritual truth is a harder work; it cannot compete with the information available to the touch of a finger on internet devices. The discipline of taking in hand a book and reading it cover to cover has become rare in many lives. The compulsive habit of perusing a screen for scattered items of unconnected interest may be an effort to relieve empty boredom. But it is also a shallow use of intelligence. Few people ever pause long enough for a silence at the depth of the soul to make itself known. Without that internal silence, we banish God into an unworldly state of unreality. His sacred name is no longer recognized. For many people, the chase after perpetual distraction has replaced familiarity with God and the search for his invisible reality. In our own day, it seems almost that God cannot be found except with a serious effort of separation from the common habits of our own time. The inability of many people to desire God can be compared to the forgetfulness that people experience in large cities who never look up to the sky at night because in a city there are no stars to be seen. They are blocked from view; the sky at night is a blank shadow of empty darkness. The stars in their vast spaces have disappeared as if they do not exist.

～

"We are destroying our ancient edifices to make ready the ground upon which the barbarian nomads of the future will encamp in their mechanized caravans" (T. S. Eliot).[6] Again, prophetic words can be heard here in a telling image for our own century. The great question of religious import today concerns not just the existence of God, which is treated with

[6] T. S. Eliot, *Christianity and Culture* (San Diego, New York and London: Harcourt, 1948), 185.

general indifference in wide sectors of Western society, but whether humanity can survive without religious principles. If God is a dying reality, what follows? Without God, no sacred understanding of the human person can persist. Idolatry by default will replace the absence of God in forms suitable to a technological age. Recall a not so distant past: technological inventiveness in the manufacture of gas chambers and crematoriums, despite their repulsiveness, sprang up when religious loyalties were transferred to the Nazi state and its Fuhrer. The creative aberrations of a new age—perhaps through biological means, perhaps through technological advancement, or a combination thereof—will be less overt, more secretive, in concealing their elimination of God. We hear these days that startling developments in the advancement in humanity are about to emerge. Technologies combining gene and computer chip manipulation will elevate humanity to a new species, making obsolete a former humanity. These proposals of modern day science, as in the Nazi period, depend on the death of God as the Creator. The whisper of the satanic voice can be distinctly heard in such talk. Most of humanity will not realize what is happening and will likely acquiesce once again in history without protest to the superior intelligence and authority of the scientists. The future decades may display instead a shocking acceptance of these supposed advances. The truth of God will be denied, and the consequence will be new forms of godless inventiveness in science and technology.

∼

The proliferation of falsehood is a significant mark of our time. But what does this daily exposure to lies and falsehood mean for a society? It would clearly seem to indicate the triumph of the satanic spirit to some unprecedented degree. The father of lies may be ascendent in our time unlike any other time in history primarily because of the universal appeal of technology in the modern age. The availability of technological distraction and media entertainment has been accompanied by a real infiltration, no doubt, of demonic entities into this modern source of obsessive interest. Technology in its many facets and possibilities has proved to be, from the satanic perspective of malice, a wonderful medium for the destruction of the minds, hearts, and souls of countless people. One of the subtler demonic efforts in the manipulation of technology is to disparage and deny reality and make unreality an attractive alternative. The desire of the demonic that we drift away from the real and entertain fantasy is strong. Pornography is a telling example. The essential seduction taking place in the vast pornographic use today rests on the necessary embrace of a lie. The demonic signature is not simply written here in the temptation to a sin against purity, but in a desire to enslave souls in the lie of sordid images whose only reality is on a screen. Satan is aware of what he is ultimately seeking, which may not be simply sexual perversities. The betrayal of reality in deceptions of this sort cannot occur without a preparation also taking place that may lead a soul eventually to deny the reality of God. The more that the perverse imagining of unrealities on a screen becomes the craving of a soul, the more likely a soul is unable to turn to the invisible spirit of a personal God. The dependency on a screen for reality is a direct threat to a deep sense that the invisible God of love gazes on one's life.

～

The loss of God in private lives naturally spills over into a contempt for God manifested in public ways. Without God, no traditional morality survives for long, as Dostoevsky observed in the nineteenth century, prophesying the amoral soullessness of Russian Communism. The reverse is also true. The breakdown of moral sensitivity, the inability to distinguish right from wrong, good from evil, truth from falsehood, testifies in our day to the radical absence of God in society. With the disappearance of God, it is not surprising that morality should descend into a state of darkness. But one sign of this moral darkness should be noted above all. The rabid obsession to protect a legal right to kill the innocent child in the mother's womb bears witness to a societal godlessness beyond all other signs. This link between killing children and societal godlessness is largely unacknowledged, nor is it recognized how perverse is the embrace of the metaphysical lie and falsehood in this horror. The denial of a human life from conception is a refusal of reality. The prevalence of abortion in a society, treated as unobjectionable by a majority of the population rather than a repugnant evil, is a satanic metaphysical triumph quietly suffocating God within souls in our day. This alignment of souls with the grave societal evil of abortion reasserts itself in every cycle of political elections in the West, and yet few recognize the consequence. The defense of abortion cannot coexist with faith in God, neither in a person nor in the soul of a society. Those who advocate for it, and those who simply tolerate it with some degree of acceptance, place themselves in league with a satanic presence actively at work in this historical period. The indifference to this crime of insult to God as Creator is a serious sign that faith in God has plunged to a dangerous state of lifelessness in our current era.

~

The significance of such aberrations as gender identity choice in our day is not simply the descent into arbitrary interpretations in conflict with reality. There is a more serious and immediate consequence. The true question confronting our time is the virulent effort to kill God as Creator. With the breakdown of metaphysical perception, and the loss of a sense of what is real, the desire has emerged to replace God with a divine power residing in humanity. The human individual has arrogated to itself the role of creator. The idea, for example, that the gender we are born with can be determined by a personal choice and altered by medical interventions is indicative of this kind of metaphysical breakdown. It is truly akin to a societal psychosis caused by the loss of God. Without God, the perception of reality has become subservient to a purely subjective spirit. We have become godlike individuals who can determine what is real rather than creatures who receive what is real from a divine source of power beyond ourselves. This abandonment of metaphysical truth is likely to accelerate in the coming decades. Technological manipulation and a willful spirit of autonomy are becoming the new metaphysical principles of our day. The serious question is whether in fact we are hearing a dramatic replay of the serpent repeating his seductive invitation to Adam and Eve again at this late hour of humanity— "your eyes will be opened, and you will be like God" (Gen 3:5). And indeed, on a massive scale in Western society, we are witnessing a claim to a godlike power to create in rivalry with God himself as the Creator. This is an intense demonic temptation in our time. No other time in history has presumed on such a grand scale to dismiss God and arrogantly supplant his exclusive prerogative as our divine Creator.

~

The raw pursuit of sensual pleasure sought today by large segments of the younger generation, with an unprecedented ease and accessibility, is another symptom of metaphysical breakdown and loss of reality. Pleasures of the flesh once identified as perversions are treated today as private matters of personal taste. Young people are soaking up a new understanding of sexuality, with its own codes of conduct. Nothing that is permitted by law can be thought objectionable; only what the civil law punishes provokes any possibility of caution or hesitation. Even then, whatever poses little danger of legal repercussions can be safely ignored. The sexual violation of innocent children spreads as child trafficking increases and pornographic internet sites acquire sophisticated ruses of concealment. More generally, the use of pornography among young people is poisoning the natural impulses of sexuality, in many cases erasing the desirability of an emotional component from sexual activity. Romantic pursuit is no longer a preliminary step to sexual enjoyment. Love and sexual pleasure are viewed as distinct experiences, not at all required in tandem. It is perhaps striking that what is taking place in the relations of men and women is beginning to parallel the understanding of sexual pleasure among homosexual men. Not emotional involvement, but bodily pleasure as an exclusive pursuit largely feeds the phenomenon of homosexual promiscuity. Sexual pleasure sought as an indulged satisfaction for its own sake may become likewise a common heterosexual option in the exercise of personal sexuality. Commitment will fade as an element typically connected to sexual life. This catching up, so to speak, of heterosexual life to the patterns of promiscuous homosexual life will be a kind of metaphysical sign of the times. Degenerate vice of all varieties will be pursued, requiring only the prudence to protect oneself from prosecution and from the transmission of disease. This societal acceptance of sexual depravity will contribute to a sense of the normality of sexual gratification as necessary for human happiness. Nothing will be denied to satisfy the human demand for pleasure. The twisting of pleasure into contortions of perverse fantasy will be another sign of living in a time of metaphysical breakdown and rupture. Fantasy will replace reality in this most sacred realm of sexuality.

~

An increasingly godless society will naturally distort the public perception of morality. Without God, no principle beyond pragmatism may be left to determine what is morally acceptable or forbidden. The notion of morality may disappear in more radical ways in areas like health care, replaced by criteria of efficiency and financial cost and the relief of human pain. The value of human life will be threatened anew in the absence of moral standards. One sign of this "advancement" seems possible before too long. It may require just a few more years for society to claim a right to protect itself against undue burdens inflicted by an aging population of greater numbers. Strangely, without much protest, unlike the heated battles over abortion, euthanasia may soon acquire a status of respectability and become a common practice. In a godless era, it will seem perfectly sensible to terminate lives that drain resources and draw repugnance from those burdened with their care. A perverse understanding of compassion toward the old and gravely handicapped will overtake society, aided by legal interventions and mandates that leave no option but to fall in line. Within a few years, it is possible that euthanasia will be widely and comfortably practiced. Decisions to euthanize in individual cases will be largely determined by those who remain alive. Perhaps a new industry will flourish as euthanasia centers partner with funeral parlors. Dressed up in the finery of wood-paneled walls, lush couches, and tranquilizing music, these euthanasia centers with their private rooms will advertise themselves as "mercy hospices" offering a peaceful passage through the gentle veil of the final surrender. The drug-induced elimination of every dreadful aspect of death will seem a development that took too long to discover. Perhaps few but the seriously religious will find the practice of euthanasia repelling or even questionable. Adjustments to the societal transformation will take place in the familiar spirit of societal conformism. The news of being designated for death will be received by the sickly who remain still alert in the manner that people do when facing medical treatments in the case of serious sickness—with initial anxiety but in due time with resigned submission. In a godless world, sinister realities can quickly become social requirements drawing acquiescence from their victims. These realities may provoke some initial resistance, but in a godless world it may not take long at all before they acquire acceptance from the general population.

∼

The period in history prior to the emergence of the Antichrist, the lawless one, may indeed witness an unparalleled ascendancy of moral lawlessness in the world. Jesus refers to this in Matthew: "And many false prophets will arise and lead many astray. And because wickedness is multiplied, most men's love will grow cold" (Mt 24:11–12). What that wickedness may mean in part is a perverse contradiction of moral laws fixed and irreversible in nature, engraved by the Creator's hand into creation and metaphysically grounded, such as the distinct identity of a man and a woman. The spirit of lawlessness will permeate a perverse conception of sexuality; it will undermine the family; it will continue to defend the right to kill the unborn and the aged and invalid. The era that prepares for the Antichrist will likely witness a breakdown of morality never seen to this extent in history. It will be a time of metaphysical despair and nihilism in which truth will be a fragile concept and self-absorbed pursuit will drive human lives. Indeed, we should watch carefully. It is certainly plausible that the figure of the Antichrist may achieve a subtle metaphysical triumph in raising minds to a more "transcendent" understanding of morality, which will be in effect a law of morality with no reference to God, with no foundation in metaphysical reality. Morality, the sense of right and wrong, will shed its reliance on prohibitions commanded by God. No longer will morality be identified with violations of a code of conduct. A single principle above all others will permeate the ethical soul of humanity—what may be called the "transcendent" idea of morality: the non-judgmental acceptance of a sacred right to all private choices. The absolute autonomy of personal choices will be declared inviolable, provided no tangible harm is done to another. This "transcendent" law of morality will transform the criterion of moral judgment. No one will be permitted to interfere with, impede, or object to the choices of another. Indeed, the sole point of a moral judgment will be to examine whether one fails in a spirit of affirmation toward others in their private choices. Parenting will naturally have to undergo a radical alteration of method in order to inculcate children in the new, necessary understanding.

5

THE DUAL DECEPTION
IN A LAST ERA

We are now standing in the face of the greatest historical confrontation humanity has ever experienced. I do not think that the wide circle of the American society, or the whole wide circle of the Christian Community realizes this fully. We are now facing the final confrontation between the Church and the anti-Church, between the Gospel and the anti-Gospel, between Christ and the Antichrist.[1]

—Karol Cardinal Wojtyła

Of all the many and serious faults of the Church, . . . the most serious would be that of passively accepting its own liquidation by a power that laughs at the Gospel.[2]

—Pier Paolo Pasolini

Indeed, the present age is the age of Judas. . . . To be sure, it is not literally with a kiss that Christ is betrayed in the present age: today one betrays with an interpretation.[3]

—Walter Kaufmann

[1] Karol Cardinal Wojtyła to the American Bishops in August, 1976, quoted in Robert Cardinal Sarah, *The Day Is Now Far Spent*, trans. Michael J. Miller (San Francisco: Ignatius Press, 2019), 136.

[2] Pier Paolo Pasolini, quoted in Antonio Socci, *The Secret of Benedict XVI: Is He Still the Pope?* trans. Giuseppe Pellegrino (Brooklyn: Angelico Press, 2019), 12–13.

[3] Walter Kaufmann, Introduction, in Søren Kierkegaard, *The Present Age: On the Death of Rebellion*, trans. Alexander Dru (New York: Harper & Row, 1962), xiii.

A great firestorm rages at the center of the satanic angelic being. The firestorm is his consuming desire to be godlike apart
from God himself. This relentless satanic obsession to replace God and assume the exclusive role of a sovereign presence in the universe gnaws at the satanic being. He knows,
however darkly, that this ambition is impossible to achieve.
Nonetheless, his endless desire is to showcase his competition with God's presence in the world by raising up perverse caricatures of divine actions. He aspires to exercise
destructive power that will rival God's display of benevolence. The hidden sign of Satan can be observed throughout history in this compulsive need to contradict all that is
true and undermine all that is sacred. His resentment toward
God and the divine attributes that are not in his nature is
a constant spur digging at his heel. Omnipotence is not in
his rights to claim, and yet his immense desire is to possess
unlimited power in himself and to use it in hatred toward
God and in malice toward humanity. What he is driven to
do in lieu of possessing divine omnipotence is to construct
caricatures of divine power in the world. His caricatures are
a form of competition with God, whereby he can draw God
into what he considers a contest of equals. And if not of
equals, which he is forced always to admit is not the case,
it is at least a contest in history in which he alleges that
he has achieved victories more often than not. Look at the
numbers, he insists, the numbers in hell, when reminded of
his final defeat at the end of time.

～

In three short paragraphs, the *Catechism of the Catholic Church*
has clear words of warning about a last era of the Church:
"Before Christ's second coming the Church must pass

through a final trial that will shake the faith of many believers."[4] The nature of this trial is not explicitly developed
in the text. An interpretation of this trial, however, as simply
a persecution of Christianity from hostile forces outside the
Church would not seem sufficient. The description speaks
rather of the unveiling of the "mystery of iniquity,"[5] a term
commonly identified as the satanic presence in history. The
ascendency of evil in that last era will climax in a spiritual
testing for believers. The testing will come about "in the
form of a religious deception offering men an apparent so-
lution to their problems at the price of apostasy from the
truth."[6] Reference to the Antichrist follows, as the one who
poses the "supreme religious deception".[7] This deception
will repeat the temptation first whispered to Eve in the Garden—"You will not die . . . you will be like God, knowing good and evil" (Gen 3:4–5). The great deception of that
time will be to seduce men to an illusion of their glory in
place of God. If such a massive deception of humanity is to
take place—in spirit or by the influence of a single historical
figure at that time—it may involve a separate and distinct
trial within the Church, apart from hostility directed at the
Church from the world. This form of religious deception
may include a final trial for the Church to prove her fidelity
to the truth of God revealing his will in the Church's irreformable teaching throughout the previous centuries. An
internal struggle of grave proportions in doctrinal matters
within the Church would indicate, for instance, that the time
of this great trial is at hand. The satanic deception might
prevail temporarily in leading many Catholics to accept

---

[4] *Catechism of the Catholic Church*, no. 675.
[5] Ibid.
[6] Ibid.
[7] Ibid.

alterations of traditional teaching that cannot change in the Church. If that were to happen, the deception would be the catalyst to an internal spirit of betrayal within the Church and cause a grave trial of suffering for those who remain faithful to the Church in her continuing truth. What is of interest is the possibility, then, of a dual deception in that last era—in the world by the emergence of the Antichrist who becomes a figure of adoration and leads men, as it were, to worship themselves; and, secondly, within the Church herself, a separate deception of grave magnitude, due to some form of partial collapse in doctrinal truths. Most certainly, at the same time, a remnant of faithful Catholics will remain deeply rooted to the unchangeable source of truth in Jesus Christ and will not waver in their commitment to the true heart of the Church.

~

The German Thomist philosopher Josef Pieper (1904–1997), one of the finer minds of the twentieth century, wrote a startling appraisal in 1952 of the Antichrist as a possible personage emerging in contemporary history. This piece of writing, in a concluding section of his book *The End of Time*, is not a digression into uncharacteristic reverie. For Pieper, the emergence of the Antichrist as a world figure is an essential part of what he termed the "catastrophic" conclusion of history—as promised by Scripture. Catastrophe in this sense would not mean the destruction of the world by war or natural disaster. Rather, before the Second Coming of Christ, we must expect a climactic period of spiritual testing that will be pernicious to the Christian faith and will deceive untold multitudes. The Antichrist himself, by his outward bearing, will be a great deceiver, a caricature of Christ:

"This power of deception, tradition therefore sees as being founded primarily in the seeming sanctity of his personal life, over which Antichrist takes great pains."[8] Despite the appearance of his refined spirituality and holiness, he will be an embodiment of evil hiding behind a façade of seductive charm and altruistic goodness. The picture depicted by Pieper depends as well on a worldwide political structure not currently in place, but also not inconceivable in the decades ahead or in a future century. In Pieper's view, the figure of the Antichrist will be the leader of a world government, posing as a savior of humanity, bringing peace and security after a time of unrest, tension, and conflict. The naïveté of the masses across the world will embrace this attractive figure, leading to a cultish idolization of his person as the grand benefactor of humanity and even to the worship of him as a Divine Presence. The satanic desire to rule over the souls of men will be finally realized through this seductive leader who "dominates history at the end of time"[9] at the head of "one single governmental structure equipped with prodigious power."[10] The exercise of this world power will be ruthless in its extension. The consequence in due time will be the imposition of severe anti-Christian regulations and laws by an intolerant absolute power. "A coercive power at the highest level of intensity . . . will confront the Church in her role of *ecclesia martyrum*."[11] The "blood-testimony"[12] of the powerless who resist the satanic power will entail a final persecution, a Church of anonymous martyrs

---

[8] Josef Pieper, *The End of Time: A Meditation on the Philosophy of History*, trans. Michael Bullock (San Francisco: Ignatius Press, 1999), 139.

[9] Ibid., 126.

[10] Ibid., 128.

[11] Ibid., 133.

[12] Ibid., 144.

resembling the unnamed early Christians who suffered the Roman barbarities of the first centuries, before the final coming of Jesus Christ as Lord of history. Pieper considered all this a realistic possibility even in our time.

~

The Russian philosopher Vladimir Solovyov (1853–1900) wrote as well on the Antichrist in a fictional work entitled *A Short Story of Antichrist*. Similar in his description to Pieper, Solovyov portrays the Antichrist as a religious imposter, a man of deep spirituality, of irreproachable morality and sympathy toward all, a conciliator able to overcome religious divisions, a vegetarian and a staunch pacifist, an upholder of ecology, an international benefactor bringing peace to the world after a time of conflict, a man honored by the multitudes. He is a person of extreme self-love, however, who sets himself in rivalry against God. At first, in his rise to prominence, he bears "no hostility against Jesus";[13] he considers Jesus a predecessor, a forerunner to himself as the world's final savior. Christ brought the sword and division; he brings peace and a new salvation to humanity, an equality for all in their needs. Shortly after he has achieved fame, however, he makes his covenant with Satan, who promises him absolute power and his assistance. Immediately he is inspired to write his magnum opus, *The Open Way to Universal Peace and Welfare*. This book, "all-embracing and all-reconciling", displays "an unprecedented power of genius".[14] Uniting in a single text a respect for humanistic tradition, for ancient mysticism, and for radical social inno-

---

[13] Vladimir Solovyov, "A Short Story of Antichrist", *A Solovyov Anthology*, ed. S. L. Frank (London: Saint Austin Press, 2001), 229.

[14] Ibid., 232.

vation, it gains for him a universal acclaim from all classes of people. The book draws an objection from a small sector of critics because of the absence of Christ on any page, but this lacuna is quickly dismissed by the appeal of religious inclusivity upheld so beautifully in a book "permeated by the truly Christian spirit of active love and all-embracing benevolence".[15] The takeover by this man of a united European single government leads to the world falling under the spell of his personality. The universal peace he brings and seems to embody in person, his great aspiration to eliminate poverty and the suffering of the poor, come to a climax in the worship of him as a divine figure. Much like a return to the Roman emperors of the past, he is honored as a god, and most of the world bows in obeisance to him. The Solovyov account, although a piece of fiction, has perhaps a remarkable prescience. The figure of the Antichrist may well emerge one day in the distant or not so distant future in just this kind of manner—a man of radiant charm and attraction, a genius who captivates all, a figure who will attain world acclaim in a godless world and be treated in effect as a god in the flesh.

～

Other than Jesus' own words in the Gospel, the most significant reference to a last era in the Church, and perhaps the most enigmatic, is a short passage of Saint Paul in the second chapter of his Second Letter to the Thessalonians. In an effort to calm anxiety about false reports causing alarm "to the effect that the day of the Lord has come" (2 Thess 2:2), Paul identifies two preliminary conditions that had not yet been met in his time. The day of the Lord, the return of

[15] Ibid., 233.

Christ, will not happen, "unless the rebellion comes first, and the man of lawlessness is revealed, the son of perdition" (2 Thess 2:3). The two conditions would seem certainly linked, the one preparing the way for the other. But what is meant by the "rebellion"? Can it refer to a spirit of internal dissension and discord within the Church in that period of a last era that will place the faith of true believers under intense trial? The word rebellion is significant. A rebellion arises from within; it would not mean a persecution of the Church from outside the Church by an irreligious, hostile society. It must signify a spirit of revolt within the Church herself. In other words, a period of rebellion unlike any other in history, incomparable to any previous period of theological turmoil that led to splintering or schism, may take place within the Church. The possibility of such a rebellion would be that the Church, in an institutional manner, might begin to contradict inviolable elements of her tradition and her identity as the sacramental presence of Christ in the world. The unstated implication is that the Church would begin to exercise decisions offensive to the intentions of her divine Bridegroom and Founder.

∽

The passage seems to suggest, not simply the widespread loss of faithful practice in the Church during a historical era, but a condition of grave unfaithfulness within a portion of leadership within the Church. A rebellion against true teaching and the irreformable tradition of the Church seems to be the implication. Such a time would not compare to the Protestant Reformation, led by figures like Martin Luther, who rose up from within the Church and sought heretical reform, but, opposed by the rock-like bulwark of the Catholic edifice of truth defended by the popes and the Magisterium, split permanently from the Church. In this case, in a last era of the Church, the rebellion may be unprecedented inasmuch as it remains internal, not leading to any formal separation or schism. It is a rebellion of unknown proportions, not a permanent triumph, surely, but perhaps a take-over of sorts that is temporary, a grave test to the hearts of true Catholic believers. In short, the "rebellion" that must first occur raises the specter of some form of apostasy within portions of the Church, perhaps a partial collapse of doctrinal life within the Church that is granted a façade of legitimacy by certain sections of the Church's teaching office. If a rebellion of this nature were to happen in future decades within the Church, affecting portions of her hierarchy, even at high levels, it does not signify that the Church herself as the Body of Christ, united to Christ, thereby ceases. Naturally not, since the promise of Christ to remain forever with his Church holds intact. The reality of the Church would prevail in the invisible presence of the Body of Christ still much alive in the Catholic faithful. At the same time, the Church in her true reality would descend to a condition of self-abasement and humiliation, much like our divine Lord in his Passion. The presence of the Passion of Christ would hide in the fervent lives of those believers, clerical and lay, who persevere in faith and love for Christ and remain intensely committed to the unchangeable truths of the Catholic faith.

∼

The second condition that follows the "rebellion", Saint Paul asserts, is that "the man of lawlessness is revealed" (2 Thess 2:3). This expression is a more than likely reference to the emergence of the figure of the Antichrist. The question remains whether this will be a flesh-and-blood human person, or whether it refers to a pervasive spirit of opposition to Jesus Christ as Son of God and Head of the Church. The passage in Thessalonians is strongly worded and suggests more than a metaphor: "[He] opposes and exalts himself against every so-called god or object of worship, so that he takes his seat in the temple of God, proclaiming himself to be God" (2 Thess 2:4). In other words, there is the possibility of a real figure in history who seduces humanity in some extraordinary manner and at his apex of influence usurps the place of God as the object of divine worship. He comes at the end of history, in a last era of the Church, to bring to a climax a perverse historical tendency in our fallen human nature to bow in adoration before idols of our own making. How this takes place in concrete terms is naturally unknown. The image of the Antichrist taking his seat in the temple of God may be only suggestive and symbolic: he will be an idol to the masses of humanity, a quasi-godlike figure who draws fawning worship of a sort. One must hope against hope that the most horrible scenario is out of the question: namely, that if some form of apostasy does occur within a portion of the Church, penetrating as well the inner sanctum of the hierarchy, the seat taken in the temple of God is the throne of Saint Peter. This possibility would seem too outrageous to consider as a future event. On that seat, metaphorically or otherwise, the text continues, this figure of lawlessness will declare himself to be God. Variations in the meaning of these words are naturally also possible. Perhaps the "man of lawlessness" will declare himself as the one who now exclusively proclaims the word of God; in other words, in a demonic imitation of Jesus' oneness with his Father, he will declare himself as the man sent to speak God's word. Or perhaps, in a variation of sorts, he will make a pantheistic claim of his own oneness with the Divine Presence unfolding in a process of historical evolution and finally arriving at its ultimate incarnation in himself. In any case, it is certain at some point in his rise to power that he will lay claim explicitly to a presence of divinity in his person. The demonic need to rival and caricature God will be on display in a supreme form.

~

The passage of Saint Paul, as it progresses, comments that the mystery of lawlessness "already at work" in this world continues under constraint, held back, as it were, presumably throughout history, until the time when the one who now restrains it is removed: "For the mystery of lawlessness is already at work; only he who now restrains it will do so until he is out of the way" (2 Thess 2:7). What does this mean? It is perhaps a significant image, since the "removal" of what is restraining the mystery of lawlessness takes place by some expulsion of the one who exercises this role of restraint. When that someone, or that principle of restraint, is no longer present, when the one who restrains it is removed, the conditions are ready to unleash the figure of lawlessness. "And then the lawless one will be revealed" (2 Thess 2:8). It is the pattern of history that the law of divine revelation, the truth of God, is at war with a mystery of lawlessness provoked by satanic forces. The Church in history fights this war of the centuries against the powers and principalities of darkness for the sake of truth, with the papal office at the vanguard of this battle under the protection of the Holy Spirit. But once the one who restrains the mystery of lawlessness is removed, which can be the pope himself, then the lawless one, the Antichrist, will be revealed. Perhaps the passage suggests once again that, indeed, apostasy to some degree in the Church is possible. The Antichrist rises in prominence in a role of deceit as the Church loses her proper legitimacy as declaimer of truth. Indeed, the lawless one, as we have heard already, "takes his seat in the temple of God, proclaiming himself to be God" (2 Thess 2:4), which would be an ultimate humiliation to the Church beyond any measure.

~

The presence of the lawless one, the Antichrist, seated in the temple of God, is likely not the "desolating sacrilege" (Mt 24:15) that Jesus mentions in the Gospels of Matthew and Mark with an explicit reference to the prophet Daniel. The desolating sacrilege "standing in the holy place" (Mt 24:15) or "set up where it ought not to be" (Mk 13:14) suggests some egregious type of idol, some grave violation of the sacred place, some form of blasphemous worship in the holy place. The mystery of lawlessness, in other words, enters inside the sacred confines of Catholic life. This could be an action in Saint Peter's Basilica, the church of the Roman Pontiff, but the desolating sacrilege could also be some form of egregious violation directed to the mystery of the Holy Eucharist and the Mass. The ordination of a woman, the "marriage" of two men, the concelebration of a Mass at Saint Peter's joined by Protestant clergymen and clergywomen: many desolating sacrileges are possible to envision, including grave violations of a formal nature to the sacredness of the Holy Sacrifice of the Mass. All this is preliminary, however, to the revelation in public of the lawless one. The mystery of lawlessness, according to Saint Paul, is bound to invade the Church herself in the period prior to the removal of the one who restrains the lawless one.

～

How striking for the present day, in the light of Saint Paul's words to the Thessalonians, is the interpretation of the last era in the Church by Tyconius, a contemporary of Saint Augustine and an influence upon his work *The City of God*, and about whom Joseph Ratzinger wrote an article as a young theologian in 1956.[16] The key ecclesial premise for Tyconius is the existence of a bipartite Church in history, a Church that throughout history will have an element of betrayal co-existing with an element of genuine holiness. This tension of darkness and light within the Church, of betrayal and beauty, will climax in the last era, he writes, with a final confrontation between these two elements. Tyconius turns to the same Second Letter of Saint Paul to the Thessalonians for his central insight. As mentioned already, Saint Paul writes that the coming of the Lord at the end of time cannot take place until the rebellion first occurs and the lawless one is revealed. The mystery of lawlessness that then gains ascendency and power, as it were, may possibly entail a corrupting breakdown within the Church as the element of darkness takes dominant control within the so-called bipartite Church. Saint Paul proclaims further, as we have heard, that the mystery of lawlessness will become manifest only after the one who restrains it is removed. The interpretation of Tyconius is that in the last era the true Church of light will in some mysterious manner withdraw in spirit from the false Church of darkness, perhaps provoked by

[16] See Giorgio Agamben, *The Mystery of Evil: Benedict XVI and the End of Days*, trans. Adam Kotsko (Stanford, Calif.: Stanford University Press, 2017).

aberrations in the public teaching of the Church. This separation in spirit from a state of coexistence in the Church
with the darker element within the Church will become the
catalyst to the temporary triumph of a spirit of lawlessness
within the Church. Possibly a rebellion against traditional
beliefs—perhaps an undermining of moral doctrines—will
become enshrined to some degree in the public teaching of
the Church. This can only happen because the true Church
has been silenced, or has separated herself in some spiritual manner, perhaps due to overt provocation, and so is no
longer able to restrain the hand of rebellion as she formerly
did, thereby allowing the contradiction of doctrine to occur in some public fashion. The idea of a separation in spirit
does not mean a schismatic action; in fact, it cannot signify
that, but rather a condition of marginalized ineffectiveness, a
defeat of sorts institutionally, due to a refusal to accept aberrant manifestations with the institutional Church. It is possible to remain in the Church while rejecting false teaching
within the Church. The Church does not disappear in this
case; she does not face ruin or collapse. What does happen
is a deceptive appearance within the Church, as though the
institutional Church in her official teaching has altered her
former teaching. The true Church, on the other hand, will
remain in a persecuted condition of concealment within the
institutional Church. She lives within the faithful followers
of Christ. But this true Church of the faithful suffers her
own passion in the days so described. Naturally we cannot
know what this suffering will entail until the events fully
manifest themselves.

~

Interestingly, Saint Paul uses the same term for the lawless one—the "son of destruction" in Greek—that Jesus used at the Last Supper in referring to Judas. "I have guarded them, and none of them is lost but the son of perdition" (Jn 17:12; i.e., the son of destruction). The unusual coincidence of this term is striking. Saint John likely did not write his Gospel until a number of years after Saint Paul's letter. The dual reference to Judas, the one who would betray Christ, and to the lawless one, a figure who will betray the Church in the last era, by means of the identical Greek expression may be a hint of the betrayal that will take place in the Church in a last era. Just as Christ is violated by the treachery of Judas, the Church may find herself undergoing an internal betrayal of her truth. There is nothing that prevents the Church from betraying her master if we mean that certain elements in the Church will act in those days in the role of Judas. The authentic Church will remain inviolate, but she will be a persecuted Church, somehow cut off from union with the semblance of the Church that is exercising a false authority in contradiction to Catholic tradition.

～

In a last era of the Church, it is possible that words of Jesus that have mystified us and resisted comprehension may suddenly expose their meaning and take on a striking significance. The history of that time will make this comprehension possible. An example might be the words of Jesus, in a reference to the end of time, when he asserts that on the last day "one will be taken and the other left" (Lk 17:34). They ask "where, Lord?" (Lk 17:37). But this question raises a further conundrum. Are they asking, "taken where?", or are they asking "left behind where"? Jesus seems to ignore the question; rather, he leaves the question aside and responds cryptically—"Where the body [or corpse] is, there the eagles [or vultures] will be gathered together" (Lk 17:37). In fact, we may perceive at some point at a future date that he is providing in these words a quite direct reply of grave significance. Several times in the Gospel, Jesus answers in words that seem to have no connection to the question or request or comment he has just received. His mind is focused on a different point of concentration, and not on the question. Perhaps in this case as well, his thought stretches beyond the question "where?" and is turned toward the dangers of that future time. If so, the phrase is very striking. For it may indicate a truth about the Church in the last era before the coming of Jesus. The Church, which is the Body of Christ in history, may be refined by fire in that last era until she becomes by purification a smaller remnant of intensely dedicated believers. Simultaneously, while the Body of Christ will be truly present in this remnant, and in the hidden saints of that time, what is identified by the world as the Church will still exercise an institutional presence in the world. The institutional Church, seeking to retain prestige and importance in the eyes of the world, will perhaps be uprooted from her true mission and even cut off from grace, like a soul in mortal sin. Instead, the true Body of Christ, which is the spiritual reality of the Church, will hide in the remnant of dedicated and faithful believers. Another body which will call itself the church, but which metaphorically is a corpse now rotting and dead, will lay claim to the name of the Church and show itself to the world. The corpse will draw the vultures—that is, those who do not really believe and who seek to refashion the

Church and her teaching in a new image. They will feed off the dead flesh of a defunct portion of the Church that no longer represents the real Body of Christ in the world. The true Church that can never be destroyed will be living in the remnant of believers who have never left or betrayed the heart of the Church and have never compromised their faith. But these souls may suffer much for their faith. They will suffer precisely by remaining faithful to Catholic tradition and persevering within the Church.

~

"But first he must suffer many things and be rejected by this generation" (Lk 17:25). The words of Jesus, taken at face value, would seem to point to his Passion, but perhaps they refer to a more mysterious suffering and rejection. He had just been asked by a group of Pharisees "when the kingdom of God was coming" (Lk 17:20). The question would seem a request for clarification about this unique phrase—the Kingdom of God—and perhaps whether its arrival would coincide with the imminent revelation of the Messiah. But Jesus, once again, does not answer this question directly. He replies with a turn to the distant horizon of a future event, namely, his coming at the end of time. "For as the lightning flashes and lights up the sky from one side to the other, so will the Son of man be in his day" (Lk 17:24). And then come the words that first he must endure much suffering and be rejected by this generation. This phrase ought to alert us to a mysterious development that takes place in the last period of the Church. Our Lord continues to be one Body, one Flesh, with his Church. He gives himself in the sacrificial offering of the Eucharist daily and makes himself one with the Church. The suffering and rejection of which he speaks may not refer simply to an indifference to his truth as God from an unbelieving world. Rather, it may identify a rejection he will undergo from within his own Church that will be singular and unique to that time. His rejection may be the wound of a betrayal unlike any in previous history. His own Spouse, the Church, or at least significant institutional elements within her, may turn against him to some degree, even as a faithful remnant within the Church remain closely united to his heart. In that case, an internal rebellion carried out within the Church, a rebellion costing much suffering to those faithful to Christ, will be a primary sign of that last era of the Church.

PART TWO

6

DIVINE VULNERABILITY: CONTEMPLATING THE WOUNDS OF GOD

God does not pretend to be what he is not or hide his true nature or masquerade under disguises alien to his being. . . . Jesus' Passion and death are not only the most extreme possible humiliation of God; they are by the same token the most exhaustive possible revelation of the depths of God's nature.[1]

—Erasmo Leiva-Merikakis

God is as he shows himself; God does not show himself in a way in which he is not. On this assertion rests the Christian relation with God.[2]

—Joseph Ratzinger

My people, what have I done to you?
Or how have I grieved you? Answer me! . . .
What more should I have done for you and have
   not done?
Indeed, I planted you as my most beautiful chosen vine
and you have turned very bitter for me,
for in my thirst you gave me vinegar to drink
and with a lance you pierced your Savior's side.[3]

—"Good Friday Reproaches (*Improperia*)"

[1] Erasmo Leiva-Merikakis, *Fire of Mercy, Heart of the Word*, vol. 4 (San Francisco: Ignatius Press, 2021), 491.

[2] Joseph Ratzinger, *Introduction to Christianity*, trans. J. R. Foster (New York: Herder and Herder, 1970), 165.

[3] Roman Missal, 2011.

The centerpiece of history is the event at Calvary, the killing of Jesus of Nazareth by a Roman execution. Christianity proclaims the hour of his death as a line of demarcation dividing all of history into a before and after this event. He is God in the flesh who dies on that Roman Cross, and so we can say properly that our God is murdered on that day. As we also well know, our Lord and God Jesus Christ cannot remain subject to death, but rather he conquers death by his death on the Cross. His Resurrection on Easter Sunday is the beginning of a new history for humanity. What we are invited to see from that day at Calvary, and throughout subsequent history, is the mystery of a vulnerability in God. The Passion of Christ opens our eyes to the choice of God to be wounded for love of his creature. This vulnerability of God to be wounded in love is likely to manifest itself in a stronger manner as the years progress. Spiritually, for those with eyes to see, a recognition of the vulnerability of God to being wounded can become a sacred insight. We love him to the extent that we are wounded in love for him as we gaze upon his wounds in the present day. These wounds are bound to show themselves more transparently in a last era of the Church, which is to say perhaps that God will show us his vulnerability to being wounded within his own Church. We ourselves can embrace a spirituality of vulnerability, as it were, receptive to the wounds of Christ that we may observe he is suffering in the present day. This receptivity to his wounds can become a means of interpreting the current day. The thought of our Lord wounded within his own Church may shine a light otherwise unavailable on events that might disturb or shake us. It is a light that can lead to greater love for God and his mystery, and for persevering in faithfulness to his Church, rather than halting in alarm and dismay.

⌒

The wounds of Jesus have a meaning beyond the lacerations of his body in the crucifixion. The ripping apart of his flesh from the brutal scourging, the nails hammered into his hands and feet, the thorns embedded in his skull, were real events in the historical life of our God as a man. The infliction of pain on his beloved body may be too difficult for a sensitive soul to ponder except intermittently. But perhaps the wound to his human heart, before and after his death, should be kept continually before our attention. Contemplation of the wound to the heart of Jesus may open a hidden path into a knowledge of love that may eventually overwhelm us. Indeed, in pondering the wound to the heart of Jesus, we may begin to see Jesus suffering his Passion once again in the present time. The mystery of our Lord wounded in heart, suffering within his Church, may be hiding secretly within the events of the present day and in the decades to come. The wounded heart of Jesus, if we can enter inside its inner recesses, is suffering still in the world today. The events of our time may be in truth a contemporary piercing of the heart of Jesus. He suffers again contempt and indifference and mockery, all the while turning his eyes openly, as he once did, toward his tormentors. The betrayal of Jesus is in fact an active, ongoing reality in all of history. Let us then realize that what we may be witnessing in our own time are not simply disturbing occurrences in the Church, but, more deeply, a grave piercing of the loving heart of Jesus who may suffer his Passion again in history during the present time and in the decades ahead.

⌒

He offered no resistance; he required no forcible effort from the Roman soldiers to nail him to a cross. He did not pull away as they stretched his hands to the wood. He opened his palms freely to the placement of the rusty nails, and they hammered the nails without a need to hold his body down. Through it all he offered no resistance. It was not a resigned passivity or an incapacity to feel horrific pain that took place. Rather, the mystery of divine vulnerability was showing itself nakedly before human eyes. The One who makes in his Passion a complete gift of himself submits to a suffering that extends infinitely beyond human rejection or agonizing bodily pain. He gives the immensity of himself as God and by giving becomes vulnerable to being treated as nothing, meaningless, his death no different from countless brutal deaths throughout history. He does not resist his executioners as they carry out this death by crucifixion, because an absolute submission in the hour is essential to his divine vulnerability. He must show forth for eyes capable of seeing the truth that God does not resist even grave evil when it is his will to manifest the infinite reality of divine love. All this embracing of divine vulnerability by Jesus is one with his Father's will. The Passion of Christ brought back to our minds will ever remain a secret path into the divine mystery. The Father himself perhaps hovers always near to souls as an invisible presence of vulnerability open to all the vaguely felt sorrows of devout men and women when they glance at the sight of a crucifix on a wall.

~

A continual desire in Jesus to disappear from men's eyes, observable at times in his public life, when he escaped from the crowds to be alone in solitude, was perhaps an inclination flowing from his divine nature. His truth as God in the flesh may have urged him in his public life to hide with regularity and remain apart. These interludes of withdrawal were not simply to step away into quiet for the sake of solitude and prayer. They were likely signs of the longing within him to lean out from his human nature as man toward his own infinite truth as God. Throughout his life, his Divine Presence remained largely concealed except to Mary and Joseph. It was never fully realized even by those closest to him until his Resurrection appearances after his death. The times of withdrawal into solitude were not, then, just a temporary hiding of sorts, but a return to the concealment that was at the core of his existence all along. Even more, these withdrawals may have been a necessary anticipation of the humiliation he would undergo when he would be despised and rejected in his Passion, completely unrecognized as God. The disappearance into hiding for One who was majestic by nature would culminate at the end of his life in the humiliation of his condemnation and death at Calvary. A vulnerability to humiliation was in a sense a necessary condition of our God taking upon himself flesh. Unseen in his truth as God, he allowed abusive contempt to confirm to all appearances that God himself had abandoned him. Yet, in this disappearance, his reality as God in the flesh manifested at last its deepest truth of humility and infinite love. These patterns of disappearance and hiding may show themselves again, but this time in the Church as our Lord relives his Passion in a last epoch.

～

Jesus lived the three years of his public life like a man on death row awaiting execution. He knew all along that he would die a criminal's death on a Roman cross. It is that truth which imparts a distinct urgency to every word spoken by Jesus in his public life. His discourses to large crowds, his private words to favored individuals, all have a deeper meaning when we realize that these words were spoken with his death clearly present in his awareness. His gestures, too, his miracles, were affected by the certainty of the eventual execution. The raising of the son of the widow of Nain is an example of a far-reaching awareness of Jesus in the hour. He was surely aware when he reached out and touched the funeral bier that his mother Mary would be a widow who would soon lose her only son. His compassion on that day for this widowed mother of Nain who followed the funeral procession of her son was undoubtedly pierced by a love for Mary his own mother. Who can know how many other moments of attention in the mind of Christ turned to the pain his mother would undergo in her union with his sufferings in the Passion? Perhaps much of the pain he experienced in anticipation of the Passion had to do with his knowledge of Mary's inner disposition of utter vulnerability in her desire to share with him completely in his sufferings.

～

Saint John the Baptist may have startled himself with the words released from his lips at the Jordan River: "Behold, the Lamb of God, who takes away the sin of the world" (Jn 1:29)! It is easy for us, knowing Jesus as God, to hear these words as a revelation of the Savior who will die on a cross for our sins. With this phrase, however, Saint John the Baptist identified a secrecy that accompanied Jesus throughout his life, including the hidden years at Nazareth. This secrecy of Jesus, his destiny to offer himself as the sacrificial Lamb, while fully present to the awareness of Jesus, was unknown to others. Saint John the Baptist became privy to the secret through a profound grace of prophecy. Jesus may love it when a soul pierces through what is ordinarily concealed in secrecy and sees an aspect of divine truth openly. The truth of his vulnerability in love would be such a secret ordinarily not seen. This piercing through to the secret of Jesus as the Lamb of God was John's privilege. But these words do not simply point to Jesus and make an identification. They were prophetic in a way that remained still a secret and could not be understood by a bystander—unless a person had discovered, like John, a mysterious hint in the fifty-third chapter of Isaiah. The phrase of Saint John harkens back to a verse in that chapter: "He was oppressed, and he was afflicted, yet he opened not his mouth; like a lamb that is led to the slaughter, and like a sheep that before its shearers is silent, so he opened not his mouth" (Is 53:7). This entire chapter of Isaiah is the most moving prophetic passage of the Passion Jesus would undergo. Perhaps this chapter, pondered repeatedly in silent prayer, may open for us the deeper secret of divine vulnerability in the Lamb whose blood is poured out for us each day in the Sacrifice of the Mass.

～

There is a further thought in this phrase that John uses of Jesus as the Lamb of God. The preparation day for the Passover is the day Jesus was crucified according to the Gospel of Saint John. On that day thousands of lambs were killed and their blood poured out in the temple precincts. The lambs were purchased by families for this purpose and the blood was spilled as an offering. At the very same time that this slaughter of the lambs was taking place, Jesus was

pouring out his blood on the Cross in a sacrificial immolation. It is as though the Father in that hour was choosing
his own lamb, his Son, to make an offering for the sake of
the sin of all humanity. This secret of the Father's sacrificial
offering of his Son is also being declared by Saint John the
Baptist at the Jordan. A clue to the greater meaning is present
to the crowds when a voice is heard proclaiming: "You are
my beloved Son; with you I am well pleased" (Mk 1:11).
Divine secrecy and the vulnerability of God meld together
in the open declaration heard in these words. It is the paradox of divine revelation always: God speaks to us and in
speaking draws us more deeply into our incomprehension
of his ultimate mystery. Saint John the Baptist surely knew
in some form of intuition what he was pronouncing and, at
the same time, could not grasp entirely what he was saying.
The secrecy of our Lord was open to his soul's view and
was closed to some degree. But even the initial piercing of
the secrecy Jesus carried in mystery called forth a great love
by our Lord for John. Anyone who penetrates a secret of
our Lord is bound to receive a return of love. The mystery
of his vulnerable heart, wounded for love, is the great secret
to be sought today. He keeps this mystery hidden except
perhaps to eyes of love that seek to pierce the events of his
Passion in a manner that discloses his Passion being relived
in the present day.

～

"And if one asks him, 'What are these wounds on your
back?' he will say, 'The wounds I received in the house of
my friends'" (Zech 13:6). We live in an age of Eucharistic
sacrilege unlike any other in the Church's history. Yet this
truth often confronts today the widespread claim of the right

of every person, properly disposed or not, to the reception of Holy Communion. It is evident today that people not in a state of grace often join the Communion line to receive the Eucharist. They step forward to take the sacred Host in a gesture of casual possessiveness that belies any actual longing for a union with the heart of our Lord. The sacredness of the Sacrament has been displaced by the false notion of communal solidarity in everyone together receiving the Host at Mass. Sacrilegious reception of Holy Communion is not just another mortal sin, but a direct act of disrespect toward God himself, unlike other sins pursued for selfish pleasure or satisfaction. It is, in truth, like spitting in the face of Jesus on the Cross at Calvary. The hidden question remains: What does God perceive in this act? In fact, the prevalence in our day of the unworthy reception of Holy Communion is a great and terrible sign of the vulnerability of God to being wounded. He gives himself fully to a soul even when he faces the cold callousness of a soul indifferent to his presence in the Eucharist. He enters the private chambers of a soul darkened by grave, unconfessed sin, and he must submit, as it were, to the soul's implicit assumption that it has no serious need for the mercy of God. Indifference to God's mercy is the usual disposition acquired from sacrilegious reception of Holy Communion. And what happens over the longer period of a life when our God can be treated in this manner? The wound to the heart of Christ in the Eucharistic sacrilege is a frightening reality. It is perhaps the most poignant sign observed today of a vulnerability in God to being wounded in the very act of offering us his immensity of love.

~

"Then he also went up, not publicly but in private" (Jn 7:10). The words refer to a quiet entry of our Lord into Jerusalem, at a time some months before his death, for the Feast of Tabernacles. He entered Jerusalem as a solitary figure, unrecognized and unidentified for a short time, before he spoke openly to the crowds in the temple area. The preference by Jesus for this mode of secrecy, for a cover of concealment while walking among men, is perhaps an essential trait of his personality. We need to acknowledge it because this preference for humble concealment continues to this day. What is above all secret on this visit to Jerusalem is the intense awareness of Jesus that he is approaching his Passion. The silent manner by which he carries the inevitability of his Passion at the depth of his heart, not speaking of it, is a clue to a deeper understanding of him. Beneath what he does speak is the concealed urgency of the suffering that he felt day by day was drawing closer. This secrecy of the Passion, unknown to those around him, and the privacy of our Lord's knowledge of it within his inner life, is a deep truth of his life in the three public years. It affected every encounter he had with people, although they were unaware of it. Perhaps the same secrecy continues, in a certain sense, in every historical era. The Passion of Jesus remains hidden from human eyes that have no interest in him, from the eyes that are blind to his love for them. But this observation does not refer simply to human indifference to the suffering he endured at Calvary. Our Lord's Passion is among us continually in the crucified Lord who does not leave this world and who perhaps is preparing the world at present for his eventual return. He is again among us as One carrying the treasure of his presence in secrecy in our midst. His heart hides itself as each day moves closer to some revelation of his suffering in a new manner. More than ever in history, it seems that he is ready to share his Passion with those who desire to receive him in love. Indeed, the Passion of Christ is perhaps soon to reveal itself in a more striking way as an event lived again within the Church in our own historical time.

~

Perhaps we do not often consider that Jesus' suffering in Gethsemane was not solely in taking on the sins of humanity. Indeed, he did make an extraordinary act of allowing the sins of all of history to carve their horror into his human soul. He sweat blood because of the sickening nausea of sin invading his human soul. But he suffered horribly as well and bled from the pores of his skin, while aware that his mother would undergo her own Gethsemane. She, too, may have faced a temptation and her own Gethsemane, in her case to ask the Father to spare her son this horrific ordeal, or at least to ease it in some manner. She may have confronted a temptation that she as a mother might ask for a reprieve, that her son might delay his time of departure and perhaps remain with her for a longer period. She may have been tempted to say "no", at least for now "no", not until more people might accept her son readily. But she answered much the same as her son did, that not her will but God's will be done. Her Gethsemane drew from her a second great "yes" to God. She refused to impede the holy mission of her son to complete his life in accord with the Father's will. She knew that her son had never denied her a request, and she nonetheless declined to make the request that he wait a bit longer before completing his life. This suffering of Mary in the temptation of her own Gethsemane, in the quiet of her private prayer, reflects the greatness of giving all to God for the sake of God's ultimate desire for souls.

~

So often God takes his initial approach to us in a divine condition of risk and vulnerability. He comes as One who can be refused and denied admittance; his tapping at the door of a human heart can be ignored. Indeed, he is a God who can be cast outside into the cold. There are countless people who at some point in life callously occupy the home in their soul that belongs to God and evict him. He is a God of unfathomable humility, submitting repeatedly to crass gestures of rudeness from his creature. Until we realize this humility of God, we cannot love him properly. He is vulnerable to being wounded and finds few people who are moved to see how, in his humility, he turns his face away, hiding it from view, not in anger, but to conceal the rejection he experiences from those indifferent to him. It is as though God is capable of a broken heart, but he does not want to show it. This vulnerability of God is known best perhaps by those who are close to the poor. The poor people give witness to the experience of God being despised and unwanted. It is hard to consider that God allows himself to be treated in much the same manner as they experience every day, yet it is true. This hidden truth of God subjecting himself to the instability and superficial whims of the human heart is a great secret within God's relations with humanity. He is a God of humility who does not seek to conquer or subdue for the sake of love. He prefers to be loved as One who will extend from his divine heart even a small request for a moment of attention, if it can draw a soul to a desire for him. On the other hand, he pours out his love in excess whenever he receives greater love.

~

Two statements of Jesus set next to each other in the diary of Saint Faustina can have a striking effect by their juxtaposition. The first reads: "I have inscribed your name upon My hand."[4] These words are not surprising. We may rightly expect that a saint should be told by Jesus that her name has been carved into the palm of his hand. But let us remember that this hand even now carries the wound of the nail mark from Calvary. And perhaps Jesus would say that the name inscribed upon his hand can be found only in the center of that wound. The name of a saint, indeed the name of each of us, hides inside the wounds Jesus received at the Passion in love for us. The second statement follows immediately after this: "You are engraved as a deep wound in My Heart."[5] Such an expression has provocative meanings. Not simply the name inscribed for lasting remembrance on the palm of the hand, but now the words speak the stronger reality that Saint Faustina herself is a wound in the heart of the Beloved Jesus. What does this signify? that even a saint wounds and causes pain to the heart of Jesus Christ? a wound due to the pain inflicted by sin or indifference or failures of generosity? That might be true; saints retain their capacity to cause suffering to the heart of Jesus. But the real mystery of this phrase must reside in the way a deep wounding of the heart accompanies love itself. The desire of God for a soul that already belongs fully to him, inscribed already in the

[4] Saint Faustina Kowalska, *Diary of Blessed Sister M. Faustina Kowalska*, no. 485, trans. Marians of the Immaculate Conception (Stockbridge, Mass.: Marians of the Immaculate Conception, 1996), 523.

[5] Ibid.

palm of his hand, is an immense thirst for that soul to unite everything in life to him. To be wounded by love is not just a human reality. God himself suffers this wound of love for every soul destined to a union in eternity with him. He is wounded and suffers in waiting for the more complete gift of our soul to his love.

~

The complaint of the Pharisees that Jesus welcomed sinners and ate with them should not surprise us. Familiarity and ease with people who openly violated the moral law, as Jesus exhibited, would suggest, in the judgmental mind of a Pharisee, a lack of concern for morality itself. The people in question, those known as sinners in that society, no longer cared to hide lives of sensuality and of disdain for Jewish law. If Jesus could be on friendly terms with such people, even sharing at table with them, it must be, the Pharisees thought, that he was indifferent to their sin, or perhaps he was privately a sinner himself and comfortable being close to sensual people. This description, however, misses the altogether different truth shown in the Gospel that Jesus as God is seen welcoming sinners. This congeniality with souls who disrespect the sacred obligations of divine commands would seem impossible at first glance. God would not give an impression that the moral law does not matter. He is incapable of forgetting the reality of sin. Indeed, these people who flocked to draw near to Jesus cannot be Jews who simply were careless about stricter rules of Sabbath observance. They were tax collectors and sinners who flouted the moral law and provoked words of condemnation from Jewish leaders. The welcome Jesus gave to them should not be misinterpreted. Jesus was not the prototype of a modern-day theologian enjoying the praise and adulation of men happy to be told that their sensual propensities no longer exist as sins in the eyes of God. His welcome of sinners did not mean indifference to sin, as though his divinity could be temporarily denied. He welcomed these souls to his heart because his heart was vulnerable to love. He drew them close to win their affection and, hopefully, their renunciation of sin. Nonetheless the word "welcome" remains a striking exposure of the vulnerable heart of God. He draws near in mysterious appeals to the souls that need him most, in signs of his real presence, in assurances that nothing is too late and no sin or vice is a reason for despair.

~

Saint Mary Magdalene received the first Resurrection appearance of Jesus in the Gospel accounts. Blinded by her tears, she does not at first recognize Jesus when she turns around from inside the tomb and sees him. But he calls out her name, tenderly, and her eyes open. She may then have prostrated herself at his feet, clinging to him, shedding tears all the while. She would likely have encountered the nail marks in his feet. Jesus is emphatic: "Do not hold me, for I have not yet ascended to the Father; but go to my brethren and say to them, I am ascending to my Father and your Father, to my God and your God" (Jn 20:17). The phrase "to my God" is unusual and notable, yet often glossed over. Never does Jesus in the Gospel refer to my God—except once. He rather identifies himself as God in several variations—"I and the Father are one" (Jn 10:30) . . . "Truly, truly, I say to you, before Abraham was, I am" (Jn 8:58) . . . "He who has seen me has seen the Father" (Jn 14:9). But there is one time he uses these words "my God", and that is on the Cross when he quotes the first verse of Psalm 22: "My God, my God, why have you forsaken me?" (Mk 15:34). Perhaps there is a hint of great mystery in the way Jesus pronounces this phrase "my God" to Saint Mary Magdalene and then tells her to repeat the full instruction to his disciples. Perhaps the "My God, my God" poured out in anguish on the Cross still echoes in the heart of Jesus as he uses this phrase outside the tomb on that first Easter morning. It is as though Jesus is telling us that he will carry permanently into eternity a human nature that has been forsaken by men when he ascends to the Father. The resurrected human nature of Jesus the Son of God will continue to pour out a "My God, my God" in prayer as a sacrificial victim. Perhaps in truth Jesus in his humanity now in heaven never sheds or purges from himself the experience of forsakenness. It becomes a perpetual cry for him to speak these words of the psalm. He carries that verse of the psalm into a timeless state of permanent victimhood poured out for us. And perhaps that same cry of forsakenness will be heard personally by some souls in its piercing depth as the Church enters her own Passion in a last era of the Church.

~

Immolation at Calvary is loss, disappearance, the removal of the visage of his divine dignity in exchange for the bruised, beaten face of a humiliated criminal. Yet under the appearance of humiliation remains the truth of God hiding in this man Jesus of Nazareth. The immolation shreds his appearance, leaving it torn and shattered. But the reality hidden inside the horror of the Passion is the immensity of divine love incarnate in this crucified man. Immolation in the last era of the Church may likewise involve a disappearance, a burning away of surfaces once radiant in the Church, so that the reality of victimhood in the Church herself may be refined as a culminating mystery of history itself. Jesus Christ crucified and at one with his Church is a truth always moving in the direction of a final testimony. When that day comes, the *ecclesia martyrium* may come forth to meet the hour of its destiny. Indeed, let us be vigilant to observe the hidden martyrdoms that may take place in the coming decades. The reality of a burning away, a form of disappearance, in the Church will entail, not at all an end to the Church, but perhaps the loss of the Church in her former prestige as the place of Divine Presence. Instead, the Church may disappear into hidden corners marked by intense faith and fervor. A great love for the Eucharist, for the martyred Christ, will hide in these corners. The external structure of the Church held up for centuries by a Magisterium faithful to the Holy Spirit may suffer great strain in a period of final turmoil in the Church. But the Church herself, in her offering of the Holy Sacrifice of the Mass and in her living faith in the crucified Lord, will not be overcome. She may undergo a rather persecuted existence, yet remain very alive in her secret "catacomb" reality. All this will reflect the pattern of Christ's own last week.

7

ONE THING NEEDFUL:
GIVING ALL IN GIVING OURSELVES

To give oneself to God, recklessly forgetful of self, not to take account of one's own individual life to allow full room for divine life, this is the profound motive, the principle, and the end of religious life. The more perfectly it is carried out, so much the richer is the divine life that fills the soul.[1]

—Saint Teresa Benedicta of the Cross

What God demands of us is not this or that; He demands everything.[2]

—Pierre Reverdy to Jacques Maritain

True Christian resignation is no apathetic affair; it is the extremity of being torn apart.[3]

—Charles Péguy

A more serious life with God may compel at times a need for a self-offering that must be made without inner strength or courage, without clear confidence of being heard, but only with the sheer unfelt conviction that we must offer

[1] Saint Teresa Benedicta of the Cross, *Thoughts of Edith Stein*, trans. anonymous (Eugene, Ore.: Carmel of Maria Regina, no date), 30.

[2] Pierre Reverdy letter, October 1924, quoted in Jean-Luc Barré, *Jacques and Raïssa Maritain: Beggars for Heaven*, trans. Bernard E. Doering (Notre Dame: University of Notre Dame, 2005), 203.

[3] Charles Péguy, quoted in Hans Urs von Balthasar, *The Glory of the Lord: A Theological Aesthetics*, vol. 3 (San Francisco: Ignatius Press, 1986), 414.

ourselves fully to God, that our soul in its entirety must be
delivered up, and that this act of offering cannot wait, cannot be delayed any longer. A sense of spiritual consequence,
of real urgency, accompanies this act. We realize that only
by offering ourselves completely can we avoid the risk of
halting on the path, of faltering in perseverance. To souls
who know the experience, it is striking how the interior life
is inclined after a time to rely on such acts of self-offering to
galvanize the spiritual life of prayer. It can seem as though a
pure act of self-offering becomes a secret doorway into the
heart of God. The power of a repeated short phrase—"I
offer myself again entirely to you"—becomes undeniably
evident. In fact, it needs to be repeated, because there is
no conclusion to these words; no offering of ourselves ever
finishes. There is a limitless depth in our heart and soul, and
in God himself, and we are tending with each act of deeper
offering to these greater depths. This need continues until
our last breath, when we can breathe out a final act of self-
offering. Let us consider as well the delight of God when
he draws us to desire sacrificial immolation and we respond.
He loves to see our soul take another step closer, without
fear or hesitation, to Jesus on the Cross pouring out his life
in immolation. He rejoices to see us offer ourselves to this
same spirit of immolation. This act of self-offering is bound
to become a primary grace extended to souls as the decades
of this century continue.

～

The need to give all and everything to God in the silence
of prayer is a demand of love itself. It can never be just
to repeat words or to renew a promise we have frequently

repeated, even when the words we habitually use are profound in themselves. The harder task is to seek a silent enclosure within the soul where the words of surrender—"I give my all to you, and all of my all"—reach into a deeper region of self-abandonment and meet God offering himself in a surrender of himself to our soul. The realization that God desires to give the fullness of himself—a truth most insistent and real in the reception of the Eucharist—urges us to plunge into a greater depth of release from ourselves in giving all to God. We discover then that only the arrival at greater depth allows us to take a step closer to the desired "all" of a complete self-giving. The "all" is the completion of a self-offering, a necessary element in any true immolation. The last period of the Church will surely draw a strong inclination in souls to offer all and join with the Christ in completing the Church's final task.

～

It is an essential habit to cultivate: To go to prayer with pure simplicity knowing that nothing else is needed but our Lord's Real Presence in the Eucharist before us in a tabernacle. Our own poverty is insignificant. He hides even while directly present before our eyes in the tabernacle, and we simply need to turn to him. "I give all to you, and I desire nothing but you." A simple phrase like this is not a small act when the words are spoken from a silent depth of soul. In fact, these words spoken slowly from our heart can be an act of pure love very pleasing to God. The great effort of prayer is to return repeatedly to the silent depths of our heart where all acts are purer. There is no technique to take us there. The path is unmarked and with no signs to lead us. A longing to cast ourselves completely before him and give all to him is what carries us into these depths of silent self-forgetfulness. Nothing else is needed. The purity of our longing for God takes over, and that is enough.

~

Not what we speak with words in prayer, not the power of any single word, but a "soul desire" inflaming our words is what carries silent prayer more deeply into the heart of God. The word "surrender", for instance, has a beauty in prayer and in our relations with God. But the surrender of our soul only takes on a deeper reality when it enters a garden much like Gethsemane, where the night is cold and the winds cast twisting shadows among the gnarled trees. There the soul must expect no rescue but from God himself. The great need in our own Gethsemanes is to discover the prayer of Jesus being prayed secretly in our soul: "Not my will, but yours, be done" (Lk 22:42). This word of surrender does not come to the help of prayer as though providing an answer to solve a problem. An act of surrender may not remove a tension felt within our soul. Rather, what may happen is that a sense of his strength, of his promise to take care of everything, may pierce a mysterious depth within our soul. The surrender to God in a brief phrase becomes suddenly, not our prayer alone, but Jesus' words to his Father spoken again from a concealed depth within our soul in that hour. This is the nature of a true spiritual fire that must invade our desire for God in prayer. Only when prayer over time carves a fire of deep surrender to God inside the deeper layers of our soul does a passion for God truly inflame our soul.

~

A paradigm shift has taken place in spirituality over the last decades. Traditional spirituality in the past stressed the centrality of the will and the essential task of becoming—becoming holy, becoming a saint—an effort of responding with a strong will to the demands of God's will over a lifetime. It was oriented to transformation and change. The human person by means of hours of prayer, by asceticism, virtue, selfless charity, generous self-giving, and so forth, can be transformed over years and become what God desires. We can place ourselves at the service of God and be used by him, depending on our willingness to give ourselves fully to him. A clear conviction undergirded traditional spirituality: our Lord's desire for souls is united to his own sacrificial oblation on the Cross; indeed, human lives that enter this union with his oblation are fruitful for the salvation and sanctification of other souls. It is true that traditional spirituality in its weaker tendencies could focus excessively on spirituality as personal advancement, on the weighing of merits and the counting of graces. But in its proper understanding, the complete gift of self to God for the sake of others was its goal and orientation. And it did not hide or soften the truth that to arrive at a depth of union with God is a rigorous and exceptional prospect. The shift in spirituality occurred as psychological categories began to invade considerations of spirituality. A kind of therapeutic notion of spirituality took over and replaced the older view. The language of brokenness, woundedness, and victimhood became predominant, in the effort to bring healing to souls damaged by life circumstances, including life in religious congregations. This approach can also be said to seek a form of becoming, i.e., becoming healed, or, in a variation, becoming fulfilled, but the core orientation is quite different. Instead of a striving forward with a gaze set on the goal of God and holiness, a goal never completed and always stretching into the future, the orientation of therapeutic spirituality tends to collapse its focus onto the self and the achievement of a state of well-being. At times this means a focus on personal pain and inadequacy, followed by efforts to find a path to inward healing. Or the concentration is on fulfillment as a human person—naturally, of course, in the service of God and one's fellowman—but the self and its fulfillment in work and life remain an essential priority. The goal of these therapeutic approaches to spirituality is to arrive at a peaceful acceptance of self as loved by God or, perhaps in time, a happy sense of personal accomplishment in life. The result, if the goal is realized, is often indistinct from the attainment of some form of spiritual complacency, either a peaceful satisfaction with being loved by God simply as one is or a basic egoism in arriving at a recognized achievement. It is not surprising that a missionary spirit and a zealous concern for the salvation of souls is not a primary motive for therapeutic spirituality. On a contrasting note, it should be said that traditional spirituality, when practiced in its hard realism, often rewarded a soul's efforts with the chronic dissatisfaction of never arriving at the goal. There are always more souls to seek, a neverending prospect. Yet this did not stop many people in history from making God and the salvation of souls their great pursuit in life. The desire to give to Jesus Christ crucified a full gift of love in the short life before us customarily permeates holy souls with a driven quality, and this is a mark of traditional holiness.

Their need to stretch themselves ever further in selfless love for God and for the salvation of souls is an essential dynamic of soul that made saints in history. A return to this spiritual wisdom has become more important than ever in our current day.

~

Perhaps the first great insight that galvanizes any contemplative vocation is the perception of a profound desire to offer one's life fully to God. This need not signify an eventual entry into a monastery or cloistered convent. The strong interior urge felt to pursue a deeper gift of oneself to God in prayer is already a sign of an awakening contemplative disposition. But this desire must be acted upon in prayer, soon after it is felt, without delay. Procrastination risks the loss of a quiet but strong attraction to giving oneself to God and replacing it with calculations of cost. If the greater act of offering is analyzed, or questioned too acutely, a soul often steps back and does nothing. On the other hand, when an act of offering our life fully to God is freely given, a dramatic threshold is often crossed quickly in the life of our soul. This is true even when that act is taken in the quiet privacy of a silent hour of prayer. Our life can never be the same when such an act reaches into some depth of a wholehearted desire. God listens to the truth expressed in our prayer when we speak from depths of the soul, and he delights in every wholehearted offering of a life to himself. There are consequences immediately. What changes quickly after such an offering is the interior ambiance of our prayer when we are alone in silence with God. The desire to belong only all to him resonates more forcefully in our soul each day. We can have a sense of a new depth within ourselves and feel a need to cast ourselves out into the deep. In short, a contemplative desire has been ignited with that offering, and it may be only the commencement of a lifelong fire of love for God. Our soul simply needs to give itself to that act of self-offering and allow it to become a daily undercurrent animating our prayer of silence with God. We can live in a certitude of God's protective presence despite any troubles of the current day.

~

An early depiction of souls in the Old Testament who may have fallen in love with God and in that love offered themselves in a type of immolation to God is not easily recognized. A friend of Jewish background, but now deeply Catholic, pointed out this story to me. It is the account in the tenth chapter of Leviticus of the two sons of Aaron, Nadab and Abihu, anointed as priests by Moses, who light a fire, in their censors, place incense on it, and offer this fire before the Lord. The possibility is strong that they are motivated by a desire to give themselves in this offering. It is not an offering that God has commanded; it is not the fulfillment of an obligatory sacrifice. Instead, they choose to light a fire not from a source in the temple, but their own fire. The phrase is ambiguous, but it may mean that they seek to make a gift of themselves to God as an offering. As a result, we read that "fire came forth from the presence of the LORD and devoured [consumed] them, and they died before the LORD" (Lev 10:2). The common Jewish interpretation is that these two sons exceeded the bounds of an offering, that they violated God's wishes by offering beyond limits, and so their lives were taken. They died, in this view, because of their forbidden offering. But this interpretation may be incorrect. The Jewish viewpoint is that one should not offer oneself beyond what is commanded under obedience. Yet our Christian understanding is that an offering of ourselves to God can never be too excessive when moved by love. The excess of love in the reality of Jesus Christ crucified has become the measure for every offering of love in Christianity. There is never too much to offer. The truth residing in this story may be found in an examination of the single sentence—"fire came forth from the presence of the LORD and devoured [consumed] them." My Jewish convert friend insisted that it is an expression in Jewish terms that never signifies a punishment. It is used only to indicate a sacrificial offering accepted by God. If so, they died before the Lord, before the face of the Lord, consumed by him, because he loved them in their offering. When Moses in this passage comments: "I will show myself holy among those who are near me, and before all the people I will be glorified" (Lev 10:3)—it is perhaps an indication of the acceptance by God of this holy oblation by the two brothers. God unites himself and manifests his holiness in the oblation of those who offer themselves completely to him.

∼

We cross a threshold of deeper friendship with Jesus Christ when we offer ourselves to become friends of his Passion. We have not asked then for a friendship of comfort and consolation, but to become one of the rare friends who draws near to him in his hours of terrible pain and final immolation. Even in our human relations, there is a different truth in a friendship when we refuse to allow a friend to suffer alone. We may know we can withdraw and stand apart from another's suffering, but we reject this option and

thereby risk that the suffering will pierce our own life. This
piercing of our own life is perhaps a real danger in offering
ourselves to be a friend of Christ's Passion. But the sense
of danger quickly disappears in the act of offering ourselves
to it. Perhaps what happens is that some hint or promise
of seeing his face, as it were, draws us forward. His love
blinds us, and we forgo all hesitation. In offering ourselves
to be friends of his Passion, we may soon find that we love
him more deeply when the sight of his Passion is near to
us, inhabiting our own interior life, returning daily perhaps
in our prayer. For some souls there can be hours of prayer
when nothing matters in the hour but the heart of our Lord
pouring out the labored breath of his love in the solitude of
his Passion. We learn perhaps over time that Jesus is sensitive to courage in prayer and delights to see courage in our
soul. It is why he turned with quick solicitude to Dismas
hanging to his side on another cross at the crucifixion. He
saw a man fearless in overcoming the crowd around him.
He will not turn away anyone who with courage and a measure of stamina wants to know friendship with his Passion.
Few were with him at Calvary in his agony and solitude,
and perhaps very few to this day remain close to him in his
solitude at Calvary. But this compelling attraction for Jesus
in his Passion may soon become more prevalent in souls as
the years of our era persist in their tension between spiritual
light and darkness.

~

"For nothing is hidden that shall not be made manifest, nor
anything secret that shall not be known and come to light"
(Lk 8:17). These words might be interpreted at times as
though they referred to bad behavior or criminal acts and

the inevitability of eventually getting caught. Instead, they have a deep spiritual resonance when understood as referring to hidden and secret aspects of God that cannot become known. The great secrecy within our Lord's Passion is a truth waiting to be unveiled to the soul that enters the heart of Jesus in his Passion. The secrecy of the Passion and its sacredness opens to the soul that offers its own suffering in life to Jesus. Our Lord may take that offering and join the soul to his heart precisely in the desolation of his Passion. If we pray in the time of serious trial or suffering—"I have come to give you my all"—we may receive from him an entry into the secret recesses of his heart. And what is secret about these inner recesses of his heart? We discover that there is no measure, no limit, to the vulnerability of our God to pain and suffering. He is unwilling to place a limit on the wounds he receives, no measure on how far he will continue to love even when receiving contempt or betrayal. The soul that exercises no measure, no limit, in offering all to God will discover that God holds nothing back in giving himself. The great entry into the secret wounds of Jesus at Calvary commences in our soul's inner life when we learn to offer ourselves from the depth of our inner being. We become one with our Lord in his own suffering of the present day.

~

The surrender of a single hour's daring, rising from a sudden interior desire, ought not to be forgotten, once we learn its importance. This surrender is never small, and a threshold can be crossed in a single hour when our soul approaches a pure act of love for God. The depth of our prayer is directly affected by a pure act of surrender. Prayer can indeed be measured by the repeated effort in silence to let go into the hands of God, as though we released our hands from a rope while scaling a mountainside, leaving us nothing to hold, nothing to secure our footing. The act of letting go does not plunge us into disaster. The interior act of letting go into God's hands does not cast us into a descent through open air. It would seem rather that something like a spring of living water from an inner mysterious source lifts and carries our soul. The great need in surrendering to God is to refrain from impeding the flow of God's presence that rises from a place of depth in our soul, before it then returns to the hidden recesses of the soul. These surrenders of pure love for God are never without effect. They may have no preparation and may seem to pass quickly in prayer, but they carve strong desires into our soul. They edge us closer to a more complete offering of our soul to our beloved Lord. The daring of an hour's surrender will always urge us afterward to disappear more entirely into the Beloved's love and to live alone for him in all ways. Perhaps this disappearing is a taste of the ultimate surrender we can expect at death. With each surrender to a pure love for God, our soul can lose itself in a greater abandonment to the Beloved, ready for greater works of love and sacrificial offerings not previously known.

~

The risk of offering ourselves to the *blessing* of God is not often realized. Most people look at being blessed by God as a necessarily desirable thing, bringing favor and happiness by the very nature of a blessing. The blessing of God is taken as synonymous with a gift that enriches life in some manner. What if this is a false notion of a true blessing from God? The possibility that the greatest blessing is to be invited into some painful alignment of our life with the life of Jesus in his Passion is hardly considered. It is an important courage to cultivate: if we offer ourselves to this deeper blessing, we are bound to taste some of the dust of Calvary in our mouth. We are going to find ourselves like Simon with heavy wood on our shoulders. If we ask for even more blessings, because we love more and want to offer even greater love, we may find ourselves more often looking up at our Lord's straining, bloodied face in his agony on the Cross. The deeper blessing of God to the interior depth of our soul cannot be granted without a union with his Passion. Yet who would desire to turn away, when in fact we experience more intense love always when near our suffering Lord and God?

⁓

Souls that are mysteriously certain of God's desire for the complete offering of their life have received a great favor from God. It happens, for instance, as I have heard recounted a few times, that a young woman or man visits a cloister or a monastery, and every minute over the course of some days seems to pronounce an emphatic truth that one has entered what is going to become a permanent home. It is truly a home that has been entered, familiar in a way that seems almost a return to a place once loved in an earlier period of life. It happens even that the other monks or nuns present there seem to recognize this same person in the way that some people at a family gathering might instinctively turn with affection to welcome a person who turns out to be a distant cousin related by blood to all there. The recognition by the soul of belonging can be mysteriously profound in such circumstances. The only way to explain this is that God is very intent on souls knowing where they fit and will flourish in his divine plan, and where they will have a door open to the great adventure of giving all to God. The sanctity of souls who look back in old age at their lives often shows this kind of initial recognition of a day still vividly remembered that they had found the place where they belonged for the rest of their life. In our own day, our Lord may be very desirous for souls to find a place for the greater offering of an immolation in union with his own.

~

The desire for a more complete gift of ourselves to God is inseparable from a need to serve God's purposes for the sake of others. Every greater offering of ourselves to God is bound to urge a greater offering for souls. "Take all, but give me souls." These words were dear to Saint Teresa of Calcutta, taught by her for many years to her congregation as an ejaculatory prayer to be used often. Every pure surrender of our entire being to God leads to a desire for souls. Love in service follows, depending on our vocation and opportunities. At times, quietly, this is a service of intercessory prayer as a soul gives away its prayer, as it were, for the salvation of others. Instead of seeking in prayer to advance one's own closer relations with God, a soul turns away from self to intercede for others far from God. The great laying down of our lives that the Gospel urges surely requires a steady disposition to give away our prayer at times for the sake of other souls in need. A love that would imitate Jesus' love from the Cross demands the sacrificial love of a selfless prayer for souls. And this is exercised best in giving away our prayer for the sake of others. Sometimes we forget that the deepest charity may be an interior charity, and certainly the offering of our prayer for souls most in need of prayer

exemplifies this quality of heart. Indeed, let us examine ourselves and test it. Cloistered nuns will sometimes say that
they are often most full of love interiorly when they are forgetting themselves and generously dispensing their prayers
as a bestowal of gifts upon unknown strangers. Prayer then
takes on a quality of love like the prayer of Mary our Mother
in heaven, who prays and intercedes constantly for desperate
souls and souls in danger. We should do the same with regularity and place the intentions of our prayers in her hands
to be used as she desires. It is a reality of love that the highest forms of love may not be seen by others. Yet they are
perceived by God, who takes the offering of a generous soul
and with the help of Mary distributes supernatural alms to
those most in spiritual need. And surely as these years continue, a spirit of generous offering for souls who have lost
God will be a great demand of love.

∼

Perhaps a pure abandonment to God is everything: " 'Father,
into your hands I commit my spirit!' And having said this
he breathed his last" (Lk 23:46). If Jesus made such an act
the culminating testimony of his life, it must have immense
significance. But what does it mean exactly for us? The need
in silent prayer to cast ourselves into the hand of God, with
a great act of interior release, letting go, throwing ourselves
blindly into the dark abyss of God's care, can become a daily
exigency of prayer. Yet to arrive at a confident sense of being
caught in the hands of another, never dropping interminably,
but held and protected, may not happen until we accustom
ourselves to the free leap, as it were, in an act of complete
abandonment to God. We must leap like a paratrooper of

prayer, commending ourselves to God, because he alone can carry us and keep us safe. In learning that leap of abandonment, we come to know quickly enough that we are by nature incapable and inadequate, sometimes learning by failing and sin, other times by the barriers we encounter in moving forward in self-giving. The beauty of the leap of abandonment to God is that he seems to show us before very long that we are in his gaze and his affection. The soul abandoned to God becomes sometimes quickly the soul overwhelmed by divine tenderness. It is as though God were waiting for this time in life when our soul would finally realize its utter poverty and need. He reaches out to us then easily, it seems, almost with divine impulsiveness, if that can be said, when we expose ourselves nakedly before him in a state of need and desire.

~

In effect, this is a great challenge for the interior life: to clothe ourselves in the blind nakedness of a complete offering to Jesus Christ crucified. We cannot know what it means to offer ourselves to something so expansive and sacred as an ocean of infinite love in Jesus Christ. The metaphors dissolve in the face of the actual reality of God offering himself as a victim of love on a cross at Calvary. But the truth remains that the God of love, Jesus himself, receives our offering into his wounds at the crucifixion. In that offering, he clings to our soul and its poverty inasmuch as we cannot fully grasp what happens in love when we release ourselves in a surrender to his Passion. We need in prayer to believe intensely that God desires our words of complete surrender. Few souls seem to recognize the power that such a surrender has over the heart of God. Our soul takes God captive in a certain sense, inasmuch as we offer our own life in captive servitude to God to use us for the sake of love. The surrender to God in an offering to our Lord's Passion cannot but unite us to his thirst for souls. The outcome is both predictable and utterly mysterious. God loves to replicate the Passion of the divine Son in souls willing to offer themselves in this manner. But he likewise loves to pour forth mysterious graces, unknown to that soul, for the sake of countless others in need as a fruit of this surrender to his Passion. We can expect that he will seek to identify souls increasingly with his Passion as the years continue.

~

Jesus makes hard demands in the pages of the Gospel. But in his own life he also honored his greatest demand that we lose ourselves out of love for him. He performed exactly this act of loss in dying on the Cross. For us, this loss of self is to die to self and disappear so that a fruitfulness for others may rise from within us. What is left behind after a conversion, and then thrown away, discarded as useless, opens a space of emptiness in us to be filled mysteriously by God himself. This loss of self cannot take place without a shallow self we have known withering slowly away until it is no more. Only then do we begin to discover a true depth of mystery in ourselves. In Jesus, the mystery of his divine identity needed no process of discovery. Yet a pattern of self-emptying in him is present for us to observe from his conception as a child. He gives away divine majesty in the Incarnation to live only for the will of his Father. He remains in his hidden years seeking only to be one with the silent presence of divinity. Then, as man, he gives away the flesh of his humanity to the awful hours of a Roman crucifixion. A humiliating loss of himself in his divine dignity haunts the hours of his Passion. By the end, near death, he became unrecognizable, so marred was his look. The loss of self in a soul's immolation may display this same pattern of disappearance and radical defacement. The abject suffering in Jesus, worse as the hours continued at Calvary, concealed the reality of God placing before us the unfathomable mystery of divine humility. This same demand of humility—after we have gazed on him in his crucifixion—is perhaps the essential need in our current day if we are to advance in love for Jesus Christ crucified, our Lord and God. We realize we are nothing in ourselves by looking steadily on our God in his self-abasement on the Cross. And perhaps we realize that this self-abasement of our God continues into the present day.

8

PURE RECEPTIVITY IN PURSUIT OF THE GOD OF MYSTERY

The mystical capacity of the human mind needs to be strengthened again. The capacity to renounce oneself, a greater inner openness, the discipline to withdraw ourselves from noise and from all that presses on our attention. . . . Let us be honest about it: today there is a hypertrophy of the outer man, and his inner strength has been alarmingly weakened.[1]

—Joseph Ratzinger

Unlike the hunger of the body, the hunger of the soul can be nourished only by more hunger.[2]

—Gustave Thibon

It seems to it that the entire universe is a sea of love in which it is engulfed, for conscious of the living point or center of love within itself, it is unable to catch sight of the boundaries of this love. . . . For the soul beholds itself converted into the immense fire of love that emanates from that enkindled point at the heart of the spirit.[3]

—Saint John of the Cross

[1] Joseph Cardinal Ratzinger, *Truth and Tolerance: Christian Belief and World Religions*, trans. Henry Taylor (San Francisco: Ignatius Press, 2004), 159.
[2] Gustave Thibon, quoted in Erasmo Leiva-Merikakis, *Fire of Mercy, Heart of the Word*, vol. 3 (San Francisco: Ignatius Press, 2012), 168.
[3] Saint John of the Cross, *The Living Flame of Love*, 2.10–11, in *The Collected Works of St. John of the Cross*, trans. Kieran Kavanaugh and Otilio Rodriguez (Washington, D.C: ICS Publications, 2017), 661.

Prayer depends on receptivity to the mystery of a personal God. These words are not a description or explanation of prayer. They speak rather of the secret magnetism that can invade the deeper layers of our soul and draw a great longing for God in the quiet of our prayer. God is the source of this longing. But it is not recognized unless we allow a pure, receptive openness to God to inhabit our interior desire. Nothing of a desire for an experience of God should be sought, even as this would seem for many the most compelling desire possible in prayer. The soul itself must become a pure receptivity, wanting nothing but God. But such a pure longing for God entails an inability to know with clarity what is being sought. God is so immensely beyond our possession in some fleeting satisfaction. Any attempt to hold him down, to keep him captive, violates a reality of relationship with the majestic One who is infinite love. We can only be receptive to him and allow his initiative to determine any mysterious intimacy with the divine heart. He takes the lead in these matters after a certain threshold of love has been crossed. We can only be receptive while ready to succumb to his allure. God loves in treacherous ways, we might say. He expects a great surrender of our soul once he has introduced us into his secrets. But he will cease quickly to show himself if he sees that we refuse to give away our desire to possess a prize in our relations with him. And then, conversely, he will seem to pour himself out in excess without concern for his effect on a soul when he sees a pure desire to receive nothing but him and his love.

~

"God's speech is the effect he produces in the soul" (Saint John of the Cross).[4] Indeed, God speaks mysteriously in the

---

[4] Saint John of the Cross, *The Living Flame of Love*, 1.7, in ibid., 643.

silence of prayer. He penetrates the depths of our spirit in silent prayer with his living presence. A deep longing for him is already a real encounter with his hidden presence, a sign already that he is speaking. We have only to exercise a certainty in faith that he draws this longing from a hidden place within the depths of our soul. A pure receptivity to him can convey at times an undeniable sense that in our longing for him we are already in contact with him, listening to him. It is then we should invite our Lord in prayer to come, to enter through the door of our longing, to enter inside the interior depth of our desire. The receptivity we cultivate as a disposition in prayer allows us to realize that our Lord accepts this invitation. He does indeed walk through the door we have opened to him. He is the guest of our soul's longing even as he remains the divine Lord of the universe. He takes possession of our longing for him as though desiring to hide there in a remote corner of his own creation. He comes, not as One majestic in his sovereignty, but as one who draws near with a familiarity, pleased to enjoy our poor company. Someone might ask, does he ever refuse the invitation that hides in our longing for him? Perhaps not, as long as we remain poor, which is a comforting truth. Our receptivity to his hidden presence may be subject to instability and strain, but our longing for him to come to us and take hold of us can be a perpetual hunger. It can be an act in prayer that is always repeatable. And perhaps it is answered fruitfully whenever we are poor within our interior soul. The Church herself in our time may find herself poorer over time, and yet precisely for that reason united more deeply to the mystery of our Lord present within her today.

∼

In almost all the Ethiopian Orthodox churches, small and large, outside the building on a wall is a life-size reproduction of a particular painting. It is a common sight around the country. This simple painting depicts Jesus standing outside in a gesture of knocking on a wooden door. Nothing else distracts the observer or draws the eye. The door, however, on closer view, manifests a defect: there is no door handle to open the door. It can only be opened by someone inside. Jesus must wait for the occupant to open the door and invite him inside. Until then, he can only wait and continue knocking. The image poses a great spiritual truth. We must invite him inside our lives, into the depth of our heart and soul. The door must be opened from the inside. The all-powerful God will not break that door down; indeed, he may not continue knocking if there is no response from the inside. But if we open the door from the inside and invite him in, there is a certainty that he steps forward into the inner domain of our life and changes this inner reality completely by his presence. This gesture of opening the door to our Lord will be important for souls of spiritual depth in the coming years. Perhaps without realizing it, they will invite our Lord and his Passion into the heart of the Church herself.

~

"No one can receive anything except what is given him from heaven" (Jn 3:27). A pure receptivity to God implies a risk of uncertainty in the hour of prayer. We receive from him, but we may not perceive what we are receiving. We cannot know what he is giving, because what he gives is the fullness of himself as a gift. It is God's way never to give partially. The gift of God in giving himself to us necessarily overwhelms us in a literal sense, although only a rare soul realizes this to any degree. The thought of the God of the universe descending in his fullness upon our small soul and hiding there can seem absurd. Yet this is the reality of his gift: he cannot divide or distribute portions of himself in giving himself. Perhaps we can have some sense of this truth only to the extent that we seek in prayer a pure receptivity to God. The gift of God to our soul may exceed our comprehension, but it is not beyond our desire. Indeed, we should pray in words like these: "I am longing to receive what you are desiring to give." We can know he answers this prayer and that we are receiving him when he leaves us empty of desire for anything other than him. At such times we want nothing but him, and there is no other desire. In an hour of pure receptivity to him, nothing is obtained from this pure desire, nothing taken away from prayer, at least in any possessive manner, except God himself. What God gives in giving himself in this manner will always be impossible to hold in our grasp or comprehend. Yet we can be aware in a pure longing for him that he is giving himself. Indeed, he may stretch our longing for him into unseen layers within the soul. It remains a concealed truth where he hides in that longing. The elusiveness of God in his love for us is inseparable from his gift of himself to our soul.

〜

"The temptation to let oneself go instead of giving oneself: that is the temptation of our time" (Henri de Lubac, S.J.).[5] Even souls of greater depth need to know that God does not force our love for him, and he does not coerce. He leaves

[5] Henri de Lubac, S.J., *More Paradoxes*, trans. Anne Englund Nash (San Francisco: Ignatius Press, 2002), 81.

us free to decide for ourselves how deeply we will receive his desires and give ourselves to him. The Gospel command "Follow me" (Mt 9:9), for instance, the first words that Saint Matthew the tax collector heard from Jesus, is verbally in the imperative tense, but in tone and appeal, it simply invites. The words, despite their strength, do not force a submission. Rather, they summon a soul to what is not entirely clear or determined. Unknown possibilities are implied in this phrase "follow me." Indeed, the phrase provokes questions: Follow where, in what direction, for what aim and purpose? Receptivity to our Lord is the primary response that Jesus seeks to elicit by this expression, and even now with us. The questions can wait for later. He wants us to lift our vision toward the prospect of a blind pursuit, ready to keep walking wherever the road of following him may take us. We are not simply to march head down in obedience to a call of strict duty. Something more demanding is required if a pure receptivity to God is present in our soul. It is only by remaining blind, accepting his invitation without knowing what lies ahead, that our Lord continues to speak his personal requests. He prefers our blindness so that he can lead us to a union with his own Passion. He seeks to draw us without a sight of the Cross and to entice us with love, so that when we do say "yes, I will follow you anywhere", we will pursue this choice to the end, wherever that takes us, into whatever taste of the Passion he wants to share with us. The form of an invitation, rather than an imperative command, is in a way a subtle strategy by God to expose the truth of our soul. We confirm our desire for a pure love of God when we step forward blindly toward a voice that seems to carry the rasping echo of the dust of Calvary into our heart.

~

Only three times in the four Gospels does a person use the personal name of Jesus when addressing him. It is not his mother, or any apostle, who calls him by name. The blind beggar Bartimaeus shouts out the words, "Jesus, Son of David, have mercy on me!" (Mk 10:47), but his cry is released before the crowd, not in the immediate presence of Jesus. When Jesus is at last in front of him, he says, "Master, let me receive my sight" (Mk 10:51). There are also the ten lepers who call out to him from a distance: "Jesus, Master, have mercy on us" (Lk 17:13). The single occasion when a man directly addresses Jesus in a personal manner by name occurs at the crucifixion as Dismas, after rebuking the other crucified criminal for his taunting words, turns to our Lord: "Jesus, remember me when you come in your kingly power" (Lk 23:42). The promise of his eternal salvation is our Lord's reply: "Today you will be with me in Paradise." There is a hidden layer of significance in this being the one time in the Gospel that a man speaks directly to Jesus using the sacred name given by the angel Gabriel to Mary and Joseph. How did Dismas know his name? Perhaps the fame of Jesus accounts for this knowledge, but I suspect there is another reason. Dismas may have been a young man caught up in the wrong crowd—perhaps an associate of Barabbas, along with his fellow criminal on the cross, for Pilate may have decided to take two of Barabbas' cohorts to their execution when they demanded the customary Passover release and Barabbas is freed. I wonder whether Jesus had very personal words with Dismas as the three men were led to their execution carrying the heavy wood on their shoulders. They may have been tied together by rope at the ankles to impede any attempt at escape. On that difficult walk, Jesus may have looked in the eyes of Dismas and asked his name, and he may have given him encouragement not to fear, despite the horror they soon would face. When asked, Jesus may have told Dismas that his own name was Jesus, and that he would be by his side, near him, throughout the ordeal. A bond may have formed on the stony path to Calvary. When this young man, full of regret for his mistakes, is lifted on a cross beside Jesus, he may be the one person at Calvary, other than Mary the mother of Jesus, whose companionship gives Jesus a unique consolation. The climax of that consolation is in the exchange that took place between them. The way he spoke Jesus' name, while suffering his own crucifixion, pierced the heart of Jesus with love for this young man. He allowed our Lord to be his comforter, and he accepted to be a friend of God in the last hour of Jesus' life. Dismas received his assurance of eternal joy in heaven, but it is possible he was rewarded as well with a great power of intercession for the lost and ruined who will find mercy on their deathbed because of his prayers in heaven.

~

The inclination to forge ahead in the interior life, crossing into an unknown territory of the soul—despite caution signs—seems to be clearly rewarded at times. Perhaps God loves to see the sheer recklessness of a soul who wants him desperately and refuses to consider any cost. Other times, our soul in seeking God may seem to get lost in a maze, unable to recognize its whereabouts, and an effort is necessary to find familiar surroundings again. On the other hand, whenever a step forward in relations with God involves a fruitful step, it is often because a passage across a barrier

with God has been courageous in our self-offering. A risk
must be taken in which all security and sense of direction
might be lost, and sometimes all security does disappear for
a while, both in the interior life and in a worldly sense. Yet
crossing a boundary of no return seems to be precisely the
kind of spiritual gamble that God likes to see in souls. There
can be an analogy in a worldly sense. The lover passionate
in love usually cannot wait long to declare a personal love
to the one loved. But this entails a risk that a door will close
in a rejection. No one who takes the first step in speaking
of his love for the other is assured of a return expression
of ardent love. The possibility of disappointment is always
present. Let us turn to God with this dilemma in mind. If
we are to pursue deep relations of love with God, there is
an absolute need to take this risk of declaring our love without reserve or caution. It may surprise our soul that God
does not answer in any prompt or noticeable manner, which
may only mean that he awaits a further threshold of love to
be crossed. We should never think, even after a declaration
of great love for God, that we have stretched our soul to
its limits. Perhaps tomorrow the tautness within our soul
snaps, our restraint is overcome, and we are unleashed to
the true gift of ourselves that he has been awaiting from us.
And only then will we begin to know what it is to love God
with real intensity.

~

What seems to be only a quiet desire for God that arrives
one day without a hint of its importance, taking up residence in a corner of our soul, as though keeping silently to
itself, may be a true picture of what can become a profound
grace. There can be a lengthy concealment of a grace before
the full impact of a much stronger desire for God displays

itself. It is perhaps not so unusual to carry the divine favor of his predilection for our soul within us without recognizing or understanding it. The recognition of the face of God turned toward us, when he finally does make himself known, so often requires a period of God's concealed presence in the soul as a preparation. But even such a recognition is never a lightning strike coming from nowhere. The quiet and hidden preliminary hints are God's usual ways, like distant thunder heard over the hills. Should it be surprising that an intervention in our lives intended by God to transform our lives, even explosively, is initially so self-effacing in this manner? In fact, God seems to favor these quiet approaches when he is slowly carving his way into the core of a soul. He penetrates the depths of the soul where nothing can be observed so directly, and he does this action silently, planting within us at his own pace a kind of labyrinth of desire within the inner recesses of our soul. All the while our soul does not know what is being prepared and perhaps does not suspect it. Then one day the flame is lit, and the explosion ignites. And soon a fire is coursing through the labyrinth caverns of our soul, and we burn with a longing to give ourselves completely to God. The almost miraculous reality of this phenomenon can be astounding. And yet God seems to repeat it again and again in souls. We should look personally for that grace at this time of the Church.

~

"In the thickets in Arabia you will lodge. . . . To the thirsty bring water, meet the fugitive with bread" (Is 21:13-14). These words of Isaiah pose a question: To whom are they addressed? The Lord who is thirsty himself, alone in the desert plain, is the One who will give living water to the thirsting soul. Perhaps the words were understood by Jesus in this manner. In his life on earth, but also after his death, he will plunge into the harsh desert of a hostile rejection and make his home there. His abandonment of himself to the desert of human indifference places him in a perpetual state of unrelieved thirst. But this parched condition does not overcome him. He who entered the desert of thirst waits to give water to every thirsty soul that approaches him. It is an encounter of the One who thirsts with a soul in its inner deprivation. Jesus draws near always to a soul of thirst and offers the water of his own life to drink. It is striking how this pattern happened in the life of the Samaritan woman. She was alone, parched in soul, scarred in her woman's heart by failed love. In the first moment of meeting her, Jesus asks her to give him to drink. He who is in the desert, alone in the scrub of the barren desert, summons her to know him in his thirst. Yet he makes this request in order to offer her living water and relieve the desolation within the desert of her soul. "Go, call your husband, and come here" (Jn 4:16). It can seem an unkind remark, since Jesus knew that she had five previous husbands and lived now with someone not her husband. He seeks to draw out her painful thirst for love. She is indeed a fugitive running from long memories of pain in her private life. And Jesus meets her at that hour with the bread of his own divine love. And indeed she seems clearly to recognize his thirst for her soul. On that day, by the end of that encounter, the desert of her soul has become inhabited by a fresh outpouring of rain and the explosion of sudden flowers.

∿

The unfathomable depth of God's immense hidden being, unknown and inaccessible to our thought, is meant, not primarily to provoke speculation, much less our doubt or questioning, but rather to draw from us a receptivity to his ultimate mystery and a great personal surrender to him. Such a surrender to God, as he is, as he exists in the timeless hour of eternity, signifies an act of unknown implication. We may wonder after an act of pure surrender to the God of infinite love and mystery what the coming days may bring as a result. A surrender to God requires that fear of the unknown be overcome and transcended. His strong desire may be that we release ourselves from the limits of passing time and cast an offering of ourselves into the immeasurable hour of God's timeless making. He wants us to forget ourselves, to forgo all calculation and prediction, in surrendering to him. The greatness of our surrender is measured by the extent to which we cast ourselves blindly into the mystery of his eternal gaze upon us. The significance of every life offered more fully to God is unknown except within the mystery of his gaze. And that truth we can never know beyond a mere glimpse into what remains a dim light in the distance. Human time means little in its external dimensions once our soul has submitted itself to God in a great surrender. And yet the same human life in even its smallest hours acquires a depth of meaning after such a surrender. A new capacity for offering and love is received as we return to the hours of passing time.

～

The paradox can be insistent with every leap into deeper spirituality. We do not get closer to God without a greater distance stretching between our soul and God. It is a painful realization, almost shocking, that in drawing nearer to God we seem so often to lose him for a time. In a similar way, his presence can seem to be most elusive and unresponsive in the hour when we have no greater desire than to meet him. It can seem often that just on the edge of a direct encounter with him, his presence disappears into a realm of impenetrable shadow. His face, as it were, vanishes at the very moment we expect his eyes and his features to come into view. We are left staring, unable to regain a focus in the darkened air. We are bound at first to be confused at these patterns. Indeed, the experience of blindness, when it extends over time, may seem to proclaim a departure of God and even a permanent absence. But with grace and perseverance in prayer, we can learn to shift our thought to a more salutary awareness, namely, of the immense distance between our nothingness and the immense hidden reality of God. The blindness we may suffer is precisely for the sake of this awareness. We need to recognize these repeated patterns if we are to turn with proper adoration toward the divine mystery of our transcendent God. This need is going to increase in the decades to come when God is denied by much of the world.

~

The patterns do begin to show themselves and become known if we persevere in prayer. Prior to every apparent loss of his close presence, his companionship is often enjoyed with some ease. We needed only to open an inner door to a private room, and there he seemed to be waiting, as though expecting our visit, eager for our words. But then, once again, we are swept back into a dark condition by a wave of incomprehension that overtakes our inner spirit. He departs to the place of hiding, and we are alone again. The

untraceable distance of the unknown God once again permeates our soul. We can only gaze through the murky haze
toward a horizon without markings or signs. Nothing we
do ourselves can bring a satisfying return of his presence
in the current hour. Sometimes that absence may extend
many days, weeks, perhaps months. But the result is that we
often long for him with painful intensity in the hours of
prayer. The endurance of unsatisfied longing becomes itself
a slowly deepening grace. The conviction of his return can
be embraced with certitude, even in the most trying darkness. Then the pattern repeats itself with his arrival again in
some gift of his presence. Soon enough, as though all has
completely changed, he is known by some word or sense of
his immediate presence.

~

Saint John of the Cross' evocation of pure faith—"leaning
on pure faith alone"[6]—has taken on an unsuspected resonance in a time of ecclesial confusion and doctrinal ambiguity. Saint John of the Cross employs the term "pure faith" in
the contemplative context of his writings on prayer to urge
the soul to walk in the blindness of dark faith, to traverse
the long path of daily silent prayer without seeing what lies
ahead, ready for lengthy periods of internal darkness. But
what does he mean by this experience of interior darkness,
and how can this metaphor shed light on a proper spiritual
response to our own time in this era of the Church? Saint
John of the Cross writes that a sense of obscurity in prayer
is an unavoidable experience as faith deepens and we begin to receive contemplative graces in prayer. We might ex-

[6] Saint John of the Cross, *The Ascent of Mount Carmel*, II.1.1, in *Collected Works of St. John of the Cross*, 154.

pect the opposite to be the case: that a radiant clarity and
more penetrating insight would be consistently enjoyed as
we draw closer to God in prayer. But deeper faith has a different effect. In silent prayer, with the gift of contemplation,
the mind finds itself more often silenced, unable to arrive
at satisfying thoughts, left in an empty void of thought. At
the same time, as contemplative graces advance, the soul
learns to be untroubled with this silent incapacity, content
to remain in the Lord's presence, longing for him with love.
Faith itself, the exercise of the pure act of faith, has this effect
on the mind in contemplative prayer. The mind finds itself
disinclined to pursue an exercise of thought or reflection,
and not out of sloth or disinterest. Instead, the immediate
presence of God draws a focused attention of love in prayer.
The simplicity of a single phrase from the Gospel, the bright
flash of a scriptural insight, is sufficient to ignite a sustained
desire for God. A sense of interior darkness may permeate
prayer, but this is not a darkness of doubt or questioning.
It is simply an inability to see what is loved intensely, like
a man who has gone blind in his late years and sits quietly
with his beloved wife. The soul rests nearer to the mystery
of God in that quiet and perhaps at times is consumed by
a longing for him. It enjoys the certitude of being drawn
inside the mystery of Divine Presence. It knows the Lord,
not by thought or imagination, but by the longing it experiences in the depth of the soul.

～

This description of contemplative graces affecting the mind
in an hour of silent prayer may be pertinent in a time when
Catholic faith confronts indifference and even overt assaults
against the faith within the Church. In such a time, the night

of contemplative faith will not be confined to a soul's interior purification. The darkness that will enclose holy souls will not be simply an experience within the private enclosure of silent prayer. There will be a different experience of darkness, coming from a source outside the interior life and encountered within the Church herself. Indeed, an important parallel may exist for us, and we should note it today. Trouble and turmoil within the Church may not diminish in our time. Rather, a dark cloud of doctrinal ambiguity may increasingly cover in shadows the public face of the Church. Souls of deep Catholic faith will naturally suffer frustration with unclear teaching. This state of affairs will have to be met with a spiritual courage advised by Saint John of the Cross when facing interior purifications of darkness. These same souls, in their dedication to prayer, will learn the importance of a "contemplative approach" to the darkness occurring within the Church. This will not entail passivity or interior withdrawal in the effort to be untouched by ecclesial events. Instead, they will cultivate the prayerful habit of a deep certitude toward the truths of traditional Catholic faith. As Saint John of the Cross insists, the certitude of faith intensifies as prayer deepens, even as clear vision diminishes and the soul experiences darkness. This same spiritual truth will be important for prayerful souls in our own time. Nothing external or public that takes place as an assault upon truth within the Church, even when it is disturbing or shocking, can touch the truth of our Lord's identification with the heart of his Church. The suffering of Jesus in bearing any form of betrayal within the Church will only deepen the surrender of souls to his wounded presence concealed at the heart of painful events. These souls will live their own sacrificial offering in union with the

Passion of Christ. The contemplative insight will be strong in that time when his Passion is being relived in all forms of unfaithfulness witnessed within the Church.

∿

"I want what you want, only what you want, nothing more." These words can be a very good prayer, and they can be a way to unite our desire to God's will, but such a prayer is not immune to illusion. Humility may demand that we pray as well, "Lord, teach me to want only what you want; help me to know what you want; do not allow me to be deceived by my own desires." Saint Thérèse of Lisieux commented to the effect that God gave first the desire to her for all he intended to give her. When God gives the desire, it comes with the sacred possibility for a deeper entry into the life of God. Desires that burn with a longing for God and nothing else can be assumed to come from God. They need to be embraced from our heart in pure acts of longing for God. When, on the other hand, we begin to desire anything other than God himself, we can never know in the moment and at that time of our life whether this object of desire is the gift God wants to extend to us. It may be true that God will give us a desire for what he plans to bestow, but we can never be sure on our own that our desire corresponds with God's desire. The best prayer seems always to be empty of a particular object of desire in favor of a desire for God himself in all his mystery. Receptive to him alone, we never fail to desire what he is longing to give us, namely, himself.

∿

A kind of riveting need for God must reside at the center of our soul. A hunger in depth for God will burn secretly inside our soul to the extent that we find no means of relief. There is always a presence of poverty in a soul that loves God recklessly and holds nothing back. When our soul in its prayer arrives at seeking nothing but God himself, we become in a certain sense a starving soul, famished in our desire for God. A choice to remain poor and refuse any relief for that deep interior hunger is necessary for every serious soul of prayer. Otherwise, we stray from a demand of deeper prayer, which is to ignore our own desire for satisfaction in order that the Lord may give us the better gift of himself and secretly take possession of us. He makes this happen more often by leaving the depth of our soul in hunger. Our task is simply to leave ourselves accessible to God and, therefore, open to the pain of this hunger. Divine love then penetrates our soul in a manner that might be unknown, beyond our realization, and yet his love is not beyond our embrace as we surrender to God. The silent awareness of his love, unfelt and obscurely known, keeps our soul poor, but the certainty of his presence leads us to leap in desire toward God. He hides beneath a vast incomprehensibility within the soul that hungers for him, but he responds mysteriously to every leap of desire for him.

～

"I will give you the treasures of darkness and the hoards in secret places" (Is 45:3). When Saint Benedict as a young monk left his monastic community to seek the solitude of a mountain cave, he was mocked by his fellow monks: "If you seek the light, Benedict, why do you choose a cave?" His reply: "Because only in darkness do the stars shine bright."[7] Perhaps Benedict sought not only the physical darkness of that cave, the stark solitude and silence, but also a kind of spiritual darkness that he sensed would be fruitful. Perhaps he had some intuition that a deprivation of feeling any closeness to God would be a path to deeper interior realms of mysterious contact with God. Perhaps he even asked for this interior darkness to descend upon him, sensing that a bold step into the unknown might become a leap into the greater mystery of divine love. And so he embarked on this quest to pursue God by hiding his life in the darkness of a cave. He sought, not darkness itself, but the possibility of piercing through this darkness into the greater truth of the God of infinite love. If so, this would be a striking intuition so contrary to the natural inclination of a soul to seek truth only in light. He may have understood a deeper truth, that the deepest path to God must necessarily pass through darkness. And there, in his cave during three years, he discovered, in the physical deprivations of his life, the secret by which a soul can attract God and draw his love and even make God melt with love for a soul. From what we know of his life after this period of solitude in a cave, he seems to have realized in ever increasing insights that there is only one way to lay siege and conquer God, which is to be vanquished by him. In that mutual conquest, the God of all love shares the truth of his love for all souls. The soul of a man like Saint Benedict came to know God's love for the inestimable beauty of each created soul, and he learned

---

[7] *Lumina si quaeris, Benedicte, quid eligis antra? / Quaesiti servant luminis antra nihil. / Sed perge in tenebris radiorum quarerre lucem / Nonnisi ab obscura sidera nocte micant.*

Saint Benedict, in Ferdinand Gregorovius, *Latian Summers and an Excursion in Umbria*, trans. Dorothea Roberts (London: Junior Army and Navy Stores, 1903), 40.

the mystery of sharing the divine desire for the most miserable of sinners to find their way back to his divine heart.
Benedict learned to love souls in his cave in a manner as
never before in his life, which is a remarkable thing, since
in the solitude of his cave he had no immediate contact with
people. Most strikingly, he may have received this great love
for souls while undergoing a complete deprivation of any
tangible sense of closeness to God and while suffering the
emptiness of solitude in his cave. He may have experienced
in his own soul the mystical pain of a separation from God,
but he suffered it as an offering of love for souls in their
spiritual misery. Perhaps we must take a strong lesson here
if we are to pursue the light of God himself in a time of
increasing spiritual darkness.

9

A PASSION FOR GOD:
SUFFERING FOR LOVE OF GOD

Suffering is the means of her penetrating further, deep into the thicket of the delectable wisdom of God. The purest suffering brings with it the purest and most intimate knowing, and consequently the purest and highest joy, because it is a knowing from further within.[1]

—Saint John of the Cross

Plenty of people he finds to share his banquet, few to share his fast . . . there are many that follow Jesus as far as the breaking of bread, few as far as drinking the cup of suffering.[2]

—Thomas a Kempis

The extreme greatness of Christianity lies in the fact that it does not seek a supernatural cure for suffering, but a supernatural use of it.[3]

—Simone Weil

A passion for God, if strong for years, tends to burn more secretly as time goes on. This may be a truth both in individual souls and in the network of holy souls united in their

---

[1] Saint John of the Cross, *The Spiritual Canticle*, 36.12, in *The Collected Works of St. John of the Cross*, trans. Kieran Kavanaugh and Otilio Rodriguez (Washington, D.C.: ICS Publications, 2017), 613–14.

[2] Thomas a Kempis, *The Imitation of Christ*, II 11.1, trans. Ronald Knox and Michael Oakley (New York: Sheed and Ward, 1959), 76–77.

[3] Simone Weil, *Gravity and Grace*, trans. Arthur Wills (New York: G. P. Putnam's Sons, 1952), 29.

love of God as history progresses. The passion of a soul is largely concealed from an outsider's view, but it is also typically unknown and unexamined by a soul's own eyes. In religious Sisters, such as the Missionaries of Charity, it is not uncommon, from what I have observed, that souls of great spiritual passion often do not know how close they are to God, and it seems they do not care to know. They do not take a measure of their love or its progress, they simply live this love as they give themselves to the Lord in the chapel and in dedication to the poor. It is in their private life of interior prayer, if we were privy to its secrecy, that we might glimpse the reason why they do not realize the true depth of their love. They have advanced in love primarily by suffering their love for God. Painful experiences of love have been the stone-laden steps on their path to greater love, much of it in interior suffering, mysteriously leading to more intense love. It may be hard for us to perceive a link between greater love and suffering, but for these souls the two, love and suffering, become in time somewhat inseparable. The one completes the other, indeed almost predictably. Over the course of years, these souls learn to offer suffering as an act of love and to suffer all things as an offering of love to God. At some point, it perhaps becomes a personal secret of love for them to make this offering. In their love for God, as it grows, a love for suffering also deepens as a chance for a greater offering of love. In many cases, I think, they seem to expect the return of suffering when it disappears, just as a lover awaits a beloved to return home eventually. They even long for this companion of suffering. They have accustomed themselves over time to a steady pattern—the stoking of stronger fires of love in times of suffering—and so they welcome suffering to a degree. All this they never look at too closely, which enhances the secret of their greater love. Unknown to themselves, the offerings they make conceal themselves largely within their interior life. Nonetheless, the truth ought to be known. These patterns of love and suffering that combine in a fusion of self-offering to God repeat themselves in souls of great love. They tell us perhaps that Jesus hides his own wounds of love within such souls. When the day eventually comes, these souls may number far more than we realize in a last era of the Church.

~

Perhaps we are fully committed to love only to the extent that we will not refuse to suffer for love. If we are committed to love, we must be equally committed to suffering for a greater love. The statement does not suggest that we should make a request to God for suffering. Such a prayer might be answered in a manner beyond a soul's strength. What the words do urge is a recognition that no deeper love exists unless we are ready to suffer for love. Here we encounter a spiritual law observable almost universally in saints: their love grew as their suffering increased. Nonetheless, this link is not inevitable, and most people will not perceive the invitation to greater love in their trials of life. There must be a fresh insightful choice to offer suffering for love whenever a new trial of suffering arrives. The commitment to suffering is not a desire for suffering. It is rather a refusal to turn back when love is tested by suffering. Often what this means is a refusal to take back an offering made in love as suffering begins again to show its face. Great offerings are sometimes made in a quiet prayerful silence when sufferings are still unknown and await us in the future. We are unaware then what God might do with our prayer of offering, even as we may give him an open invitation and make ourselves

vulnerable in this act. The commitment to love, despite the
suffering that may occur, or, rather, united to the suffering that may come, is a promise to remain on a path that
heads in the direction of Calvary, knowing that greater love
awaits our life precisely when the taste of pain begins to be
felt more. The inseparable union of love and suffering then
becomes an insight, an encouragement to stretch farther in
the offering of our life in love to God.

~

In the late afternoon on the last day of her life, a few hours
before Mother Teresa died in the Motherhouse of the Missionaries of Charity in Calcutta, one of her sisters was walking past the open door of her small room and stopped in
the hallway to observe her. Mother Teresa was leaning over
a table, her back bent and her head down, with her hands
pressed on the table, clearly in pain. In her last year, she
suffered severe pain caused by the bones in her spine collapsing on the nerves of the spinal cord. At times it kept
her in bed or confined her to a wheelchair. The sister hes-
itated, anxious at the sight, and then heard these distinct
words: "Jesus, what are you asking from me?" The inseparable bond between love and suffering exposes itself in these
words. Mother Teresa did not cry out: "Why, Jesus? Why
are you doing this to me?" Her question does not suggest
the cry of a soul looking for an explanation, or possibly even
for relief, but rather that of a soul seeking to know God's
desire for a particular intention to be offered in this suffering. The lack of knowing likely accentuated her suffering.
Incomprehensibility toward the Beloved's exact purpose in
that hour was possibly a cause of pain to her heart greater
than the physical suffering. A cry like this to know what

to offer could arise only from a woman whose love accustomed her to offer all suffering into the hands of God.

~

The authority of the Cross of Calvary within our interior lives, carved within us as a rule of love, is an essential element of holiness. This is not just to accept the need to bear our crosses patiently. The authority of the Cross speaks of a wisdom long known by saints. It refers to the authority of Jesus in his Passion to demand surrender from us in an absolute manner. If we want to love him, he says, we must say "yes, I will offer this in love for you, I will offer this for souls." The authority of the Cross can become in time an unfailing interpretation of all events that cost us any degree of suffering. The wisdom of the cross has no other primary meaning than this interpretation ready at hand: the deep recognition that suffering offered in love for our Lord and for souls is never wasted. The suffering becomes an offering and a donation, and no longer simply a painful experience to pass through and endure. Instead, a living truth lights up in our soul. The offering of any suffering, under the authority of this rule of offering, transforms a painful experience into a singular gift offered to God. We may learn over time that we have nothing greater in life that can be given back to God than the offering of ourselves in times of pain or suffering. Placing ourselves under the rule of offering and the authority of the Cross of Calvary hastens the awareness that this is precisely our primary purpose in life—to offer for others, as Jesus did on his own Cross. This effort of offering is becoming all-important in our current era in the Church.

~

There can be in spirituality a misguided idea that a soul seeking God can never suffer unhappiness. The thought can be that no one desiring God and living virtuously can be unhappy. Afflictions of the interior life, trials of darkness and solitude, yes, but not unhappiness. This word unhappiness seems to convey a failed state of the soul, something twisted and distorted in a person who has found nothing to love in life. But this is a mistaken view. The reality of every soul passionate for God may be that there is a corner of soul where the wound of unhappiness cuts at the soul repeatedly. It is not a sign of aberration or failure; rather, it is a sign of a deeper unmet need in seeking God. It is a sign perhaps that will be felt and experienced more deeply in our time. The corner of our soul still unhappy is the place to cry out as a beggar before God. Unhappiness will continue to afflict the soul when it remains stifled and locked away from entry to that corner. The poverty at the soul's core is still too concealed. The result is a sense of incompletion, an unhappy irresolution at the heart of our life. It is the pain of not arriving yet at a deeper passion for God that he still expects and awaits from our soul. But this condition can be corrected. We must accept, in the trial of darker circumstances, the need to offer ourselves fully to God in the privacy of prayer. The Church herself can survive in her holiness in the coming decades only with this offering by souls from the depths of their interiority.

~

The healings of Jesus in the Gospel took place before his Passion. After he suffered at Calvary, however, and rose from the dead as our God, it may be that he prefers a better gift for a soul than the healing of its illness or disease. He wants to draw a soul that suffers bodily into a deep offering in union with his own oblation on the Cross. It is a far greater thing to become holy than to become healed. The bodily sufferings that are not removed from us invite us over time to this holiness. We learn a mysterious lesson in suffering when it is not simply endured, but offered for the sake of others, for the return of souls to God and their salvation. With the destiny of souls at stake, and our own capacity to offer for them, we may learn not to focus on pain, particularly our own, but to concentrate our desire on the release of souls from spiritual loss and despair. In effect, a vulnerability to love begins to awaken in a deeper manner when suffering pierces our life with illness or disease or any other hard pain. We learn to respect our Lord's desire to give himself in suffering to every soul that is willing to offer itself as he did on a Roman cross at Calvary. There may be an important truth here for the current day. The presence of suffering in personal lives is bound to increase in tandem with the Church herself suffering in a last era.

~

"I have not come to bring peace, but a sword" (Mt 10:34). Yet despite these words, how many treat the search for peace and tranquility as a motive for their religious faith. It is true that religious faith may bring inner peace to some degree, but if our faith is lived with greater interiority, it may also entail hard trials in life and serious experiences of purification within prayer. The sword that Jesus mentions here may be the cutting to the core of the soul by which we are tested whether we really desire to give ourselves fully to him. It is possible that peace is not necessarily a steady presence within the saintly soul. The holy souls of history may have suffered in their souls much more than they enjoyed peace. Their prayer is the first indication of this truth. The certainty that our Lord is truly present in silent prayer, listening and giving himself, is not the same thing as enjoying the comfort of peace in prayer. The certainty of his deeper presence does not in itself soothe a soul with warmth. Something else perhaps is the stronger reality. A sword of divine fire may instead slice through the heart in prayer, even unfelt and too deep for sensitive awareness. This sword brings no comfort of peace, but rather a splitting of bone and marrow in order that we may cry out painfully with a more intense love for the Lord. And he most certainly hears that cry and turns toward us, even in a deafening silence.

～

The soul that loves God intensely will find itself increasingly powerless before divine love and, for that reason, open to a greater suffering in life. Love means in part to become powerless to refuse God when it is certain that a request comes from him. The long habit of surrendering to God out of love for God removes all but the barest capacity to say "no" to God. These souls may experience reluctance and the strain of a greater surrender to God. But if they love much, they do not speak this word "no" to God. To an outsider, they may seem submissive in giving up a strength and independence that ordinary people will exercise thoughtlessly. But these are souls of greater love, and it is the nature of love to abase itself before the beloved even when this love brings suffering. And yet there is another aspect to this quality of greater love. What is increasingly powerless in us may be an inability to understand our afflictions. We may suffer incomprehension toward our suffering. Suffering can seem at times to be a wound inflicted by the hand of God. Much can be endured if the meaning of suffering is clearly present and the eventual fruits of our suffering are known. But when all is dark and silent? The powerlessness of love has no recourse then but to offer to God with an uncomprehending love, with intensity and a blind trust in Divine Providence. This habit of offering blindly, without comprehension, is a mark always of deeper love. It is an exercise of the true power that some souls never lose even in the depths of their apparent powerlessness before the trial of suffering.

~

In the opening chapter of the First Book of Samuel, Hannah's misery as a barren Jewish wife, her humiliation before the reproaches and mockery of Penninah, the second wife of Elkinah, with whom she must share a household full of children that are not her own, is a heartrending account. The long years of begging in prayer for a child have been fruitless. She has come to know the impenetrable barrier of divine silence: no answer to her pleas; nothing but the same silent refusal. Her sense of unworthiness has carved a deep scar of bitterness into her spirit. All this leads to a day of abject tears poured out in the temple and a promise that, if the gift of a son is bestowed, she will consecrate the boy at birth to the Lord. She is at a point where she cannot voice aloud her prayer. In her grief, she only mouths words in the temple with no sound heard. And she is reproached again, this time by the priest, Eli, for her appearance of drunkenness as he watches her moving her lips while speaking no sound. Her tearful protest of misery at the words of his rebuke, however, provokes his compassion, and he blesses her. And what happens is worth noticing. Finally, her prayer is heard after it has passed through the heart of the priest, Eli, who feels a terrible pity for this sorrowing Jewish woman. Can it be that sometimes our own prayers, long unheard, desperate prayers that seem long ignored, cast against the barrier of a divine silence, are waiting as well to pass through the pitying heart of another person, perhaps a priest or cloistered nun, before God finally answers with his favor? An intervention beyond ourselves must occur. Then, in a moment, and sometimes so easily, we receive what we have long begged for in sorrow. The desire of God when we are suffering and prayers go unanswered may be in part for us to learn the lesson of a resigned patience in suffering. Or, more likely, God's desire is that at some point, even frustrated, we expose our sorrow fully to another soul who will pray for our need. We may have little awareness of how intensely God loves to see the charity of intercession for others in prayer. And at times this intercession may be for our own need. It is likely that fervent souls in the Church will need in future days to cry out for intercession for the Church from her saints in heaven.

~

Perhaps the fullness of a great offering by our soul can be contained in a small fragment of suffering offered with a pure love for God. The small fragment hides immense possibilities, just as the smallest particle of the sacred Host conceals God himself in the flesh. Let us not miss this truth. There is nothing small when the love is great, and there is no small offering when the sacrificial intention burning within our soul is to offer ourselves with great love to God. The prayerful action, for instance, of offering even a small suffering for the sake of a soul dying in that hour and in need of grace is no paltry thing. Perhaps this prayer is used by Mary as the last needed intervention to break open a heart on the edge of an eternal tragedy. In this regard, we should keep in mind what awaits us as we age. The end of a life is often a continuous series of small moments of suffering. They pass one into another, and an older person may suffer from an inability to shake free from unrelenting discomfort and pain. Suffering of this nature offered for souls is not without fruits; it is not a sacred abstraction, a pious and wishful hope, to offer these sufferings. The offering contains a real promise concealed in the heart of God. The divine release of love to souls in need of a last grace may have a necessary link to the suffering offered for that soul. God in his infinite love can take the small suffering offered in love and use it to bring a soul in danger safely home. Much more, necessarily, is the power of intercession in greater offerings of suffering. When we turn to God, completely overcome, stripped down to the shreds of a desperate appeal, it is perhaps a state of soul that God has been awaiting in us. It is no small thing to offer ourselves to God in that state, just as it is no small moment, despite the short time it takes, when the priest consecrates bread and wine into the Body and Blood of Christ. Let us remember this truth especially today. There is a power of love that takes captive the heart of God when from our need we pour out a cry of offering for souls in much greater need than our own. These souls in need surround us constantly and will increase even more as this century continues.

Saint Paul was thrown to the ground, blinded by a piercing light, as Jesus spoke audibly: "Saul, Saul, why do you persecute me?" (Acts 9:4). The identification of Jesus reliving his Passion in the persecution of his followers is the implicit truth contained in these words. The Passion and death of Jesus did not end his suffering. Rather, he continues to live his Passion through the simple souls who suffer in a mysterious union with him in their lives. The persecution he suffered in a betrayal by Judas and in a decision by Jewish leadership to seek his Roman execution did not conclude with his death. It is living on in the period in which Paul has become a fanatical figure seeking to crush the incipient religious movement of Christianity. After the encounter with Jesus, Paul is blind for three days and eats and drinks nothing, not because he enters a period of fasting and mortification, but because he is utterly overwhelmed. And the true reality of this crushing experience for him may be to realize, not just that Jesus is the Messiah and the resurrected Son of God, but that his Passion continues in his followers. Paul will discover this truth in a personal manner. He will write later: "I have been crucified with Christ; it is no longer I who live, but Christ who lives in me; and the life I now live in the flesh I live by faith in the Son of God, who loved me and gave himself for me" (Gal 2:20). He came to know in his own sufferings, in the persecutions he endured, that the Passion of Christ was living again within his own life. It is a profound realization that is repeated throughout history in every saintly life. There is no great love except that the Passion of Christ mysteriously unites our soul to the heart of Christ. The saints became saints because they understood at some moment the need to offer themselves and their suffering to this sacred union. It is a truth we are likely to witness strongly in the last era of the Church.

∼

The conduct of God with souls follows definite patterns. Our Lord enters more deeply into souls that, unknown to themselves, become a hiding place for the wounds of his heart. He seeks out souls in which he can keep these wounds secret, so that no one, not even at times the soul itself, comes to know of them except by the favor of the Lord. His vulnerability to being wounded afresh in a life is a secret he prefers to conceal until a soul has grown much in love. Until then, he hides his wounds by entering, unobserved, into the personal suffering of our soul. He makes his home inside the suffering of our soul and offers us his own Passion. But he does this secretly. He lives his Passion again in a mysterious manner in union with our soul's own suffering. As much as he desires secrecy in this, his greater desire is for our soul to come to know by love the wounds of his heart in the very mystery of suffering. This occurs by some resemblance to his Passion in a personal way. We can come to see this truth only perhaps by accepting a taste of the humiliations, the loneliness, the isolation of his own last week. "He was despised and rejected by men; a man of sorrows, and acquainted with grief; and as one from whom men hide their faces he was despised, and we esteemed him not" (Is 53:3). These words convey one preeminent example by which Christ in his Passion can be mysteriously present in a life, wounded in love for a soul. And, in fact, many hidden souls do know personally the experience of these words from Isaiah. A real taste of the Passion of Christ hides at the core of their lives, and they sense this the more they love him in his Passion. Through their love for Christ crucified, they gain access over time to the vulnerability of God being wounded by love. Their suffering is the mysterious replication of Christ's wound of the heart penetrating their own heart in time.

～

The hollowed-out path of wooden planks that slowly climbs up a mountainside in northern Ethiopia has aided countless passing pilgrims making their upward journey. Few people would think to extend gratitude to the empty, indented spaces in that wood. Yet without this winding path, the ascent up the mountain would be dangerous to navigate. The hidden souls of spiritual depth are often like that wooden path—hollowed out and indented with poverty's bruises, but indispensable for our effort to climb to a higher level of understanding in our encounter with the mystery of God. We can only ascend by placing our steps in the hollow trail of their teaching and example. No one has become holy without friendships with holy people. Most of us require to find these friendships in our reading of the saints. But blessed is the soul that finds a holy friend over a lifetime, and even a saint, especially in a marriage or in religious life or in a priest who has become a father of love to their life. It may be that the humbler our soul becomes, the more likely we will perceive the soul placed hiddenly in our path to aid us on the way to God.

～

There is a vast difference in offering our personal sufferings to the Lord for the sake of others, and the far greater act of love by which we offer ourselves to the interior sufferings of his Passion. Perhaps only after a long period in life of drawing close to Jesus in his hours of darkness in Gethsemane, in his condemnation by the Caiaphas and the Sanhedrin, in his trial before Pilate, in his scourging by Roman soldiers, in his terrible immobility on the Cross, do we sense the need for a different offering of soul. An entry into a depth of love otherwise impossible can then take place. The offering of our soul to know him in his Passion can become after a time a compelling fixation. Perhaps quickly at that point we feel a desire to enter inside the mystery of pain in his heart during his Passion. The inner recesses of his heart can then become the great focus of our longing for him. The indifference of callous spectators at Calvary, the mockery and disrespect, the jeers and laughter, are a torture to his heart far beyond the pain of his torn flesh. Those who embrace the call to become victim souls of his love need to know these internal wounds. They want to know these sufferings within their own experience of prayer. They seek that knowledge as an entrance into the very heart of God. If they take hold of it as a knowledge, it always leads to a fruitful desire to intercede for souls in spiritual danger. The granting of this knowledge of his heart by Jesus to a soul always compels a profound urgency to intercede for other souls. And Jesus seems to accept the prayer of every soul that thirsts with his own thirst for the salvation of souls at risk of eternal loss. But he perhaps does it with greater solicitude toward our requests when we have asked to be united to his own internal suffering for souls who in the end of their lives are at risk of rejecting him.

∼

It is a good, loving effort in prayer to consider the look in the eyes of Jesus during the pain of his crucifixion. What did he stare at, what held his gaze, from what did he refuse to avert his eyes? Did he lock eyes with some individuals who surrounded him on the uplifted Cross? These divine eyes of Jesus could not be detached from the human heart of love that burned in him. Nor could his human pain be separated from his gaze of divine longing. He looked with searching eyes for the return of sympathetic eyes, and perhaps he found some there at Calvary. We ought to place ourselves beneath that Cross, leaving our own eyes ready to meet his, ready as well for a piercing realization that the wounds inflicted on our Lord by the mockery and contempt at Calvary are real in our own day. He looks into our eyes as God and wants to find a kindred soul, someone capable of recognition and courage. He wants to see in us a soul overwhelmed by a desire to be united with him in love. He longs to hear a soul gazing at him declare quietly that no fear of suffering for him will turn these eyes fixed on him to an easier path.

～

There are secrets in the internal suffering of Jesus on the Cross that await our discovery. But only love, indeed a very personal love for Jesus, allows the entry into these internal wounds of Jesus at Calvary. Our love must be a beggar's cry of pleading. The plea that we cannot love him as we desire without knowing more deeply the secrets of his inner pain seems at times to be what releases the door to the inner recesses of his heart. The Lord of suffering is almost incapable of refusing a soul requesting to love him more intimately by coming to know the secrets of his suffering in love. He does not say no to this request, even perhaps when it is naïvely pronounced. There seem to be hidden souls today who are seeking this kind of relationship with

Jesus crucified. They have in common a prayer that his Passion in all its sacred mystery might invade their heart and wound it to the depths. They pray that Jesus might carve the mark of his Cross into their own heart and engrave his Passion into their own soul. "Let your Passion live in me; let your wounds of love abide in me; let us be heart in heart, wound in wound; let your offering become my offering." It is a heroic prayer, we might think, inviting unknown consequences. But perhaps it is more accurate to say that it is a prayer of a soul in love with a crucified Beloved. It is the prayer of a soul who does not want to stand apart in the gaze of a spectator, able to walk away when the ordeal is completed. A soul that prays in this way wants to the touch the actual suffering of Jesus in love for souls even to this day.

10

JESUS AND HIS PASSION:
STILL NEGLECTED, STILL SCORNED

The contemplative life becomes awfully thin and drab if
you go for several days at a time without thinking explicitly of the Passion of Christ. I do not mean, necessarily,
meditating, but at least attending with love and humility
to Christ on the Cross. For His Cross is the source of all
of our life and without it prayer dries up and everything
goes dead.[1]

—Thomas Merton

I say to you the best and holiest thing is to think of the
most holy passion of our Lord and to pray over it, because
this is the way to arrive at union with God . . . in this holy
school the person finds true wisdom. Here is where the
saints have gained their knowledge.[2]

—Saint Paul of the Cross

Every time that I think of the crucifixion of Christ, I commit the sin of envy.[3]

—Simone Weil

Jesus spoke openly about his Passion prior to his crucifixion
at Calvary, of being handed over to the Gentiles, of being

[1] Thomas Merton, *The Sign of Jonas* (New York: A Harvest Book, Harcourt, 1981), 261–62.
[2] Saint Paul of the Cross, in Martin Bialas, *Mysticism of the Passion in St.
Paul of the Cross* (San Francisco: Ignatius Press, 1990), 209.
[3] Simone Weil, *Waiting for God*, letter 4, trans. Emma Craufurd (New
York: G. P. Putnam's Sons, 1951), 38.

mocked, spit upon, flogged, then killed. Only once, however, in a verse of Saint Matthew's Gospel, did Jesus men-
tion the word crucifixion. In every other reference, he an-
nounced only that he would be killed. One can ask whether
in fact in his public life he may have been entirely silent
about a crucifixion. He certainly knew that a Roman execution by crucifixion awaited him. But his silence about the
manner of his death, nailed miserably to a Roman cross, is
worth pondering. Was it a sign of a mysterious reserve in
Jesus, a quality of divine discretion that continues to this
day? And if so, the discretion of God in our current day
may be quite the same as in Jesus' lifetime, when our Lord
did not reveal openly what was to be his manner of death.
A simple thought is initially important in this regard. When
Jesus spoke of his death, the event lay still in the future. He
knew what would take place, but he carried this knowledge
of a death by crucifixion as a secret within his heart, perhaps only speaking of it to his mother. If he was silent in
his predictions about the exact mode of execution, despite
knowing it, there may have been a reason. He would not
expose the crucifixion as the manner of his death because
it had not yet been decided by the Jewish leadership at the
time of these predictions. While keeping his reserve, he allowed the decision by Caiaphas and the Jewish leaders to
seek a Roman crucifixion to play out in all its actual malice. He would not allow the crucifixion to appear afterward
as a *fait accompli*, predetermined by the hand of God. The
malice of human men would be lived out in all its tensions
and ultimate freedom. Perhaps we might ponder whether a
divine reserve is operating in our own time to keep secret
the exact mode of suffering that the Church must undergo
in the coming decades. The Lord may allow men once again
the freedom to decide how they wish to crucify him within
the Church herself.

~

The determination by the Jewish leadership to seek the death of Jesus came to a climax shortly before the Passion week. Soon after the raising of Lazarus, as Saint John tells us in his Gospel, Caiaphas met secretly with the elders, and at that meeting the decision to eliminate Jesus was taken. Caiaphas' famous remark settled the matter: "You know nothing at all; you do not understand that it is expedient for you that one man should die for the people, and that the whole nation should not perish" (Jn 11:49–50). Nonetheless, all was not decided. Risks and repercussions about the manner of his death still faced them. Saint Matthew's Gospel will say that they conspired to remove him by stealth and kill him. It is likely that a smaller group plotted in private conversations how to accomplish this. They likely considered other options besides a Roman crucifixion. The desert surrounding Jerusalem offered easy possibilities, where to take a man on a dark night and make him disappear was not difficult. On the other hand, a Roman execution by crucifixion offered advantages, even scripturally. Someone knowledgeable in these meetings must have read to the gathering the passage at the end of Deuteronomy 21: "And if a man has committed a crime punishable by death and he is put to death, and you hang him on a tree, his body shall not remain all night upon the tree, but you shall bury him the same day, *for a hanged man is accursed by God*" (Dt 21:22–23; emphasis added). Surely, this legal scholar argued, these words could prove useful with the Jewish crowds. A public execution by crucifixion, a man hung on a tree in agony, would confirm the fraudulence of the man nailed to a Roman cross. No one hung on the wood of a cross can be holy if God's words in the law are truly sacred and trustworthy. Let him be crucified for all to see, and clearly this man can be proclaimed in league with the devil and under God's curse. The argument was persuasive, and the decision to seek from Pilate a Roman crucifixion was made. They needed only to settle their legal strategy to win their case before Pilate. The accusation that Jesus was claiming to be a king and therefore a rival to the emperor proved to be a clever tactic in the praetorium. It may have surprised some of the Jewish elders how smoothly it went, with help from the crowd. When Pilate finally pronounced a death sentence by crucifixion, there were likely a few minutes to observe congratulations pressing in on Caiaphas and his own triumphant face of pride.

~

The sensitivity of the skin of Jesus after sweating blood in Gethsemane made the kiss of Judas a dreadful source of pain. It was not just a painful acceptance of his betrayal that caused suffering to our Lord. The kiss itself was extremely painful to the touch. The satanic presence that had overtaken the soul of Judas participated in this kiss. It must have burned the cheek of Jesus. Jesus had not had physical contact with malicious evil prior to this hour, only confrontation with the devil as a combatant in the desert temptations. Now he was compelled to experience the attempted deception of the demonic in inflicting a kiss upon his sacred face. He may have turned often in thought during the remaining hours of his life to that kiss. It was a defining moment of exposure to the malice of evil. Without any possibility of remaining hidden and unknown, the evil one nonetheless exercised his desire to pay contemptuous respect to one whom he desired to destroy. The whole history of humanity is present in this gesture. The satanic presence is insatiable in its effort to bow in deceptive respect before a humanity it despises with immense hatred. And he does the same to Jesus in that moment because he cannot do otherwise. The gesture of the kiss is an image, too, of the Church in history. The satanic presence will continue to offer a kiss of betrayal throughout the centuries. Unfortunately, in many periods of time, like our own, that kiss leads to a confusion and a lie that is embraced by many. The effort to undermine sacred truth in all its forms is simply a replication of the kiss of Judas on the face of Jesus.

~

After the examination and trial before Caiaphas and the Sanhedrin, and the determination to put him to death, there were still some hours left in this night before Jesus was brought before Pilate in the early morning. During these hours, Jesus was likely taken by Jewish guards to a prison cell under the authority of the Jewish police. There, locked up in a cell, he went through a kind of second Gethsemane, alone and forsaken again. He was aware that they would seek from Pilate in the early morning a sentence of death by a Roman crucifixion. He knew well that a crucifixion awaited him. And it is possible that in departing from Caiaphas and the others, he caught some whispered reference to their desire and perhaps overheard some of the strategy in the plan for a Roman crucifixion. But then he was plunged again alone into darkness and isolation, as in Gethsemane. This time, perhaps, his internal suffering in solitude was not caused, as in Gethsemane, by embracing the sins of humanity upon his human soul. He did not sweat blood this time. Instead, he may have suffered in knowing the souls in history who would unite their lives to him in his torture on the cross. It was a suffering of great love to him to know the almost reckless desire of souls who would offer themselves in union with his Passion. During this night in his isolation, he perhaps cast his inmost thought upon them and saw them with his divine eye. The Roman scourging and crucifixion were certain, and he knew that nothing would take place to avert them. But he was perhaps moved in these hours alone in that prison cell to contemplate in his vision the loving souls who would gaze on his Passion and beg to suffer in their own souls his suffering in the Passion. In that darkness, before the morning light, he may have pronounced a resounding "yes" into history to embrace these souls to his heart and allow them a share in this privileged suffering. It was a second Gethsemane, but very different in its solitude, with his interior eyes focused on the souls who would seek the core of his heart in suffering and receive an answer to their request in love.

～

The forcible stripping of Jesus first took place when he was scourged. Roughly divested of his clothing, he stood for a moment before the Roman soldiers as God in the flesh in his naked humanity. The humiliation for Jesus, a Jew of pious modesty, to stand unclad before the eyes of Gentiles, naked before mocking men, is a significant revelation of God. In truth, the moment encapsulates the humiliation of God before his creatures. The presumption to strip God of his mystery and display him to open view will occur repeatedly in history. The reduction of God to an exposed target of vile disrespect can find its telling image here in actions of the Roman soldiers. Then he was tied to a pillar, and the brutal scourging commenced. By the end of it, he had received 120 stripes from the three-pronged whip, two-thirds on his back and a third on the front of his body, according to scholars of the Shroud of Turin. They covered him with clothes again, which quickly soaked in the blood of Jesus. Then a second stripping of Jesus took place at the site of the crucifixion. They divided his clothing among them, and for his seamless tunic, they cast lots. It is a terrible question to ask whether the humiliation of Jesus extended to a complete nakedness on the Cross. The desire of the Romans to humiliate a crucified victim permitted that possibility. But in the case of Jesus, crucified on the preparation day for the Passover, with thousands of Jews already in Jerusalem for this holy week of remembrance, it is very doubtful that the Romans would have risked the offense to the Jews of placing a man naked on a cross just outside the walls of Jerusalem. In fact, the humiliation of Jesus did not require nakedness on a Roman cross; it was quite complete already. He was wearing a crown of thorns on his head in mockery of his kingship. He was nailed in the nakedness of his silent abjection while receiving the taunts and mockery of the crowd.

～

The thorns that pierced the head of our Lord were inflicted as a gesture of mockery. The Roman soldiers in the praetorium knew that Jesus was accused of making himself a king. The malicious action of wrapping a crown of thorns around his head is understood to be an act of humiliation. If it was shaped as a crown, he wore it in mock imitation of the laurel leaf crown the emperor wore in Rome. They may have placed, however, not a crown, but a kind of headdress or basket of thorns upon the head of Jesus. And, indeed, they may have slammed this headdress of branches and thorns upon his head with a piece of wood. All this violence was accompanied by shouts of mockery and derision. This action also introduces the possibility, as some mystics have mentioned, that three of these thorns pierced the head of Jesus with mortal wounds. They penetrated blood vessels or arteries that would slowly bleed and not stop bleeding, and perhaps the thorns even reached the brain when the head-dress of thorns was pressed into the Lord's head. The image is striking if that is the case. The Logos, the mind of God himself, is subject to a terrible wounding even unto death in the human brain of Jesus the Son of God. The Logos, the Word made flesh, not only allows himself to suffer humiliation and to bear violent contempt from his creation in the Passion. His sacred reality as a God vulnerable in the flesh is even open to a piercing of the human brain of the Son of God. He wishes us to know him in his Passion as the Logos, the Word, who receives silently in the depths of the divine mystery all human gestures, the gestures of love and the gestures of deadly malicious contempt.

~

The Virgin Mary's first sight of her Son carrying the heavy crossbeam across his back on the way to Calvary was shocking, and it may have flooded her mind with an immediate remembrance. Many times in her life she may have read alone and also with Jesus the description in Genesis of Abraham accompanying his son Isaac on the steep climb up Mount Moriah, where Abraham had been commanded to offer his son in sacrifice. "Take your son, your only-begotten son Isaac, whom you love, and go to the land of Moriah, and offer him there as a burnt offering upon one of the mountains of which I shall tell you" (Gen 22:2). Abraham laid the wood for the burnt offering on the back of Isaac, who carried it, while Abraham carried the fire and the knife for the sacrifice. During her life, Mary may have meditated deeply on her own maternal role in the offering she would have to make of her son, Jesus, which she very likely realized early in his life. She is another Abraham in this sense, as she carried the fire within her heart for the burnt offering that she would consciously make of her son Jesus. When she sees Jesus with the wooden beam across his back on his way to Calvary, the connection is immediate. But she knows that this time there will be no last-minute intervention by an angel calling down from heaven and halting the sacrifice. Instead, at the sight of Jesus pushing forward under the weight of that crossbeam, she saw the sacrificial offering that was soon to consume Jesus on the hill of Calvary. And she makes this offering herself of her son as the Lamb of sacrifice. The story in Genesis concludes, after the intervention by the angel to stop the hand of Abraham raised with a knife over Isaac, with the promise that Abraham, because he did not withhold his only son, would be blessed as the father of offspring as numerous as the stars of heaven and as the sand on the seashore. Mary, in looking at Jesus carrying this wood of the Cross, surely realized that she was hearing these words of promise as well, but as mother of the generations to come who would embrace her divine Son in love and surrender.

～

The violent stretching out of the hands of Jesus so that the Roman soldiers can nail him to the wood of the Cross, the immobility of his arms in an outstretched gesture as he is raised to a vertical position, invoke images from the life of Moses. Moses stretched his arms out in prayer and intercession as the Jewish armies faced possible defeat by enemies. The arms were held up by others, and while they remained outstretched, the Jewish armies succeeded. The arms of our Lord on the Cross are held in place by nails transfixed into the wood. The nailing of Jesus in an utterly painful immobility of his hands to the wood is an image of the triumph of his prayer of immolation. Nothing can defeat him as he hangs nailed to the Cross. He will not dislodge himself from that fixed immolation; he will undergo his immolation to the end. But there is another significant image. Moses held his hands outstretched when he turned the divided waters of the Red Sea back upon the Egyptian charioteers and soldiers, destroying the enemy army. The outstretched arms of our Lord on the Cross may be also an image of the ultimate defeat for the satanic enemy that seeks the ruin of souls. The waters of the Nile flowed back upon the Egyptian enemy, and the power of grace descends on the world to defeat the infernal enemy as Jesus offers himself in suffering to the immolation of crucifixion. Satan is indeed conquered, and we must know this great truth in our struggles with the evil one as they intensify in the days and decades to come.

∼

The silence of Jesus on the Cross, his lack of speech for most of the three hours, hid a deep, mysterious reality. His silence coincided with an intense prayer of intercession for history and all sinful humanity. We can hear it certainly in these words: "Father, forgive them; for they know not what they do" (Lk 23:34). Perhaps we interpret this statement as an act of forgiveness toward the Roman soldiers and to the crowds taunting and mocking him. But the words stretch far beyond the immediate context of Calvary. We are hearing a prayer by the Son of God immolated in sacrifice on the Cross. These words are spoken from a deep cavern of mystery within the mind and heart of Jesus. He is speaking to his Father, not just regarding the hostile presence of people who surrounded him at Calvary. His words are a private prayer appealing to the Father for all sins in history committed without awareness of inflicting a wound on the heart of God. Jesus' own heart suffers for the failure of souls to recognize the piercing of his heart. We might say that our God in his fatherly tenderness is revealed in this brief sentence of merciful appeal by Jesus. Jesus seeks almost to make excuses for the offenses directed against himself. "They know not what they do." The implication in those words is that we human beings are not so malicious as it seems. If we knew what in fact we were doing, we would reverse our actions quickly and beg forgiveness. It is an appeal of infinite pathos within the heart of God.

~

Blood flowed freely from the thorns that cut into the brow and head of our Lord. The blood dripped down his forehead into the eyes of Jesus as he hung on the Cross, clouding his eyes and causing a partial blindness, forcing him to blink this blood away to gain any sight beyond a blurred vision. Half-blinded by this blood, unable to remove it as he hung nailed by his hands to the wood of the Cross, he could not see clearly the persons who were present in the crowd beneath his Cross. His partial blindness may have led him to enter more deeply into an interior prayer of oblation while he hung on the Cross. This image of his prayer in blindness on the Cross is a truth of history. He wants us to know that the blood in his blinded eyes is an image of the vulnerability of his love for souls. He is blinded, not by blood, but by love. He desperately wants souls simply to turn to him in love, which is why he prayed for those who mocked and taunted him at the crucifixion, even while unable to see their faces clearly. The bloodied eyes of Jesus are perhaps, in a sense, how he looks at us even now. He cannot gaze on any soul except through a prism of the blood shed for that soul. He sees through the veil of his own blood covering the soul, the precious blood of his crucifixion flowing over the soul, whenever he looks at a soul who is close to him. We need to perceive this veil of his red blood shimmering before us when we turn our eyes in his direction. The blood of Jesus that filled his eyes must penetrate the eyes of our own soul with love.

~

The breathing of Jesus on the Cross became increasingly labored as he neared death. Yet this is the breath of God being exhaled at Calvary in the human nature of Jesus Christ crucified. The breath by which he poured forth his image into the creation of man at the beginning of time is now constricting within his collapsing lungs. From the Cross this breath of love continues to be poured out from the heart of God for all human persons in history. What is most striking is that it is not a last sigh of breath that will end Jesus' life on the Cross. Rather, a loud cry is emitted. The last breath is identical with a dramatic release of an outpouring of love from the heart of Jesus as God himself. The love of God for his creation is expressed at this climactic moment of the loud cry from the Cross. The longing of God in tenderness to pour himself out into death for his own beloved creation ought to shatter our hearts, which typically remain too cold to this last moment in the life of Jesus at Calvary. He is showing us by the loud cry as his last breath that he dies making an extraordinary oblation of himself. His love is beyond measure, unfathomable in its extension and reach, even to the most miserable of souls, which may indeed be ourselves on many days of our life, if we have the wisdom to perceive it.

~

The loud cry of Jesus at the time of his death may be the most significant unexamined phenomenon in the entire Passion. Yet its spiritual importance is profound. Sometime before this cry at his death, Jesus spoke the opening words of the twenty-second psalm: " 'Eli, Eli, láma sabach-tháni?' that is, 'My God, my God, why have you forsaken me?' " (Mt 27:46) His cry of forsakenness drew mockery from the crowd, as someone shouted that Jesus was calling on Elijah. Sour wine was ordinarily kept at the Roman crucifixion sites to torment the crucified when they began to lose consciousness by splashing the vinegar into their wounds and lacerations. This vinegar was now placed on hyssop and brought to the lips of Jesus. But if we read the four Gospels as one, as a single description, we realize that Jesus, before or after pronouncing the verse of the psalm, spoke his words "I thirst" (Jn 19:28). The vinegar brought to the lips of Jesus in Saint John's Gospel near the end of Jesus' life is the response of the crowd to his thirst on the Cross. The loud cry of Jesus in the Synoptic Gospels may be linked to this gesture of extending vinegar to his lips after he pronounced his thirst on the Cross. If so, his loud cry at death is a final outpouring of the forsaken One, mocked in his last hour of isolation and need, offered vinegar by a callous crowd, which includes all the centuries of history. His loud cry at death is in effect a reply to the vinegar extended to him when he has just expressed his thirst for love. The vinegar to his lips becomes emblematic for all of history. The vast majority of mankind will offer our Lord the taste of vinegar in return for his complete immolation for us. Yet those lips at the very moment of death could pour forth in a cry of love his longing to give himself to the end in an act of infinite love for us. Only a God in the flesh could do so, which the centurion quickly recognized.

~

When in Saint Luke's Passion account Jesus with a loud cry at his death uttered a short phrase from Psalm 31:5—"Into your hands I commit my spirit!" (Lk 23:46)—these were not just last words that would carry him securely across the threshold of death. They were a spiritual testimony to us, a final lesson held back until the very end, a lesson of the way of abandonment to God as the only path to great sanctity. What we might call the culminating moment of the crucifixion of Jesus on the Cross is a loud cry of his own abandonment to the Father. It was Jesus teaching us to cast ourselves in the same way into the hands of our God. Abandoning ourselves to God comes only when we experience something close to death in our own existence. The inclination to let go and release completely into God's hands does not happen unless we are experiencing some desperation and great need. The death of Jesus can be the catalyst for realizing this state of need. If we place ourselves before this final act on the Cross, his loud cry of filial abandonment to his Father can become our own act in prayer. We need to cast all things in our life into the Father's hands. We need to remain utterly dependent on him. This is a deep disposition of the interior life. The abandonment to God of ourselves does not take us across the threshold of death. But it does lead to the death of any illusion that we can control or direct our own path to God. This last word of Jesus on the Cross, in the Gospel of Saint Luke, is a strong, definitive statement of the demand to offer ourselves blindly, in abandonment, to God's desire that we die completely to our own control over our lives.

~

Perhaps the cry of Jesus at death is, as it is described, long and sustained, and so an unnatural phenomenon. What does it tell us of the final moment in the life of the Son of God? Mary received this cry into the depths of her heart, and indeed it tore her heart open, and so we must ask her what she understood. The loud cry perhaps reveals to us the inner heart of God himself in love with his own creatures, with his lowly ones, who have little awareness of his love for them. It is a loud cry as though God is releasing his innermost heart to be glimpsed for a moment in the death of the Son of God. His cry is to shake us into an awareness that we have not understood. Indeed, the earth itself trembles with an earthquake at that very moment, and the temple curtain is torn in two. The cry of Jesus on the Cross pours out in a single syllable of groaning love the Lord's infinite desire to be recognized for his infinite love. He speaks his longing for souls to let go of their blind attachment to this world and to belong only to him. He shows us in effect a violent gesture of love to take captive our heart in a manner beyond any further desire of release. We should remember that God's way is always to overcome and flood a willing soul when the opportunity is present to give his love to a soul with a greater release of divine love upon it. The immensity of infinite love, indeed, demands the overwhelming expression of love as a natural expression of the divine nature. We need ourselves to acknowledge this longing of God, so that we may surrender ourselves more completely to his desires.

~

The tearing of the veil in the temple at the very instant when Jesus breathes his last on the Cross at Calvary is not just an image of the end of the Jewish temple worship. A violent tearing is taking place within the heart of God as his chosen people, the Jews, enter now an exiled state of blind ignorance. Their Messiah dies on the Cross as the divine incarnation of God in the flesh, and they do not recognize this truth. The failure to perceive is a piercing wound to the heart of God. It is not just that the malicious Jewish leadership at the time of Christ causes lamentation in heaven at that hour. The awareness is deep in the heart of God that the Jewish people, the faithful good Jews of history, will embrace a stubborn refusal to reexamine the ultimate question whether in truth Jesus of Nazareth was indeed the incarnate Son who came as Messiah. The veil tears in two, and the painful separation cuts the heart of God almost in two. He will continue to love his own, his Jewish people, but with a pain always that they love him and honor him without paying attention to his ultimate tenderness toward them. They have become like children who quickly kiss the outstretched hand of their father and then flee when he holds out both his arms to embrace them and pull them close to his heart in a lasting manner. But they turn away and run in a direction of foolish ignorance. Such is the pain of God for his Jewish children, ever loved by him.

~

The tearing of the veil in the temple at the exact moment of Christ's death has another meaning that can speak to our own time. The tearing of the veil is ordinarily interpreted to signify a termination of the temple worship as the locus of adoration for God. But the tearing might have other important meanings. Jesus' own heart is torn open in death as a Roman soldier pierces his heart with a lance to ensure his death. Blood and water flow from his opened heart as a result of that action. This tearing open of his heart in the lancing of his heart becomes an invitation to enter his wounded heart, a heart torn by the humiliating rejection he received in the Passion. But the tearing of the veil, taking place at the very same hour, may have a deep meaning in the last era of the Church, when it may link the pain of the wounded heart of Jesus to a tearing and rupture that is going to take place in the Church herself. The tearing apart of a sacred presence until then protected within the Church may occur in that last era. It will not mean the termination of the Church, which cannot happen. But it may point to a rupture into two halves of what has for centuries been identified as the Church by faithful Catholics. The Church may undergo a division within itself while remaining institutionally still one Church, as though she has been sliced from within by a terrible wound of the heart. Perhaps those who remain in love with Jesus Christ crucified must embrace a terrible truth in that time. They will have to face an insight of great pain. The Church will have a need to return to the wounded heart of Jesus pierced with a lance, not of a Roman soldier, but of callous betrayal. It will have to find its home in the wounded heart of Jesus. Then all things will be clear and understood, all things linked to wounds he is currently receiving from within his Church.

~

The sight of dried blood streaking the face of Jesus in death, his head swathed with thorns, his eyes blankly staring, must have crushed the heart of Mary. Yet she would not turn her gaze away from him. The sight of his dead body on the Cross, his hands transfixed by the nails, leaning down in death toward her, was a shocking vision. She felt the terrible departure of his soul from the immediate vicinity of the crucifixion site. The sight of death in his face stunned her and caused her to gaze on his face with a longing for his voice and the radiant eyes she knew in life. But his body remained lifeless, and she lingered in her fixation on him as others went to request the bodies to be taken down from the cross. The lack of movement in his features made her focus on the eyes, now dead, and she perhaps felt that mystical suffering that certain souls will undergo in history when the eyes of God are vacant and closed, unresponsive to their searching desire. She understood in that moment the suffering of the souls of love who would seek her Son and be left waiting in a silent death of unanswered longing. She heard nothing of the crowds around her in that hour of waiting because she was pulled inside to the profound mystery of a silent death by God who desired to speak now only in a beloved face given over to death. She turned not at all to her own heart's suffering at the loss of her Son. She was consumed rather with the divine mystery. God in her womb and now God hanging in the brutal reality of her crucified

Son leaning his crowned head down toward her, his blank staring eyes inviting her to see the infinitude of divine love in his transfixed gaze looking at her with love even in death.

～

The piercing of the heart of Jesus in death is a brutal act. He was already dead, but the Roman soldier had to fulfill his duty. His violent thrust to the heart of a man nailed to a cross confirmed the execution of the prisoner. The action enters history as a profound invitation to souls in love with the heart of Jesus Christ. He may have been physically dead at that moment, but the violent gesture of the piercing is emblematic of all of history. The piercing of the heart of our Lord in death continues after his death to the end of time. Perhaps the great realization for us is to see in the piercing a truth of suffering that will come from within his own Church. He suffered the violence of his Passion as an immolation and offering for the sins of humanity through-out history. But he undergoes the piercing of his heart af-ter death to show the pain of his heart in subsequent his-tory from the betrayal of his loved ones who will choose to deny him in any serious manner. The piercing of the heart of Jesus has a direct link with the history of the Church. Jesus will continue to receive a piercing lance to his heart whenever the Church in any historical time refuses to give herself faithfully to his truth and his teaching. A last era of the Church may be marked by piercing of the heart of Jesus in a stark manner of betrayal. Even in our own time, the piercing of Jesus' heart is a profoundly real possibility. This piercing is, indeed, likely to penetrate the history of our time in greater ways as the years ensue.

11

THE HOLY EUCHARIST:
THE DIVINE OBLATION OF LOVE

Is the sacred untouchable? Yes, certainly, and yet we touch it. Is the grandeur inaccessible? Yes, and yet we are raised up to him; he is that *tremendum*, the object of a religious fear? Yes, and yet he draws us to himself by opening his Heart to us.[1]

—Henri de Lubac, S.J.

The Being I am is a Being of fire. . . . My fire does not destroy. . . . And my flame has no need to be fed. It imparts itself, gives itself. I am the Gift that never ceases to give itself.[2]

—Lev Gillet

My soul longs for your body; my heart is athirst to become one with you. Give me yourself—that is all I want; apart from you there is nothing able to bring me comfort. Without you I cannot exist; without these visits of yours I cannot live.[3]

—Thomas a Kempis

The great reality of the Holy Eucharist is that it is a new form of created existence that did not exist prior to the institution of the Eucharist on Holy Thursday night. In the

---

[1] Henri de Lubac, S.J., *Theology in History*, trans. Anne Englund Nash (San Francisco: Ignatius Press, 1996), 240.

[2] Lev Gillet, *The Burning Bush* (Springfield, Ill., 1976), 17.

[3] Thomas a Kempis, *The Imitation of Christ*, IV 3.1–2, trans. Ronald Knox and Michael Oakley (New York: Sheed and Ward, 1959), 188.

disguised appearance of a Host is the fullness of our Lord Jesus Christ in his body and soul and divinity. Praying before a tabernacle or monstrance, we are in a physical proximity to the same body of Jesus that endured the horrific sufferings of his Passion. The wounds in his hands and feet and side are present for view, even if we are blind to them. Although they cause no physical pain to Jesus, they are signs of a suffering and a vulnerability in the human heart of Christ that did not end at Calvary. And what is that suffering extending beyond his death at Calvary? The immense inner depth of his wounded heart hides this mystery. No words can convey an adequate understanding. It is only our secret entry into his heart in prayer that can lead at times to a sense of a silent communication by means of his wounds. Simply, directly, he repeats—"I suffered for you and suffer still for you." In this silence we gaze on wounds inflicted on our God. He asks us to enter inside these wounds and to await a deeper recognition when we pray before him in the Eucharist. And then we may come to realize that Jesus Christ continues to suffer even now in his human heart from wounds of rejection and indifference. These wounds are likely to intensify in the Church in the coming years. Perhaps he asks us personally, with a very tender request, to accept within our own heart his wound of love when we receive him in the Eucharist. The reception of his Body and Blood at Mass, if it is a true act of love on our part, is to discover that we are receiving the Passion of Jesus into our lives.

~

"Do you believe . . . that in the Sacred Host, where I seem to be doing nothing, I am working? I work by the immolation of Myself to the Father's will. I work imperceptibly but efficaciously on souls!" (Jesus to Sister Mary of the Holy Trinity).[4] The immolation of which Jesus speaks as a work is the entire giving away of himself. He completes his offering to his Father's will by an act of immolation in which he sheds his majesty as divine Son and assumes in appearance the fragile nothingness of the sacred Host. What we are really seeing in the Eucharist, if our eyes are open in love, is the mystery of divine humility. Concealed in the sacrificial action of transubstantiation, at its core, is the descent of God into the immolated humility of the consecrated Host. Divine humility in the Eucharist is inseparable from a work of immolation; indeed, an immolation is the essential feature of the sacrificial humility of God in the Eucharist. And how so? Immolation demands an offering, a stripping down, a burning away, until the immolated offering disappears. An immolation requires that what is immolated disappears. This is exactly what does happen in the Mass, in one sense. Jesus gives himself to us in the Eucharist to the extent of fully disappearing when he allows himself to be consumed by us and seen no more. The immolation completes itself as we consume him in the reception of Holy Communion and become one with him through this reception. He disappears as we take him into our own body. The disappearing into a presence now within us completes the work of his immolation. His presence in us, with the disappearance of the Host, allows his work of immolation then to continue in us. The reception of the Eucharist invites us to our own sacrificial immolation out of love for Jesus. It is the Father's will that his Son reveal God's humility in this perpetual act of immolation. But it is also the Father's will

[4] Sister Mary of the Holy Trinity, *The Spiritual Legacy of Sister Mary of the Holy Trinity*, trans. anonymous, ed. Silvère Van Den Broeck, O.F.M. (Rockford, Ill.: TAN Books, 1981), 199.

that Jesus draws us to the same desire for immolation and disappearance. Jesus in the Eucharist shows that God knows no greater love than to give himself away in an outpouring gift of himself. He disappears into those who receive him, and he desires that we become one with him in a work of our own immolation out of love for him. This oneness with the wounded heart of our Lord is perhaps the great spiritual challenge of our time.

~

"I glorified you on earth, having accomplished the work which you gave me to do" (Jn 17:4). Yet still another work awaited Jesus when he spoke these words at the Last Supper. He would soon plunge into the desolation of Gethsemane and struggle to take upon his human soul the sins of human history. It was a hard work indeed to surrender himself fully to his Father's will. And throughout the hours of that night and into the next day, until three o'clock in the afternoon, he would be at work in a sacrificial oblation of unfathomable mystery. His work of love extends into eternity, because he will take this same work of oblation to the right hand of the Father and continue to offer himself for us there. The unbloody sacrifice of the Mass is the perpetual work of self-offering by Jesus as he gives himself in infinite love for us. The work of Jesus in his sacrificial oblation has another dimension. He makes a perpetual effort to draw us to offer ourselves to a sacrificial oblation of our own lives in love for him. He wants souls who are one with him in his own sacrifice. This is not a small question of making sacrifices as a sign of our love for him. He desires souls that pierce a threshold of recognition and realize the need to offer themselves to a real taste of his Passion entering their own lives. He wants comrades in arms, so to speak, courageous souls who do not fear to make the ultimate offering of themselves, knowing that all things in a life will now be completely subject to God and his disposition. The expectation can only be that a burnt offering of one's life is going to take place. There is no need to fear or be anxious, because this same offering will necessarily reveal how deeply our Lord delights in a soul when it gives itself to him without reserve. This may be precisely why the many martyrs in history, documented numerous times, did not suffer terrible physical pain in their tortures. The sword of divine fire pierced and pervaded their hearts with love, and they were conscious far more of this reality of love than of physical pains. They had offered themselves completely to God, and he filled them with a great consolation of delighting him in that oblation.

∽

The public life of Jesus displays a quietly climactic revelation as it draws to a close. Only at the conclusion of three public years when he is near his Passion does he strip away more fully the disguise of his identity. "And he who sees me sees him who sent me" (Jn 12:45). It is a remarkable admission, almost the removal of a mask of concealment, as it were. He tells us in effect that his human face hides the presence of the Father. They are one, as Jesus affirms, and yet distinct as persons. The words that Jesus speaks, he says, do not come from him but from the Father, who is doing his works in the words Jesus pronounces. The significance of this double truth—an encounter with Jesus is simultaneously an entry into the mystery of the Father—is essential for spiritual life. The capacity to cross the threshold of an encounter with divine mystery, whereby the humanity of Jesus becomes a door opening into the living reality of God himself, is a key truth of spirituality. This lifting of the veil of appearance into a direct encounter with God himself is not a pursuit after mystical experience. It is rather a daily dimension of engagement with the sacraments, especially in the Eucharist. In fact, the words of the Consecration heard at Mass are subject to an analogous recognition. Whoever hears the words of Consecration spoken by a priest at Mass hears the One who pronounces these words in a divine act. Jesus acts *in persona Christi* in the priest. His voice is present in the Mass, not as an echo of a distant memory from the past, but alive in the present hour. We hear in the words of the priest the voice of the One who poured out his Blood and first pronounced this offering in the same words we hear on this day at Mass. The act of Consecration is an immediate entry into the heart of Jesus Christ crucified and immolated in the current hour.

~

"For my flesh is food indeed, and my blood is drink indeed . . . so he who eats me will live because of me" (Jn 6:55–57). The flesh we consume is the crucified flesh; the blood we drink is the hemorrhaging blood poured out in offering. What Jesus may be saying in the second phrase from Saint John's Gospel is that in eating his flesh and drinking his blood, we will live his Passion in us because of his presence now inhabiting our heart and soul. The reception of the Eucharist is an entry into the Passion of Christ for all who accept this invitation. And, indeed, God extends this invitation to all who embrace the deeper truth of taking the crucified Lord into their soul by means of the Eucharist.

The consumption of the Eucharist is not primarily for our consolation or for peaceful intimacy with our Lord. There may be times when our Lord is close to us in a comforting presence. But the primary reality of the Eucharist is to unite us to Jesus Christ crucified, and there are always consequences in that union. For one thing, we are drawn to a love for his Passion in receiving the Eucharist. All the great souls of love found in the Eucharist an irrepressible desire to be one with him in his Passion. They left any time with him in prayer before a tabernacle or monstrance with a desire to offer themselves to their own passion of love. And our Lord was often quite availing in providing the desired taste of suffering out of love for him and for souls.

∼

"We must try to love without imagining. To love the appearance in its nakedness without interpretation. What we love then is truly God" (Simone Weil).[5] Under the appearance of mere nothingness, of a common wafer of bread, he is seen in the Eucharist. But the manner of perception is everything, for he is seen only with love. Many people who would not deny the doctrine of the Eucharist receive the holy presence of our Lord with coldness and distracted apathy. It is terribly wounding to our Lord to give himself to a heart that has no interest in his desire to be close for a privileged moment of sacred contact with that soul. He is there, and the soul is elsewhere. Yet when we perceive in deep faith how concretely real is this sacred contact with the living Christ, all is different. The perception of love begins to grant deeper insights. We may realize, for instance, that

[5] Simone Weil, *Gravity and Grace*, trans. Arthur Wills (New York: G. P. Putnam's Sons, 1952), 102.

the fullness of the Passion hides in the smallest fragment of a consecrated Host. The complete immolation of Jesus Christ in his Passion is united to the mere fragment of a Host still clinging to one's palate. The repercussion of this awareness is to know that we receive his Passion into our souls with every reception of the Eucharist. Our own desire for immolation, for a complete offering for souls, intensifies, and we realize there is nothing more important than to live for souls. The mere nothingness of a fragment of a Host suddenly can burn us with an immense consuming desire to give a complete gift of ourselves to God for souls.

～

Those who seek primarily a comforting peace in the reception of the Eucharist are perhaps guarding themselves from the deeper entry of Christ's Passion into their lives. They may be safe for now from any greater divine challenge. But over a lifetime, it seems that our Lord will seek the inner depth of our soul and challenge it with his own Passion. Indeed, we may find that a sword of divine fire cuts mysteriously into our soul in the reception of the Eucharist when we realize we are receiving Jesus Christ crucified and his Passion. A threshold may be crossed in our spiritual life when we become truly vulnerable to the sword of divine love. This sword does cut us and exposes the illusions we may have adopted of his closeness to our soul. It should be a hard conviction, for instance, to maintain that a great love for our Lord in the Eucharist can combine with a passionate attachment to material wealth. Yet people do manage to hold contrary pursuits in place. We might think it impossible for God to be resisted in the long run, but, in fact, he is easily blocked and turned away. An egregious example of this, common enough today, is to be at peace in the reception of the Eucharist while indulging gravely in immoral behavior that apparently provokes no sensitivity of conscience. Such is the state of the Church in our time. The peace of soul is a false assurance in that case, whatever the felt experience might be. Feeling some form of closeness to God is in fact no confirmation that a soul is not wounding the heart of God. The sword of divine fire cutting into our soul, and asking more from us, is the true taste of the mystery and sacredness of the Eucharist.

⁓

There is a need on some days of prayer before a tabernacle to realize the presence of an unseen radiance leaning out toward us almost as though we had just stepped into the light of a noonday sun. When we are close to a tabernacle, his personal gaze pierces all things we may ponder in an hour of prayer. While it is true that he allows us to roam freely in his presence during any hour of prayer, never constrained, even to the point of losing attention or allowing desire to dissipate, nonetheless he is there, nearby, watching us throughout this time of prayer. We are inside the enclosure of his gaze even when our thought turns away from him in distraction. On the other hand, to the extent we are pure and receptive to him when we are near a tabernacle, his presence may truly inhabit our thought, not as a spectator of our momentary thought, but touched by every turn of our attention toward him. He looks not from afar but watches from within us even the smallest gesture of a need for him. Every loving thought of him receives a return of love. We can never see this so clearly, but we do need to know this truth with the inner certainty of faith. All the passing movement of thought in an hour of prayer can become sacred, even the infinitesimal moment of a fervent desire for him. The small moment watched by God can make every full hour of prayer before a tabernacle an immeasurable privilege that passes too swiftly. We belong to him by giving ourselves to him. Even a brief minute within an hour can burn with desire for a complete giving on our part. And then some days his desire for us comes unmistakably alive within us, and we can stretch our own desire to give to him for an extended time a concentrated longing for him.

~

Quiet attention to the silent presence of God in a tabernacle is more than a practice of prayer. It is a path to love itself. A real encounter can take place with the mystery of being drawn by our God in love. There is no need of words when the presence of God is felt, inviting our soul to take a leap of desire toward him. A certitude of love as a reality beyond mere human experience draws our soul. No understanding, no insight to the mind, is given how the reality of God is known in mystery in his concreteness as a real presence in that hour. The truth of his presence simply pierces through the veil of a separation from him. Perhaps he speaks in and through the silence of an hour, but it is hard to know, and the silence seems to hide a deeper truth. A wisdom of sorts is bestowed on our soul in such hours of silent prayer, and yet nothing perhaps articulates itself to our understanding. If a barrier seems to lift in our awareness, it happens more often when we are prostrate in a silence of incomprehension. A type of wisdom incapable of arriving at words nonetheless conveys a certainty. It is a wordless certitude given in prayer that a love other than our own is drawing our soul to a depth of silence. What can words add to love's preference for silence? The silence hides everything that can be spoken. We can only turn our eyes toward the Divine Person concealed in his living presence behind the doors of a tabernacle.

~

Difficulty in prayer can come on some days from an absence of a clear attraction, from having nothing before our mind to draw out the deeper hunger within our soul. It is true we have our faith to keep us steady in prayer, and perhaps we have the presence of Jesus Christ before us in a tabernacle. But this is not enough. We must be moved by a strong interior desire in an hour of prayer. Something concrete in attraction must initially ignite a fire of desire in us. In this need of prayer, the combined impact of faith and love has a significant role to play. At first, exercising our faith, we can remain alert and receptive to the Real Presence of Jesus silent and watching before us. We can search out a Gospel passage or a verse of a psalm that lights a desire within us. The conviction that our Lord is with us in mystery can then fill our soul, just as he permeates with his reality the small confines of the chapel or church in which we find ourselves. In the hours of prayer that are inflamed by deeper faith, they often begin with a spark lit from Scripture. He uses this means to lift our interior vision, drawing us to his presence. A blind incomprehension may be experienced as the time continues, but the certainty of his presence is the truth of the hour. We love him in realizing how inexplicably close he is to us in his Real Presence in the Eucharist. Our attraction for him may intensify precisely because he remains beyond sight, available to our contact only by our longing and our love.

❧

It would seem impossible to love God with intensity if we neglected to meet Jesus in his humanity as a consistent need in prayer. A great longing for God will correspond always to a great longing for an encounter with the humanity of Jesus in the silence of prayer. Sometimes this requires a return to the thought of his human presence invisibly in front of us in prayer. For that we do not require imaginative exercises or some form of conversation with him. But we must sense with a deep faith that he is near in his humanity, that he is with us physically and wants immediate, direct contact with us. For this reason, the gift of the Eucharist in a tabernacle is really not optional for a life of serious prayer. We have to find our way to a need for time before a tabernacle. He is a human presence of real physical flesh and blood when we pray before a tabernacle or before a monstrance on an altar. He is the same Jesus who was pierced with wounds and crucified at Calvary. He would prefer that we do not forget this truth in the vicinity of a tabernacle.

❧

"Why do you call me good? No one is good but God alone" (Mk 10:18). The holiness of God, his unutterable mystery of infinite transcendence, is implied in these words. No one is holy but God alone, and no goodness is comparable to the immensity of love that hides in God. God is holy, and this truth must be sought in our prayer. It is overwhelming to engage the truth of an encounter with God's holiness while praying before a tabernacle. The goodness of God is felt as we realize he makes himself available to us for personal contact with the divine mystery through the holy presence of the Eucharist. He does not withhold his mystery, nor does he leave it entirely enclosed in shadows, but rather he places his hidden presence in an immediate proximity to our blind eyes. The simplicity of the tabernacle as a material object that nonetheless encloses the reality of God himself in the flesh—this is the truth present in every Catholic church. The lit lamp next to it burns with the fire of truth in testimony to God's goodness. He is utterly different from us in his divine immortal being, timeless and uncreated, separated from his creation. Yet he humbles himself in the goodness of his profound love and places himself in our midst. He opens himself to those who long for him. He draws our inner desire and releases upon us the cool waves of his utter holiness. The holiness of God eventually becomes undeniably evident in long hours spent in prayer before the Eucharist. The holiness of God, we learn, is inseparable from a divine humility that gives itself to the fragility and nothingness of the sacred Host. The small nothingness of a consecrated Host hides the greatness of the infinite reality of God. In the fragment is the fullness of God. The infinite holiness of the almighty God conceals itself in the mere particle of consecrated Bread on a paten in a state of Oneness with the Godhead. God is holy, infinitely holy. We must adore him, prostrate ourselves before him, worship the immeasurable truth of his humility as God. This effort must concentrate our spiritual life surely in a last era of the Church.

～

The recovery of a love for prayer after a long period of observing mere routine in going to prayer may come by an unexpected reentry of Christ's suffering into our awareness.

A priest I have known for many years told me that one day
he found an old prayer card inside a back page of an unused
sacramentary in his sacristy. The prayer card depicted Jesus
crucified on the Cross raising his face toward the heavens.
The priest placed this card in his breviary and began to look
at it each day. He said to me that at times in prayer he could
not take his eyes off the face on that faded card. The thought
of the card's burial in a book for some unknown lengthy
time, neglected and forgotten, until he chanced on it that
day made him think that it was waiting for his discovery.
And he attributed to that card a desire for prayer that he had
never embraced so fully to that point in life. He soon began
to spend an hour in silence before a tabernacle each day.
Always, he said, after some initial prayers, he would take
out this holy card and lock his eyes on the figure of Christ
crucified and on his face with its open eyes. And this habit
remained with him. From that time, it was his practice to
seek out first the Passion of Christ each day. This habit had
lasted, he said, for many years.

~

The lack of trust in a soul already close to the heart of God
is a wound to God which we may not realize. Yet it is common that people at times question too much what is the state
of their relations with our Lord. There is a need to let go
of such worry and simply trust in the presence of our Lord
soaking our soul with his presence. We belong to him entirely, a truth that must be lived and accepted, not measured
or evaluated. The union of our soul with our Lord entails a
steady, unchanging truth. Why do we question this reality?
The tendency to desire assurances of his presence, tangible
signs of his affection, testimonies of his love in some overt

manner, is wrong. We are in relations with a God of unfathomable magnitude and love. It is enough to love him; it
is the one thing needful, and it is the guarantee of his close
presence to us. The drawing power of love, especially in the
Eucharist, is the steady testimony of his near presence. We
do not need dramatic confirmation of this truth. The truth
of his presence in the Eucharist is indisputable for a serious
soul of prayer. The experience of his presence in praying
before a tabernacle or receiving him at Mass cannot be separated from the surrender of ourselves to his love. He loves
the souls who are simple in their love, who simply know
him in truth and never question, despite every opportunity
for a doubt or a question. He loves souls that simply proclaim again in any distress or darkness—"I belong to you,
everything is yours."

~

Once prayer crosses a certain threshold of surrender to God,
our longing for him cannot be held in check. In our yearning for God, we become in a certain way like a poor beggar seized by a hunger that returns predictably each day. A
desire to be alone with God in the presence of a tabernacle
begins, even imperceptibly, to invade the hours of our day,
not so much interfering with activities, but making our soul
at times impatient for the return to prayer. In that longing
for God, we may begin to resemble the poor in their bodily
hunger, except that ours is a hunger of the spirit. Have you
ever stopped to observe a poor man outside on a snowbound
street in the cold of winter waiting in a soup kitchen line for
entry inside a building? The line moves slowly, and when he
arrives at the entrance, he leans across the doorstep out of
the cold, already caught by the aroma of hot food reaching

him from inside. He is longing for warm food and a hot drink. What is served does not matter, provided it warms him. A desire for prayer before a tabernacle can be like a poor man's need in winter. In a mysterious way, the tabernacle draws our hunger. But often, even in prayer, as we kneel before a tabernacle, the hunger for God remains unsatisfied. Our prayer can feel on some days as though we were forced to halt at the door, unable to enter inside. Days when there seems to be no entry inside the heart of God carve into the soul a deeper longing. And yet, even then, still in the cold, still waiting, we are near his presence in the proximity of a tabernacle, held close to him, and often we can know this truth with a deep certainty. His living presence in the Eucharist becomes an undeniable truth of mystery the more we surrender ourselves and offer our hunger and poverty as a gift to him.

~

People who receive Holy Communion at an occasional Mass attended during the year, on a Christmas day, for instance, or at a wedding or funeral, are not so unusual. They seem to take Holy Communion with no thought they are receiving anything other than a wafer of bread as part of a ritual that everyone present at a Mass does. It is likely that in many cases they have no faith in the reality of the Eucharist as the Body of Christ; nothing prompts them to fear making a grave act of disrespect toward the sacred. They simply join the Communion line and take the Host as a participant in the ceremony, as it were, thinking nothing of it. Not uncommonly, they reach out a single hand to take hold of the sacred Host as though they were being given a religious souvenir. In all this casual indifference to the sacred reality, the wound to the heart of Jesus must be real, and perhaps quite terrible. The callousness of an unbelieving touch in this manner when in tangible contact with the Divine Presence is a wound to the heart of God that recalls the roughness of Roman soldiers stripping our Lord at the crucifixion site. It is emblematic of our time in this era of Eucharistic sacrilege that these are not non-Catholics who have strayed onto a Communion line, but baptized Catholics who in their childhood may have made a pious First Communion. Faith seems to have ebbed away and faded from their lives, and they do not realize their grave danger of soul. Rather, they likely claim a relationship with God on their own terms. But true faith disappears, turns to ashes and smoke, by paying no attention to truths of faith. These truths, such as the reality of the Eucharist, require a choice, a willed act of believing and committed practices, including the obligatory Sunday Mass. When there is no thought of these truths, and no proximity in a life to them, the truths seem to evaporate from the mind. They become a memory in the external aspects alone, like a foreign land looked at in old photographs but never more visited.

～

The question of whether Judas received the Eucharist at the Last Supper cannot be definitively answered. The Gospel leaves this unclear. As Saint John's Gospel in chapter thirteen portrays the scene, when Jesus dips a piece of bread in the bowl and hands it to Judas, this would not be the reception of the Eucharist. Scripture scholars speak of this action as a sign of affection and tribute extended by a host to a guest. If so, it is the gesture of a last chance offered to Judas to halt his intention of betrayal. As we know, Judas remains unaffected and stays committed to his plan. After he takes this bread, Judas departs into the night, his soul occupied by a satanic presence, and carries out his plan for the arrest of Jesus in Gethsemane. But did Judas receive the Eucharist earlier at the Supper, before this exit? Would Jesus invite Judas to receive the Sacrament while knowing Judas' intention of betrayal? Or did the Consecration of bread and wine into the Body and Blood of Jesus take place only after Judas' departure? It might at first seem improbable that Our Lord would give the Eucharist at this first Mass to someone in grave sin, a man who is preparing the great betrayal of the Lord. And yet Judas likely did receive the Eucharist. It was necessary for the ordination of Judas as a priest that he be present at this first Consecration and receive the sacred Eucharist. He is not fully an apostle unless he, too, shares in the priesthood. And he will not be a priest unless he is present at the Last Supper for the Consecration that institutes the sacrament of the priesthood. All this is necessary because it is precisely as a priest that he will violate the heart of our Lord with an act of betrayal. It is as a man who has received sacrilegiously the Body of Christ in that first Mass that he will cloak his deception in Gethsemane, offering the fraudulence of a kiss of respect to identify Jesus as the man meant for capture. The pain Judas causes our Lord is incalculable, and yet this pain and vulnerability to betrayal by priests has continued throughout the centuries to afflict the heart of Jesus. It is a pain that will burn the heart of our Lord especially in a last era of the Church.

∽

Those who attend daily Mass and receive our Lord in the Eucharist every day, and make a special effort to do so, are different as Catholics. They do not live a more elite version of the Catholic faith, as though worthy of particular honor. Many of them live quite ordinary and hidden lives in their love for the Mass and the Eucharist. To an outsider, it may look as though they are simply following a personal routine in rushing to Mass at the lunch hour in crowded cities, or on the way to work, jostling with the crowds; and yet submerged inside these lives is often a great hunger for God slaked in no other way. They are a quiet testimony to the startling power of truth in the Catholic faith and in the power of the Eucharist. These souls, never so numerous, have been swept up and seized by the divine presence of Jesus in the Eucharist. He drew them in love at some point in life, and they submitted to that drawing power. This truth of a sacred attraction in some souls to enter a Catholic church each day where God hides in the Eucharist is beyond description. These souls are moved without being able to convey an explanation. They know that they belong to our Lord more than to any other occupation and commitment in life. The mysterious comfort of returning to his presence in the reception of the Eucharist each day rules a portion of their life that is incomparable to anything else in life, including marriage. In his presence, whether gazing from a pew toward an altar or savoring him inside their heart after receiving Communion, they taste a sublime sacredness that is not found in any other reality of life. When I return some days from early morning Masses in convents, I see these souls in their pews, spread around the large expanse of Saint Patrick's Cathedral in New York, solitary in their love for our Lord like monks and cloistered nuns in solitary cells overcome with love. They are often immovable in their positions, kneeling before the Divine Presence, small in themselves and conquered by the vast infinity of holiness hidden before their blind eyes, concealed in their hearts.

PART THREE

12

THE IMMEASURABLE MYSTERY
OF DIVINE HUMILITY

For our God has chosen to reign in humility, and it really seems as if he wishes to show himself only just as much as is necessary in order that the visible Church shall endure to the end and that the gates of hell shall not prevail against it.[1]

—Raïssa Maritain

God is Almighty. But what is his power? It is the All-Powerlessness of Calvary that reveals the true nature of the All-Power of the infinite Being. The humility of love is the key: to show off, there is little need of power; to efface oneself one must be very powerful. God is unlimited Power of self-effacement.[2]

—François Varillon

Our incarnate God is a crucified God.[3]

—Henri de Lubac, S.J.

A mystery of humility exists in God. At first the idea of divine humility may seem an unsuitable notion for God. It is thought to be a virtue solely for human or angelic natures

[1] Raïssa Maritain, *Raïssa's Journal* (Albany, N.Y.: Magi Books, 1974), 158.
[2] François Varillon, *The Humility and Suffering of God*, trans. Nelly Marans (Staten Island, N.Y.: Alba House, 1983), 44.
[3] Henri de Lubac, S.J., *Paradoxes of Faith*, trans. Paule Simon and Sadie Kreilkamp (San Francisco: Ignatius Press, 1987), 67.

dependent on God. Yet there are clear signs of God's humility, even as we are limited to a description of this virtue in a human context. The truth is that all we say of God must bow down ultimately in incomprehension. The limits of human language to speak accurately of God affects our engagement with every divine attribute. His goodness, his mercy, his love, all conceal realities infinitely beyond our human understanding of these terms. The same can be said of divine humility, which in God extends incomparably beyond the human virtue. Indeed, divine humility is perhaps the greatest mystery of all attributes in God. It is revealed to a fuller extent only when we gaze more fixedly in love at Jesus Christ humiliated in suffering on a cross, but, even then, we can only walk away from that sight more overcome by incomprehension. The reality of humility in God, shown at the crucifixion, is inseparable from his love for us at Calvary. Divine love and divine humility become one at the Cross, and in a certain way indistinguishable; it is the nature of both love and humility to abase itself. Perhaps in a last era of the Church, God will manifest humility's abasement within the mysterious sufferings of his Church. He will hide, as all humility hides, in a concealment unrecognized except by those who perceive him as one in his love and humility with the Passion undergone by his Church.

～

The humility of God is indeed a great hidden truth revealed in the Passion of Jesus Christ. We need to enter with love inside the internal suffering of Jesus in his Passion to embrace this truth. God is humble, and he asks us to recognize this divine attribute for deeper intimacy with his divine mystery. We cannot separate the truth of God from his willingness

to be despised and rejected, publicly mocked and humiliated, scorned as an offensive nuisance to the eyes of the
learned elite of his time. The humility of God invited this
rejection almost as an inevitable necessity stemming from
his vast transcendence to his creature. He who is all in all in
his divine being allows those who are nothing in their creaturely existence without him to treat him in his human flesh
with contempt. It is an extraordinary contradiction within
history that God permits himself to be crushed by humanity
while still holding the world in place and keeping it in existence. This humility of God is a profound self-effacement, a
silence in the face of insult, a refusal to withdraw his tender
love despite the lashes of venom and the opprobrium he received. God's humility continues as a truth in his relations
with souls. He seems not to be overcome by our insuffer-
able vanities and pride. He waits like a humble beggar for
mere throwaway gestures, as though this is enough to keep
him satisfied. The God of infinite love and majesty is a God
who has embraced his own disguises of nothingness. He has
chosen to draw himself down to our lowliness and love us
even in our meager desire for himself. He is in truth not
satisfied with such little love on our part, but his humility
keeps him from turning back from the lowly returns he receives in love. It is as though for God any sign of recognition
suffices to draw from him a kiss of love for a soul.

~

Mother Teresa used to repeat insistently that God is humble. What was she seeing in God, or perhaps in herself,
to affirm this claim so strongly? One time she asked the
late Father Benedict Groeschel, the much-loved founder of
the religious community of the Franciscan Friars of the

Renewal, why he thought God had chosen him to be a priest. Father Benedict answered that he had not given it sufficient thought. Mother Teresa did not hesitate with her own reply: "He chose you because he is humble." It is provocative to reflect that God's humility shows itself in his selection of people for special treatment or favors. Of the many possibilities at his disposal, he chooses the unlikely figure, the inadequate person, the untalented one, for a special mission. Mother Teresa repeated this often about herself. Of course, we may see it differently, because we know that person after their accomplishments. We think that God has chosen the extraordinary candidate; after all, he must know that he has his options. But the truth is that he often is inclined to make use of helpless, incapable, or wounded souls to place at the center of his serious works. Mother Teresa knew with deep saintly certainty from her own life that God uses the most abject nothingness of a person to advance the power of his hidden presence in this world. This inclination on God's part is an essential truth of his divine humility. It goes hand-in-hand with his desire to remain hidden and concealed in the midst of his world.

∼

" 'My God, my God, why hast thou forsaken me?' There we have the real proof that Christianity is something divine" (Simone Weil).[4] The mystery of divine humility is forever hiding in the historical event of Jesus spit upon, blindfolded, slapped, crowned with mocking thorns. The face of Jesus covered by a man's spittle is the face of God humiliated in that hour. God himself receives this horrendous abuse and

[4] Simone Weil, *Gravity and Grace*, trans. Arthur Wills (New York: G. P. Putnam's Sons, 1952), 139.

offers no resistance. Jesus may even have turned his face toward his abusers to receive their slaps and spittle more directly. The mystery of humility is starkly present in this divine gesture of accepting human ridicule. That God makes no effort to prevent the most contemptuous disrespect is a hidden revelation of the nature of God. We need to ponder the deeper mystery of it in the present day. He submits as though incapable of resisting those intent on humiliating him. The impression of a certain passivity is extraordinary, for as God he could have stopped all this horror in a moment. Instead, he steps forward into humiliation as though longing to suffer even more. In fact, what we are seeing is the nature of love itself. Again, there is no deep love without self-abasement and humility at its core. God teaches this truth in the Passion of Jesus, and we must learn to respect its mystery and to love God in this mystery, allowing the mystery to soak into our own lives.

~

An insight into this humility of God may come in noticing how our Lord shows himself to us. If we are observant, we will perceive an ongoing pattern. When we desire him most intensely, his manner of showing himself is often with great discretion, almost with shyness, as though he does not want to draw attention to himself. He prefers a concealment that can easily be missed, precisely because he is so adept, so careful, at keeping himself hidden at the very times when he is close to us. He does not like to give away his hiding places, even when he is right next to us. This inclination toward effacement is a notable divine trait that is not often acknowledged. Nothing we can do seems to overcome it. It remains undiminished and intact all our life as though it is essential to our relations with him. He protects his hidden presence by enclosing it in secrecy, even when offering signs of his close presence. No amount of effort on our part to overcome this concealment seems to change that perduring condition. And how, we might ask, is divine humility evident in these patterns of concealment? Let us remember that if God so desires, he is more than capable of manifesting his divine power in quite fearful displays, as happens in a tornado or hurricane, or in majestic displays by the beauty of sunsets or rainbows streaking the summer sky. But more commonly with souls who love him with some intensity, he follows the patterns of the sheer whisper of the wind in the cave where Elijah stood waiting. He keeps to the quiet corners of the heart, not giving up his hiding places, preferring to communicate the subtleties of his presence in subdued tones rather than to make dramatic pronouncements. All this concealment behind a veil of discretion is evidence of a beautiful attribute in God and most attractive for our love, if we allow ourselves to be drawn into deeper love for him and for his inclination to hiddenness.

～

The providential interventions of God in this world, or in our personal lives, can be interpreted as mere chance events or fortuitous occurrences, but this view would be erroneous. It is important on our part to recognize accurately the hand of God in events that we can be tempted to explain away too easily. His speech to us, more subtly, follows a similar pattern. When God speaks personally to us, he seems quite averse to making speeches or issuing forthright commands. The language most suited to his personal taste seems to be rather the silence that lingers after a quiet whisper has been extended to our soul. He seems to love silence as a home where he returns to rest. And are these ways and manners to be taken as signs of divine humility? Naturally God does not expose his infinite depths to us. He waits for the progressive effect of piecemeal and step-by-step recognitions, for a slowly emerging realization of his personal presence to take place in our knowledge of himself. He does not want us to run away from him in fear, which might happen if we were to perceive even momentarily the magnitude of his majestic presence to us. He is humble and wants us to relish his company, even in the infinite separation of our nature from his. And despite that separation, he wants us to accept an invitation extended to us to be one with him and one with Jesus in his Passion. This desire for oneness with us is why he took our human nature and united it in Jesus Christ to his own divinity. It is the reason he gives himself to us in the disguise of the holy Bread in the Eucharist. His desire for a oneness with our nothingness is the great expression of a divine humility that is truly unfathomable.

~

Perhaps there is no real humility in us until Christ's humility in his Passion overcomes our own illusion of being in any way humble. Most of us misjudge humility. The real measure of humility is not a matter of timidity in human relations, for instance, thinking always less of ourselves in comparison to others or pursuing a constant sense of unworthiness. The only truly deep understanding of humility comes after a long gaze on God humiliated by corrupt men inflicting abuse and mockery on Jesus Christ crucified in the hours of his Passion. The silence of God in the face of the insults, the jeers, the cackling mockery directed at Jesus in his Passion is an extraordinary thing. The choice of God to be treated with contempt, to be spit upon by men—and yet still to love them as pitiful and lowly sons—is the reality of the most genuine humility. Until we face revilement and answer with love for the favor of being disrespected to any degree, becoming more forgetful of ourselves, praying for those who bruise us, we need to grow more in this essential virtue. Divine wrath, divine resentment, was completely absent from the Passion, despite the satanic actions of disparagement toward God. This divine choice to refrain from a response of justified anger is a truth of God in his relations with men to this day. God will not react to arrogance and mistreatment from his creature. He bears it quietly as though continually returning to the humiliation that he underwent in Jesus' suffering during his Passion. It is his nature to be humble, and he does not alter his desire to reveal this truth to those willing to see it and embrace it as a pursuit for their own souls. Perhaps, unfortunately, we will perceive our God bearing some of this same humiliation from his own beloved Church as the years ensue.

~

The humility of the Virgin Mary is overlooked too much. She herself does nothing to alter this, preferring often to remain concealed in her companionship with us. This is no different from during her earthly days when she was aware of being the Mother of the Son of God. She turned her exalted privilege into a humility of relations with a Son who at times carved deep fissures of pain in her motherly heart. She did not always understand the actions of Jesus, for instance, when he remained behind in Jerusalem at twelve years old during the Passover, leaving his parents in great anguish for three days. As the years went on, Jesus and Mary must have had immense layers of unspoken communication between them. They spoke words that concealed their deeper significance behind casual remarks. But for Mary this manner of conversation was at times a source of humbling incomprehension. Many times she may have been left not knowing at first the significance of what her Son meant, especially if he referred in some oblique manner to his Passion, as he did at the wedding feast of Cana: "O woman, what have you to do with me? My hour has not yet come" (Jn 2:4). Her pondering of her Son's words and gestures, of his silence and his absence, of his signs of affection and his possible withdrawal of them, entailed the humility of this pure woman before the mystery of God. Humility deepened in her through all the days of her life with Jesus. This humility led her eventually to the horror of incomprehension at Calvary, overwhelmed by the magnitude of suffering that Jesus freely embraced. Perhaps some of this same humble incomprehension will fill the heart of Mary in days to come if she observes the Church wounding her Son in grievous ways.

∼

Humility is perhaps the most elusive virtue, rarely embraced in its deeper truth. It is elusive and often unknown, because it is more than a virtue. When it is present in a saintly person, it has become a state of soul, but not in a way that can be confirmed by obvious signs. None of those who arrive at this interior state of soul would claim to perceive in themselves a possession of humility. It is the nature of humility to hide itself, most of all perhaps from those who are humble. What, then, is it, this humility? The question is not answered by a definition or description. The truth is that humility only begins in a soul as we come to recognize our spiritual need. We must plunge in time into a desperate need for God, which at times arrives only after suffering much from ourselves. Sometimes this means disappointment with self, other times it means long struggles in which God does not seem to provide help. The sense of elemental need that gives rise to humility is always tied to a state of poverty in the soul. A realization of soul that extends beyond the idea of a mere virtue may result: the absolute dependency upon God for everything in life. The elusiveness of humility is due to the fact it cannot be strictly practiced as a virtue. Rather, it begins at first to root its presence in our soul as we recognize the truth of ourselves in a painful remembrance of sins and failures. For that reason, humility is never so real in youth. It takes some time before we accumulate regrettable choices, and even more time usually for these grave mistakes to afflict our soul. But the real reason why humility cannot be practiced as a virtue is that it always leads to a great self-forgetfulness in a soul. The humble person thinks nothing of self and turns attention beyond self. There is no way to practice self-forgetfulness, strictly speaking, other than to be attentive to the needs of others as a servant acting in love for others. The humblest souls are likewise souls of great offering for others.

∼

Humility is badly misconceived when it is identified simply as modesty in human relations, which often has nothing to do with real humility. Modesty, in fact, is quite capable of serving egoism and self-interest. Avoidance of displays of conceit, for instance, or of vain boasting can be a useful discipline for gaining admiration from others. No, humility is rather something of a quality of soul, a measure of the soul when it is standing nakedly before God. This truth hides within the inner depths of a man or woman. It is considered correctly only when it is understood as a mystery inaccessible to our own vision. We are what God sees in us, and this is unknown to our knowledge. What does God see when he gazes into the secret depths of our soul? Are we aware that our sins, our negligence, our indifference, wound the heart of God? Yet, despite sins, perhaps he has a much greater love for us than we realize? The soul that prays for the descent of God in his humility upon its own unworthiness is asking for what the Lord himself desires. This recognition would seem essential for any authentic humility of soul. We must realize that each day we are the ones who have wounded him by our lack of effort to love him. The truth of humility is inevitably an awareness of having loved God insufficiently to this point in life.

~

Humility is truth, the saints tell us, the truth of our soul naked in its need before God. It is above all a truth of prayer, but encountered there only by shunning both exaggerations of unworthiness and the excesses of unreal aspirations to holiness unmatched by deeds. It is precisely the inability to know the truth of ourselves before God that may be the most humbling reality we encounter in prayer. The path to humility lies, not in a deliberate crushing of self, but more in simply forgetting ourselves. Those who turn to God in a steadier manner, seized more often by his presence, will naturally lose attention to themselves. Humble persons are humble because they take little interest in themselves. This is also a need in prayer. And then we may become, without our observation, what is always the fruit of humility. Less attentive to ourselves, we will attend to the needs of others.

The desire to be a servant, ready for the call of another's need, forgetting ourselves in the moment, these are signs of true humility.

~

The uncertainty whether, after so much time, we are getting any closer to God may be hard to bear, until we realize that our Lord would prefer that this question disappear from our concern. It is essential to humility to refrain from taking a measure of our progress with God. In fact, we cannot know what God perceives when looking at our soul. But if there is an inner yearning for him, even unfelt and emotionless, this is what he sees. We need to recover our deeper longing for him whenever we have a sense of inner uncertainty. What discourages us as setbacks in spiritual progress may be stepping stones in the direction of God, on the condition we are humbled into a greater depth of soul. Disappointments and failures, the frustration to achieve desired fruits, the impossibility of triumphs in the spiritual realm have their purpose in God's plan. They are not what they appear to be. Mistakes and mishaps of every sort point to a truth we often ignore too long. On the last night of his life, Jesus spoke this truth—"Apart from me you can do nothing" (Jn 15:5). These words are engraved in bold print as a signpost over the doorway into any greater humility. They require more than a nod of agreement. Nothing fruitful for the sake of souls takes place without the Lord's choice to use us, and our own willingness to be used, at times in what may seem to be small, negligible ways. Our nothingness without God, indeed, our nothingness without his Passion living in us, is the key to our spiritual fruitfulness for souls. Perhaps only in view of our incapacity without God, keeping ourselves near Jesus in his Passion, do we stop trying to please ourselves

and thereby offer ourselves for others with a purer intention. Poor and empty-handed is the preferred disposition for
a work of God, ready to let him use us when it is clear we
are unfit for the task. Without making them wait long, our
Lord seems to answer quickly these spiritual beggars who
give nothing but the emptiness of themselves to him.

~

There are hints in the Gospel that a simple phrase spoken
in prayer, spontaneous, unrehearsed, may draw an immediate reaction of love from Jesus. We cannot plan such words,
calculating their effect. We must simply speak with abandon
when the occasion occurs, perhaps in response to words of
Jesus in the Gospel, allowing our own words to escape our
lips with hardly a thought behind them. Prayer may then
light up as though a lamp, without our action, suddenly
turned on and filling a room that until then was full of darkness. When, for example, the Canaanite woman begging for
help for her demonized daughter heard the sharp refusal of
Jesus—"It is not fair to take the children's bread and throw
it to the dogs" (Mt 15:26)—she did not turn away in anger,
but offered her inimitable reply—"Yes, Lord, yet even the
dogs eat the crumbs that fall from their masters' table" (Mt
15:27). The unexpected words seem immediately to take
captive the heart of Jesus; in an instant her words lay siege
and conquer divine love. Perhaps only deep humility, with
no contrived piety, can vanquish Jesus so unfailingly. Humility of this sort, in words or gesture, cannot be planned,
only spontaneously released. But what if we were to imagine
a slightly altered exchange with Jesus, in this case perhaps
after experiencing a lengthy time in aridity and emptiness
in our prayer. Rebuffed repeatedly, longing for contact with

his presence, meeting every day a barrier of stiff silence, we might imagine Jesus finally speaking: "It is not fair to take the food of the saints and give it to the dogs; do not expect to receive what I reserve for those who are favored in the higher places of sanctity. . . . 'Yes, Lord, but even the dogs eat the crumbs that fall from the table of the saints'." Yes, even I, unworthy of favors, need the scraps that fall to the floor, for I hunger for you even as they do, and in my poor hunger I can be satisfied, if it comes from you, with even the small and meager gift.

~

"Love is the faculty of seeing" (Richard of St. Victor).[5] Love affects the eye; we see differently. But in what manner is vision altered by love? And should we not also say, transformed by humility? Genuine love always humbles us inasmuch as we realize we have not loved enough. If we love more, with a greater depth of soul, we ought to realize in humility that we have received a strength and a power of vision that is beyond our nature. In loving more, we gain insights and receive the unveiling of truths we could never uncover on our own. There is, for instance, an inner truth of another person that becomes available to our vision only with humble eyes of love. Often this truth is concealed under layers of disguise, but it is seen once we gaze with eyes of love. The soul who has love for another person may perceive, almost mystically, what that person is meant to become spiritually in God's desire, a truth closed to the other person's recognition. This graced vision of another is accompanied

---

[5] Richard of St. Victor, quoted in Joseph Cardinal Ratzinger, *Behold the Pierced One: An Approach to a Spiritual Christology*, trans. Graham Harrison (San Francisco: Ignatius Press: 1986), 27.

by a sense of the fruitfulness that awaits this soul if only it would arrive at an awareness of what God sees. Love desires this expansion of another to a deeper recognition of its greatness in God's plan. It longs in love for another that this realization should come to fruition. But it can happen only if the person awakens spiritually to a deeper sense of his truth before God. Love seems to grant at times a privileged vision into this truth. It is essential to love that we often desire this good of the other to be realized and encourage it in very concrete ways. There is surely no harm done by speaking boldly to a soul that God may desire much more from that life, especially when that person is still young and uncommitted in vocation. In some cases, such a challenge will be decisive for the salvation of a soul, at other times, it is for the vocation of a soul to give itself completely to God.

~

The unused and wasted person in the life of the Church is a real phenomenon, perhaps more so in the era of the Church in which we now live. But this possibility requires a careful interpretation; it can have contrary meanings. It is certainly true that there have always been people in clerical or religious vocations whose natural talents never developed in a manner they might have under more encouraging circumstances. Surely this observation holds as well in worldly circumstances of career and profession. But the reality of unused talent in the Church takes on a significance that extends beyond the question of a notable or visible contribution. The native talent of a person may mean little in the divine plan for souls. Everything that is given by God to a life is for the sake of a fruitfulness directed to the salvation and sanctification of souls. And, for that purpose, an offering of the soul is ultimately what matters, and sometimes all that matters, which may demand the painful frustration of a person's natural abilities. An age disinclined to value sacrifice for others may be likewise less disposed to perceive an underlying divine purpose in the unused natural abilities of souls who become holy. But there have always been hidden souls of humility in the Church whose greatness has been concealed behind apparent uselessness to the worldly aspects of the Church's mission.

~

The capacity to fall violently, crushed to the ground, when all seemed morally steady and strong in a spiritual life, may not be as surprising as it seems. It is best not to fall, but God has his mysterious desire that souls arrive at an ultimate gift of themselves to him. The souls that face a moment of upheaval and failure ought not to conclude they have become unfit for a great love for God. The ways of God are numerous and incalculable. He seems to allow even grave failures at times for the sake of a deeper recognition. When souls have begun in a serious manner to seek him with fervor and love, he does not expel them from the school of higher pursuit and union with him because they fail a test. Rather, at times, he seems to lead certain souls past an impediment of an overconfident reliance on themselves by means of a fall of some sort by which they are plunged into a deeper sense of their nothingness before God. In all this he does not give up on them. Rather, he encourages by grace the truth of their absolute need for him in all ways. We are nothing without God, and in fact all of us are ready to step over the edge of an abyss into the loss of God if we do not realize that God is everything and we are nothing. The great desire of God is that souls are humbled in seeking him. He will use what is necessary to engrave this awareness in a soul. Perhaps the failures of a life do not mean so much when God finds that his desire for a soul to depend entirely on him is violently awakened and finally embraced in a much deeper manner. There may be many such reversals and deep conversions in the coming years as God readies the Church for a final period of testing.

~

Perhaps there is no real humility in a life unless we have been worn down and reduced to a weariness that our soul carries after a certain point without any expectation of relief. Humility is a threshold of truth for a soul. It comes only after the realization that God is humble and that he desires the souls he loves to accept this same humility into their lives. But, again, what is this humility of God? Jesus allowed himself to be disrespected and humiliated by coarse, uneducated people. He permitted insults and aspersions cast at him while remaining silent. In the three years of his public life, he carried a weariness of knowing he was being weighed and measured, his every word examined under a harsh light of questioning. He was despised and rejected by many and persevered in the heaviness of knowing that he was offensive and unwelcome to many. Humility is to embrace all these realities and to remain silent in spirit and gentle. The humility of God will always find its translation in the acceptance of humiliation within the lowly creature of God. Mother Teresa commented that we will always find humiliation in life, but the greatest humiliation is when we know in prayer that we are nothing, and this we come to know when we truly face God in prayer. The humility that a saint like Mother Teresa exemplifies is the weariness of a soul that plunges nonetheless into an increasing depth of a great offering to God. The complete gift of self is possible only for the humble soul. Such a soul has realized it has nothing more to give in its weariness, and so it offers its emptiness and nothingness. And God is quite pleased, it seems, precisely because he has led the soul to this hour in its life, when it has nothing left to offer as a gift but the shards of a burnt immolation. The heart of the Church herself in a last era may reflect precisely this image of a burnt offering.

~

The essential task of spiritual life—after a certain time—may be to throw ourselves with a certain desperation before God and leave all else behind. But when do we arrive at such a state of need and leap toward this abandonment into the hands of God? Nothing happens of great moment in a spiritual life too quickly. We need to be humbled by life, even crushed by its harsh reversals of our expectations, reduced to weariness and strain, and only then do we perhaps awaken to the need to cast our life completely into the hands of God. Humility as a truth of the soul is perhaps inseparable from arriving at such a state of desperation, when we are completely alone with no one to turn to but God, nothing but God as a last option. The humility of the lowly who stand openly before the face of God has its first moment perhaps when they cast themselves before his gaze as a last desperate gesture. This humility necessarily is united to the humility of Jesus in his Passion, when he threw himself down into a forsakenness of abject loneliness and an absence of any protection. He cried out in the agony of his isolated human soul his offering to his Father, emptying himself until a last cry poured out his completed oblation to his Father. Humility is this spirit of self-emptying oblation, the complete pouring out of a soul, when it invites the almighty God hanging on a cross in Calvary to take all and make this offering fruitful for souls.

13

THE SECRET FIRE:
PRAYER IGNITED BY
THE WOUNDS OF CHRIST

Besides, I want you to go fishing sometimes. How? I will tell you. The most holy passion of Jesus is a sea of sorrows but, at the same time, a sea of love. Pray to God that he teach you to fish in this sea; then dive into [its depths]. No matter how deep you go, you will never reach bottom. . . . This divine fishing is done without words; faith and love will teach you this.[1]

—Saint Paul of the Cross

In order to have the strength to contemplate affliction when we are afflicted, we need supernatural bread.[2]

—Simone Weil

Can there be a mystical life without death?[3]

—Raïssa Maritain

Incomprehension of the crucifixion of Christ is a terrible ignorance of the present day. Crosses are worn as decorative or devout items, but few realize the spiritual impact a simple

[1] Saint Paul of the Cross, in Martin Bialas, *The Mysticism of the Passion in St. Paul of the Cross* (San Francisco: Ignatius Press: 1990), 232.

[2] Simone Weil, *Gravity and Grace*, trans. Arthur Wills (New York: G. P. Putnam's Sons, 1952), 52.

[3] Raïssa Maritain, *Raïssa's Journal* (Albany, N.Y.: Magi Books, 1974), 227.

cross can exercise when held in one's hands and treated with love. A sustained gaze on a crucifix, refusing to avert our eyes, can change our lives completely in a single hour. I have known this to happen in souls, and I have experienced this power of the blessed crucifix myself. An hour of holding a crucifix in one's hands invites a recognition that God himself was nailed to a Roman cross. No one can submerge his soul deeply in this thought and remain the same. A hunger for knowing Christ crucified as God himself suffering the Passion may suddenly awaken before that hour concludes. Our eyes will never look at a crucifix in the same manner again. And then we may find ourselves closing our eyes at the sight of a crucifix, loving him blindly, realizing that the suffering of Jesus on the Cross takes place in the present hour of a timeless eternity. This love for the crucifix is in truth a measure of love itself. His suffering continues mysteriously even now, in the wounds afflicted upon his body the Church. He joins himself to those who are stricken with love for him and approach him as One who still suffers. The gaze on a crucifix brings to life this thought—that mysteriously he still suffers, that he still asks for the eyes of souls beneath the Cross to seek his gaze and unite themselves to his suffering. We may be entering a period of the Church when this realization will become more acute.

～

"When evening comes, you will be examined in love. Learn to love as God desires to be loved, and abandon your own ways of acting" (Saint John of the Cross).[4] These words compel us to ask what is love, what is its essential truth in a

----

[4] Saint John of the Cross, "Sayings of Light and Love," n. 60, in *The Collected Works of St. John of the Cross*, 90.

soul? What does a profound love do to the core of a soul? Does it always produce clear dispositions and strong interior desires within a person? The saints are the best measure of love. They understood that love is sacrificial, that it seeks an outpouring and release of itself in giving to a beloved. But if we ask how this came about in their lives, there is likely a common answer. They resonated with familiar longings over time at the sight of Jesus Christ on a crucifix. On their knees, praying before a crucifix, they experienced an intense desire to offer themselves completely to God. Mysteriously, if we give it lasting attention, a crucifix will compel a desire for some form of immolation. Perhaps there is no great depth of love without this experience. The sacrifice of Jesus on the Cross can overwhelm our soul after much time spent before a crucifix. We may seem to have no choice but to offer ourselves in poor blindness to this God who died on a Roman cross at Calvary. We will probably not find a saint in the Church's history who did not at some point in life become fixated, consumed, conquered by the sight of Jesus as God on a Roman cross of crucifixion. It can be so with us as well. The gazing on the crucifixion of Jesus remains a sacred entry into greater love for God. The door can be opened simply by lingering in love for him at the event of the crucifixion and desiring to offer our own life in union with his oblation on the cross, come what may.

~

A mystery contained within the Passion of Christ is the awareness he may have suffered that he would relive these hours of his trial before the Sanhedrin, his violent scourging, the mockery, his crucifixion, in a perpetual return to the suffering of Calvary through the Holy Sacrifice of the

Mass. We speak as Catholics of the unbloody sacrifice of the Mass. The physical tortures are not repeated. But who would say that the internal wounds of Jesus in his Passion are not experienced even now in a mysterious manner as he unites flesh and spirit with his Bride the Church? Inasmuch as the Church suffers betrayal within her, he suffers again the kiss of Judas. Inasmuch as the Eucharist is profaned and received sacrilegiously, he suffers again the abuse of his body scourged with violence. Inasmuch as doctrinal truths long upheld and protected in the Church are questioned and undermined, he suffers again the mockery of thorns embedded into his skull. The awareness of Jesus as he hung in silence on a Roman cross may include the knowledge of what he will suffer from his Church in the future. The last era of the Church may indeed pierce his heart in a profound way. The knowledge that he will once again be treated with contempt, spit upon, scorned, and vilified, but this time by a disrespect for the truths of tradition forged through his own spirit acting in history within the Church, is perhaps a suffering that awaits our Lord as the decades of this century continue. Perhaps he knows our own time in the Church as the preliminary period before a great test of pure souls within the Church who will love him and remain united to his Passion as the Church suffers her own internal betrayals.

～

"The wound of the body also reveals the spiritual wound. . . . Let us look through the visible wound to the invisible wound of love!" (Saint Bonaventure).[5] These are words of great importance spiritually, if indeed they speak of an invis-

---

[5] Saint Bonaventure, *Vitis mystica* c 3.4, quoted in Joseph Cardinal Ratzinger, *Behold the Pierced One: An Approach to a Spiritual Christology*, 53.

ible wound of love piercing the heart of Jesus throughout history and into the present day. The Resurrection appearances of Jesus, as recounted in the Gospels, give the impression, on the other hand, that Jesus has passed through his ordeal of horrific suffering once and for all and no longer can undergo pain. The wounds in his hands and feet and side cause no physical pain, but remain only for our sake. In observing them, we are invited to remember the infinite love for us poured out at Golgotha. Moreover, we declare dogmatically that the divine nature cannot suffer. The Son of God suffered only in his human nature. But a question for a more profound spirituality is whether in fact there is in Jesus Christ a mysterious capacity for undergoing internal pain in his resurrected human nature. This nature after the Resurrection is a mystery beyond our limited comprehension. The possibility that our Lord continues to be wounded in pain even in heaven—in his human nature—seems not impossible. There may be an ocean of suffering that submerges his heart in affliction when he confronts rejection and betrayal and gazes at a cold indifference from those who are much loved. Saint Faustina wrote of an ocean of mercy ready to cast waves of forgiveness across countless souls in need of God. But in the deeper waters of this ocean, far below the surface, may be the pain of our Lord in looking in sorrow at the souls who refuse him. It is a crucial consideration for a serious soul of prayer. Only a soul full of love for the wounds of Jesus, for his love rejected, is willing to offer itself to be wounded in a secret manner with Jesus' painful love for souls. It is a special vocation to offer oneself to be a victim soul suffering the wounds of Jesus that in some mysterious manner of his human nature he now experiences in heaven. And this offering to his suffering for souls cannot but draw an immense depth of union with his heart's love in heaven. The willingness to offer ourselves to his suffering for souls may indeed be profoundly desired by him in our current day.

~

The inner recesses of Jesus' heart, where he hides the most piercing wounds of his Passion, are a privileged place of prayer. There is a secrecy about these inner recesses of his heart that opens to us as we realize a deeper mystery at Calvary. The mystery must be sought in silence before a tabernacle, namely, that Jesus undergoes his wounds at Calvary still to this day. What he suffered at Calvary was not subject to the limitations of time. Our own present day contributes in a fresh manner to the wounds of Christ on the Cross. These wounds must be sought with love in our silent prayer and with a particular focus for our attention. The indifference, the sacrileges, the disrespect toward the Eucharist taking place today are not simply offenses of our own time against God, but piercing wounds to the heart of Jesus that he suffered at Calvary. We come to know these sufferings of Jesus afflicting him in a timeless manner by seeking the inner recesses of the heart of Jesus. The depth of our prayer may correspond to this effort to enter inside the deep recesses of his heart. In an era of widespread sacrilegious reception of the Eucharist, a mysterious longing can take hold in our soul to be united to the wounds that Jesus suffers at Calvary from the misuse and disdain for his love in the Eucharist. In the silence of prayer, we may find ourselves burning for a union with the wounds he carries upon his Body in the Eucharist. The desire to disappear in a life of sacrificial hiding can inflame our soul in the same way his timeless suffering conceals itself in the Eucharist. This desire to pierce the secret wounds of his immolation at Calvary may alter our sense of the Passion as a focus in prayer. We are no longer spectators observing the horror of his crucifixion, but participants partaking of his Passion, offering our own oblation in union with his. His action of immolation at Calvary will tear open the inner recesses of our own soul and convey a singular realization. The wound of love piercing the depths of his human heart at Calvary—in the mistreatment of the Eucharist—is stretching across the centuries from the hours of his crucifixion to our own day.

~

"No one can enter the heavenly Jerusalem by contemplation unless he enter through the blood of the Lamb as through a door" (Saint Bonaventure).[6] A soul that feels a strong desire to identify more deeply with Jesus Christ in his Passion should ask to penetrate the profound secrecy at the depth of his heart. It is a true doorway that must be crossed. There is a sacredness, an unfathomable mystery of the holy, in what remains unknown within the internal experience of Jesus on that last day of his life. The wounds he suffered in his heart do not draw from him a great release of words. He suffers in his inner being silently. But this silence does not prevent an entry by our soul inside his silence and the possible reception of his personal word. Once we are inside this silence, his agony of love for souls during the crucifixion may come alive in a profound manner. There are secrets of divine love that are revealed only as they convey a wound of love to our souls. One of these insights is preeminent, which is that a

---

[6] Saint Bonaventure, *The Soul's Journey to God*, Prologue, 3, in *The Classics of Western Spirituality: Bonaventure*, trans. Ewert Cousins (New York: Paulist Press, 1978), 55.

much deeper suffering took place in the heart of Jesus than in any of the physical tortures. The wound suffered in his heart is the timeless pain of his love pouring out in excess and finding few souls willing to receive this great love. The soul that desires to know him in his Passion must accept to become a receptacle of this excess of love. We might even beg for this favor, since Jesus knows how often souls turn back after their initial appeal. For this gift comes necessarily with a price. The secrecy of his sacrificial oblation will be no longer so secret. Our soul will be drawn mysteriously to desire the same offering. Prayer will become a need to offer our life as a sacrificial oblation in union with his own death on the Cross at Calvary. The reward of this act is beyond the question of a fair exchange. Our soul is granted entry into the holy wounds of God's love for souls buried beyond sight in the inner recesses of the heart of Jesus in his Passion. Nothing costly we might experience in life can outweigh the treasure of this gift.

$\sim$

If we are determined to enter inside the wounds of Jesus Christ, it is only a matter of time before his Mother's im- molation at Calvary also invites us. An entry into the inner recesses of his heart unites us to her heart as well. Prayer then shifts its contours and steps closer to a deeper mystery. A wordless, unspeakable pain hides within Mary's heart, which may be deeper than ever today. It is a wound of love she has received throughout history in seeing the indiffer- ence of souls to her Son, which she may suffer today in a more pronounced manner. Indeed, from what we know of her apparitions in the last two centuries, the wound of love concealed in this Mother's heart may be approaching in the decades ahead an hour of a climactic resolution. Perhaps we need only turn to her heart pierced at Calvary to realize more intensely the drama of our own age. And what in truth happened there at Calvary in the silence of Mary's soul? Standing beneath the Cross during Jesus' suffering, she was offering herself in union with the hours of Jesus' oblation. Then, after Jesus had died, while he still hung on the Cross, a spiritual event of great magnitude took place: the spiritual piercing of her own heart as a Roman soldier thrust his lance into the side of Jesus in death and penetrated his heart. She must have both felt and understood immediately that an irreversible wound to her heart had taken place. The offering she had made in union with Jesus while he remained alive on the Cross now acquired a depth previously unknown to her. She understood in a timeless intuition the sacred wound of immolation she would now carry perpetually in her pure heart. As she watched the two criminals dying in agony on either side of Jesus, their legs broken, the fact of souls throughout history choosing or rejecting her divine Son, embracing his mercy or plunging into a dark condemnation, carved its truth into her soul. This realization wounded her heart with depths of suffering that she would carry with her across the threshold of death into heaven. The coming decades in the Church will see this tension between souls for or against Jesus Christ magnified in stark ways, with Mary's wound of immolation at the center of this tension. Perhaps our own era may witness as never before an intensity within souls of passion who seek an immolation of their own lives within the recesses of Mary's immolated heart. These same souls may come to know vividly her power of intercession for souls.

~

The intercession of Mary follows no rules of law or logic. A young man I taught many years ago in the seminary told this story to fellow students in the seminary and to myself. He grew up in a Midwest Protestant household, but his family had little interest in anything religious. He was baptized as a child, but the family did not attend any Sunday services, even on Christmas. When he was graduating from high school, his father urged him to join the U.S. Marines, and he did so. After the boot-camp training, he was assigned to a naval aircraft carrier docked in San Diego, a famous naval base that saw many American men embark for missions to the war with Japan during World War II. More than 5000 men worked on the ship, which required staggered meal times in the constantly active dining hall to feed this large number of men. One night this young man had permission with others for a free night outside the enclosed confines of the ship. The young soldiers made their way to the "redlight" district in San Diego, where bars and prostitutes were readily available, and the young Marine found himself eventually going to a cheap hotel with a Mexican prostitute. By his own description, he said that when he had finished with the girl, paid her, and was about to exit the door of the hotel room, he glanced back at this young woman on the other side of the room. He saw her holding beads in her fingers while sitting in a chair with her head down. Standing at the door, looking across the room, he addressed her a bit roughly: "what are you doing?" Lifting her head, staring into his eyes with a piercing look, she raised the rosary beads—"This is all I have now"—before lowering her dark eyes and settling back into her prayer. He said he left feeling ashamed, aware of having used this young woman for his selfish pleasure and regretting the night. Three weeks later he went into the large dining hall of the ship, feeding five hundred men at a time in shifts, and he sat in an open seat, next to a man about ten years older. This man, wearing a military uniform, turned out to be the Catholic military chaplain of the ship, the only Catholic cleric on board, and they immediately became friends at that meal. Within two months he was asking for instructions to become a Catholic. And in time he entered the seminary and became a priest. One might ask whether that young Mexican woman prayed for this young Marine as he left the room on that night? It appears to be very possible. And who is willing to deepen their belief, after hearing this story, how spiritually miraculous may be the impact of the Rosary on a life, if only we would surrender to this most certain truth of Mary's power of intercession for souls.

～

Jesus' silence on the cross at Calvary is the silence that at times we may experience in the grace of contemplation. It is not a comforting silence of tranquil peace, but a silence of desolation and inner, unmet need. The silence of Jesus on the Cross extended for lengthy periods of time: three hours of torture hanging on the wood of a Roman cross, and just a few spoken words, primarily at the end. The silence of Jesus in his pain on the Cross is an invitation into the depth of divine mystery. What does this silence speak? What single word from the silence of his heart at Calvary may be waiting for us in prayer on this day? His language of suffering in the silence he keeps on the cross may speak to our soul if we ask for it. He speaks to us the silence of a longing to be known in love, of a desire that we should know his wounds of love in the present day of the Church. He remains silent in this longing, without a word of

articulation, because perhaps even in his suffering he is reserved in a mysterious way, refusing to say that he desires
to be loved. Without words he speaks to our soul, suffering
in silence, and he waits for the rare soul that will suddenly
hear and understand this language of longing. We should
beg him to allow us entry inside his silence on the Cross.
Jesus longs that we should desire to experience this same
silence and know him in his excess of love. It will always
be true that his great love can be externally observed in the
tortures of the Passion. But the greater truth of his love is
waiting for us in the silent secrecy of his heart and its interior longing. His wound of love in desiring to be loved can
be a silent reality of daily searching in our prayer. It can be
sought as a destination of our love, a great longing in every
day of prayer. There we can penetrate the secrecy of his
suffering in silence for souls who will ignore or betray him.

∽

We know that Jesus carried our sins, all the sins of history,
upon his human soul as he suffered on the Cross. While
freely accepting the sickening ordeal of bearing sin upon
his soul, he offered himself as the sacrificial Lamb in atone-
ment for sin. The burden of all the sin of history was placed
upon him, and by his act of oblation he transformed the torture at Calvary into a release for us from the deadly consequences of sin. There is another suffering that he carried on
the Cross, however, more secret, not often recognized, and
a great truth also of his love. He took upon himself as well
the suffering of souls who would undergo abandonment and
rejection by the world. He embraced this suffering, just as
he embraced the pain that pierced his soul from the sins of
humanity, by a free act of surrender to his Father's will and

a desire to be united with souls who would undergo any resemblance to himself in his Passion. It is a striking thing to consider that Jesus perhaps goes in search of souls throughout history who resemble in some mysterious manner the hours of his Passion. He pursues them because he wants to unite himself to their suffering. Even more, he desires to take their suffering to his own heart and to inflame them with a mysterious sense of their oblation joined to his own. The cleaving of Jesus to souls is mysteriously strong when he can relive his own Passion in a life. Even though unknown to them, they replicate some portion of the Lord's Passion and become dear to him as a result. In his suffering on the Cross he already knew them at Calvary.

~

"Just as the passion of Jesus is a sea of love and of sorrow, allow yourself, when you are entirely penetrated with love, to become a mixture of sorrowing love and loving sorrow" (Saint Paul of the Cross).[7] Jesus crucified on the Cross at Calvary may have gazed mystically from a knowledge of eternal truth at the sufferings we carry in life. But he did more than observe these sufferings or pity them. By the nature of his love, he is unable to see suffering in a soul and remain detached from it. Indeed, it would seem he cannot hold back from uniting himself to a soul in its suffering. As God he turns with predilection toward the soul of suffering and sanctifies its suffering by becoming mysteriously united to it. The crucifixion at Calvary offers an endless provocation to deepen our perception of suffering in life by realizing a divine companionship in these hours. As Jesus

[7] Saint Paul of the Cross, in Martin Bialas, *Mysticism of the Passion in St. Paul of the Cross*, 201.

plunged inside the depths of his torture on the Cross, he
turned his awareness mystically to the souls who would be
identified with him in suffering. This truth requires a deep
pondering on our part. There is a suffering at Calvary that
remains hidden from our eyes in looking externally at him
crucified; yet this hidden pain of our Lord is the most significant suffering of his Passion. He drew into himself and
freely absorbed on the Cross, in the solitude of his human
soul, all the ravages of rejection, humiliation, and utter loneliness that humanity would undergo in history. These sufferings of Jesus on the Cross are tasted to some degree by
souls who seek to unite their lives more fully to God. They
are a real entry into the internal experience of Jesus nailed
and hanging from a Roman crucifix. The crucial insight is
to realize that when Jesus sees our soul longing to love him
more, begging to love him more, he reaches down to us
from that Cross, as though his hands were temporarily released from the nails, and embraces us in our own suffering.
The embrace is a union of our wounds with his wounds.
If we have suffered in our lives, we have suffered for the
chance of a secret exchange with Jesus speaking his heart's
longing for our love at the crucifixion.

∼

That Jesus as God takes certain souls in a privileged way to
his own offering on the Cross and reveals to these souls the
inner secrets of his heart is not to be doubted. The secret he
exposes in silence is the truth of his choice of that soul for
a particular taste of his pain at Calvary. It is surely true that
Jesus in his internal experience at Calvary united himself
mystically with the suffering of holy souls in history. He
became one with every type of holy suffering that would

replicate in some manner his experience of his Passion. On the Cross, in his silence, he drew near in love to souls that would undergo in pain a resemblance to his affliction on the Cross. The soul desiring a greater union with our Lord ought to remember that truth. There is an open invitation to perceive our suffering as an offer extended from the heart of Jesus. In almost a kind of hesitant discretion, not desiring to reveal himself too explicitly, he waits for the soul that will beg for his love. He in turn may show us, after we beg for love and to know his love, that the offer of our soul's love has been accepted. At first, he does this by drawing our soul to gaze on him and his suffering at Calvary and to leave our own suffering aside, outside our concern. The more we forget ourselves in suffering, the more he seems to reveal the mystery of his love for the immense needs of souls in our own time. The reality of his offering in love for souls can then become the greater focus of our attention, and we become small and insignificant in our suffering. Our soul may learn then to place the complete offering of ourselves in his hands, to let go and release ourselves. The result is a mysterious union with him in a love for souls in need of him. The desire of God for souls becomes our own desire to see souls come to know and love the crucified Lord Jesus Christ on the Cross.

～

There is a secondary stage to this. As a soul continues to suffer in any manner, in sufferings that cannot be ignored, Jesus allows these sufferings to be seen in their truth as a sacred gift. They become the means of recognizing the crucified Jesus in a different way, in a more personal manner. Rather than being diminished or alleviated, the suffering becomes something sacred. It does not belong solely to our own life, but it belongs to Jesus himself. As a consecrated woman wrote to me once, her suffering had become for her "almost like a precious royal garment that is given to me to wear—and it's an honor to do so—but which actually does not belong to me." This awareness intensifies the selflessness of a soul in its love. We forget ourselves in our pain because the suffering experienced is no longer centered on ourselves, but concerns our Lord and his expansive desire for souls. We realize perhaps in time that the suffering was never in the first place simply ours to bear. It was the Lord Jesus crucified resting himself in our soul and suffering within it. It is crucial at difficult times in life that we come to this understanding—to see the suffering of Christ hiding within our own suffering. This naturally elevates any personal suffering to an entirely different realm of love and self-offering. We sense deeply that all suffering must be offered, as Jesus offered his, for the sake of souls and their salvation.

~

"He told me that I should look at his wounds."[8] These were the words of Jesus in reply to Saint Angela of Foligno, when she asked him in prayer what she could do to please him more. Was this response simply a request to dedicate more time and focus in gazing on the sufferings of Jesus in his Passion? Perhaps a deeper insight is possible. But it requires first that we acknowledge our own wounds, our scarred flesh and aloneness, and recognize the shattering truth that we have

[8] Saint Angela of Foligno, "The Memorial", in *Angela of Foligno: Complete Works* (Classics of Western Christianity), trans. Paul Lachance, O.F.M. (New York: Paulist Press, 1993), 127.

loved little even in asking the grace to love him more. The wounds of Jesus need to be perceived as a suffering caused by our own refusal to offer ourselves to a greater love for him. He has been wounded by our lukewarmness in love, and only in the vision of that failure of love can we gaze openly on the wound piercing his heart. That we "should look at his wounds" is not calling simply for a meditation on his Passion. The words ask us to perceive that we ourselves have inflicted a terrible pain upon his heart, not just by sin, but by meager and paltry efforts in love for him. Once seen in a spiritual vision, we cannot but desire to embrace the wounds he receives from a lack of love within our own heart. "What then can you do", he asked, "that would seem to you to be enough?"[9] The result is a compelling need to love him more deeply and perhaps to offer ourselves to be victims of his love in this time of the Church.

~

It is possible that the apostles, after Jesus showed them the wounds in his hands and feet and side on Easter Sunday evening, returned often in their private thoughts over the next weeks to that sight. The resurrected bodily presence of Jesus was stunning, an immense mixture of delight and stupefaction, but in the days that followed, these men likely felt a need to ponder the wounds still carved into the flesh of Jesus from his Roman crucifixion. They were the first to experience the mysterious inner attraction to Jesus that can come from gazing on these wounds. Their initial thought might have been to question why he still carried the nail marks of these wounds when he had returned to a recovered

[9] Ibid., 127.

state of bodily life. The wounds hinted at some divine rid-
dle, a secret word from God hiding in these wounds that
needed to be discovered. It is indeed possible that for fifty
days, until Pentecost, the apostles, each in his own private
manner, contemplated the mystery of these wounds still
visible on the body of Jesus. Then at Pentecost they may
have been given the light they were seeking. The wounds of
Jesus Christ crucified are the entryway, the threshold that
must be crossed, before receiving the living presence of the
Holy Spirit. The Holy Spirit is given at Pentecost so that
these men might shout in various languages the truth of the
divinity of Jesus Christ crucified on a Roman cross. The
long gaze in the fifty days until Pentecost on the wounds
of Jesus led them to proclaim his death by crucifixion as a
divine offering on the Cross. The wounds were the catalyst
to the fire of an immense desire to pierce hearts with the
truth that Jesus Christ crucified is our God wounded with
a thirst for our love.

~

The heart of Jesus at Calvary carried a concealed knowledge of calamity, and it pierced his awareness throughout
his hours on the Cross. There is a sacred reflection for us to
ponder in this secrecy of our Lord on the Cross. He hides in
silence his knowledge of the souls throughout history that
will be lost despite his torture at Calvary. He knows them
by name, and he knows his own efforts to draw them to
himself, and he knows his failure, as it were, to win them.
It is a terrible suffering of our Lord as God on the Cross
to know that souls will be lost to the enemy because at the
end of their lives they refuse his grace. Perhaps the suffering
of Jesus on the Cross includes an appeal to his Father to act

more forcefully in grace with these recalcitrant souls. The Lord in his suffering does not want to lose them, and he prays intently for them, but the persuasion of grace is not enough. This suffering of Jesus at the loss of souls ought to overwhelm us at times in prayer. The mystery of divine humility hides within this suffering. God refuses out of humility to exercise an act of forced or exorbitant omnipotence on behalf of souls. He will not coerce souls into a submission to his mercy. There is no mercy by trickery or entrapment or sheer power, no violation of a soul's freedom. He wants a true desire for himself and a recognition of his personal love. But when a soul resists his final offer of loving mercy, it may be that a dreadful silence descends upon it at death, much like the immensity of silence that fell upon Calvary after Jesus died. It is a silence that perhaps pierces the heart of God in eternity at the sight of any soul rejecting him at the end of life. The immortal destiny of every soul is unfathomably significant for God. In our prayer we need to enter inside this tragic knowledge of Jesus at Calvary that souls refuse the divine offering of a last reprieve, the final offering of grace. We will perceive the truth of human life with a different vision of seriousness. It will intensify in our soul a desire to seek the salvation of souls with every effort of our love and sacrifice as the Church and the world enter more difficult years.

14

GIFT AND TRIAL ON THE
PATH TO DEEPER INTERIORITY

God and humanity are like two lovers who have missed their rendezvous. Each is there before the time, but each at a different place, and they wait and wait and wait. He stands motionless, nailed to the spot for the whole time. . . . The crucifixion of Christ is the image of this fixity of God.[1]

—Simone Weil

He comes, approaches, then retires forthwith. He shows himself for an instant only to stir up desire. His furtive visits seem like unkept promises.[2]

—Henri de Lubac, S.J.

The Gospels insist upon two antithetical truths which express the tragedy of the human condition: the first is that if you do not love you will not be alive; the second is that if you do love you will be killed.[3]

—Herbert McCabe, O.P.

"Behold, you desire truth in the inward being; therefore teach me wisdom in my secret heart" (Ps 51:6). The truth

[1] Simone Weil, *The Simone Weil Reader*, ed. George A. Panichas (New York: David McKay Company, 1977), 424–5.
[2] Henri de Lubac, S.J., *Medieval Exegesis: The Four Senses of Scripture*, Vol. 2, trans. E. M. Macierowski (Grand Rapids, Mich., 2000), 160.
[3] Herbert McCabe, O.P., *The McCabe Reader*, ed. Brian Davies and Paul Kucharski (New York: Bloomsbury T&T Clark, 2016), 149.

sought and loved must be nothing less than God himself. This truth of God given in the depths of silent prayer can be conveyed only in ultimate secrecy, in a wisdom without words, in the speech of divine love spoken to the heart. In this phrase of the psalm, we are praying for a gift beyond any measure of satisfaction. In silent prayer, the gift of wisdom accompanies our love for God, our longing for God, our yearning for contact with his near presence. This longing for him is often a love unfelt and untasted, a reality of the interior heart beneath every layer of taste, not something that we can call forth or recover at will. It is God who perceives this love at deeper layers of our soul, not ourselves, and we may be quite unaware of it. We begin to acquire a secret wisdom when we trust this divine perception of our love at deeper layers of soul. When our soul advances in prayer, a deeper longing for God is almost always present, drawing our heart to surrender to God, and God does see this. He sees it because the longing of our soul at these unseen depths has its source in God's own longing for our soul. God calls forth this "soul thirst" within us by his own thirst for our soul. Perhaps we may feel in prayer like a poor beggar, unable to love, incapable of speech; yet underneath this poverty, the fire of divine love is drawing us. More than we can realize, God hides at the concealed depths of our soul at such moments. The certainty of this fire of his Divine Presence is a truth we must embrace in faith in the long stretches of silent prayer when we seem to taste little of God. Certitude of his presence is a true wisdom, and it stretches outside of prayer and begins to affect everything in our lives. We become wise in every hour we embrace the truth of God's longing for our soul, even when we seem to enjoy nothing tangible to confirm it.

~

We may come to know his greater favor of love when our own love has been hidden from us for a long period of time. For it is in those times that we have no eyes for themselves and no desire other than for God himself. And he may turn to us in the time of self-forgetfulness and favor us with a certainty of his gaze on our soul. The poverty of an empty heart is the catalyst to this grace. The absence of self-interest in prayer seems always to draw the stronger gaze of God. It is as though he is curious to see whether our soul will become inflated from the favor of his love or will descend humbly into a deeper unconcern for self. A need to forget ourselves for the sake of love is the great lesson we must learn from every period of lonely vacancy in prayer and interior poverty. It is perhaps only those poor in the unseen depths of their soul who will discover God giving himself to these silent depths. But this lesson must be embraced in mystery, without looking for an easy confirmation. We cannot walk away from a favor of God as though we are no longer as poor as ever. We remain always, perpetually, still a hungry beggar for his love. And it seems that he is much pleased by that begging for a pure act of love to inflame our heart and unite us to divine love. He sometimes answers such begging readily.

~

What is consistent over long periods in some lives is a spiritual passion that hides itself when these souls turn silently to God in prayer. They have no access to the depth of desire within them, and indeed no soul does. They may consider themselves merely stubborn souls in their prayer, refusing to give up, souls who cling with a tight grip to their need for prayer. The uncertainty of their prayer leaves them unsure at times of their relations with God. For the most part they do not realize the true depth of their love for God. Yet some days, perhaps infrequently, these souls do sense an inner flame for God burning in their soul beneath the absence of feeling, and then their insecurity disappears. In those hours they enjoy a mysterious awareness of their love united to a far greater mystery of love. A yearning for God, even unperceived and unfelt, draws their surrender to his hidden presence. In those hours it is as though they arrive at the destination they have awaited, even if it is a temporary stop. It is perhaps what God loves in these souls, the hours when they recognize a longing to surrender themselves again to the beloved of their soul. He loves them perhaps even more when they fully embrace this surrender with a complete release from themselves.

∼

"When I did not seek Him with self-love, He gave Himself to me without being sought" (Jacques Maritain).[4] A certain type of contemplative wisdom descends on a soul only when it is empty of any pretension to receiving special favors from God and no longer has any desire to seek them. This wisdom comes more often in an hour of lowly abasement in prayer when our desire is dry and our thoughts are impotent and vacant. Such prayer can seem a failure of love on our part, until an insight into deeper love arrives. The insight is a crucial one for contemplative loving, namely, that God often hides his immediate presence in prayer when our native

[4] Jacques Maritain, *The Degrees of Knowledge*, trans. Gerald B. Phelan (New York: Charles Scribner's Sons, 1959), 364.

human strength and ability are overcome and useless. The turn away from ourselves, even in dry misery and empty thought, while still certain of our Lord's presence, remaining attentive to him, must become a habitual disposition. The initial frustration to arrive at an experience in prayer satisfying to our spiritual ambition must give way to the poverty of nothing so memorable taking place as we depart from prayer. We may find that it is precisely then, when we hold nothing in our hands, that we leave prayer favored by God. This is not the favor of enjoying a friendship with God at ease with his close presence. It is the wisdom of knowing that only one favor is worth seeking—God himself and the self-abasement of Jesus Christ crucified hiding within our life, drawing us to a greater gift of ourselves to his Passion.

∼

The pure radiance of our Lord's presence opens to us only when we do not try to take possession of him within our experience of prayer. And yet we may at times be tempted precisely in this way, as though we might hold him securely inside the enclosure of our soul, where he will remain in waiting until our return. There is no such thing as making God a prisoner of our love, with no chance, as it were, for escape. Clearly prayer does not operate in accord with our wishes or expectations. The idea that an experience of God requires only our choice to meet with him again is shallow and shortsighted. Perseverance in prayer may be a sign of love, but it does not mean that we are rewarded by easy contact with his presence. The great need in prayer that we need to recall often is something different. It is to surrender ourselves completely, entirely, totally to the Lord. No act of surrender is so deep unless at the same time we are inviting

God to give and take from us as he desires. What he may give in return for a deep surrender to him is a greater entry into self-abasement and a sense of his hiddenness. What he may take from us is the sensible fervor we may have enjoyed for a time. The exchanges, at times swift and strong, are difficult to manage until we realize that God is asking us to release ourselves from a desire to possess him in some manner. To let go of him at the same time we long to take hold of him can be a hard demand. The desire of love is to hold on tightly to what is loved, guarding it, protecting it for ourselves, in a fear of losing it. The beloved who is God, however, must be released from our possessive grasp so that the greater truth of his love is realized. His presence as an infinite being of loving mystery extends beyond every experience of him within a passing encounter in prayer. If we are to love God in his transcendent truth, prayer demands this spirit of releasing and letting go, allowing him then to free us from ourselves. The fruitful sign of this freedom is a deeper desire for self-giving toward others and a love for the Passion of Christ. Prayer is never simply for union with God. It flows out toward others as a sign of its genuine quality, seeking fruits that will perdure for the good of souls.

∿

The temptation of some souls is not to think that God has rejected them—they have no illusions of a mystical trial—but that he finds them dull and uninteresting. Their inability to communicate beyond a bare silence wearies them; how much more, they think, this inarticulate muteness must tire God. They would wish for more. Yet these souls, without realizing it, often have a great purity in their longing for God, which is what brings them to prayer each day. Their desire to be alone with God is never crushed, despite real suffering at times in prayer, and indeed the perseverance in silent prayer confirms their deeper passion of soul. The subjective sense of inner emptiness and futility in prayer means really nothing. The truth of a soul transcends the shifting experiences undergone in prayer. And when that truth is a desire to give to others and to sacrifice and pray for others, this steady selflessness expresses their true greatness of soul. Many souls of deep spiritual quality are unaware of this. The hunger of their soul may be unknown to them. The selflessness of their sacrifice and prayer for others is their truth, and it is well known to God. And this quality of soul he does not find dull or uninteresting.

For some souls, a sense of personal ineptitude with God in prayer nonetheless seems to lead consistently to a renewed strength of soul. Perhaps the strength they receive is due in part to their return to prayer each day as an unquestioned habit. These are souls who yearn for God and cannot live without prayer despite the experience of the difficulty of prayer. A passion for God draws them, and there is no turning back. They go to prayer and often find inner emptiness and unsatisfied need, and yet they come away desiring God more intensely. Can that be a sign of unfruitfulness? In fact, the desert of the soul is sometimes the place of the richer fruits. The power of intercession in a soul offering itself with no taste of a return for its offering may be very great. And if the desert is their home in prayer, sometimes, in fact, these souls are not so alone as they think. An unseen presence draws near when their prayer has no purpose but to offer selflessly for the needs of others. They might prefer to receive some personal favor or comfort for themselves. It would be a delight to find on some days an oasis in the desert where they could drink of God directly. But it seems he chooses not to satisfy these souls except as they pray with love for the needs of others. He makes them burn in their thirst to love, leaving them lost to the knowledge of the fruits they bear. Yet he hears their requests for others, and he answers their intercessions, many times without their knowledge. For all this, when they arrive at later years, they are often grateful, knowing with a certainty that divine favors were extended on many unknown occasions to others. It is why elderly cloistered nuns are sometimes so very full of gratitude at the end of their lives.

~

The deserts of Africa can bloom in a brilliant array of radiant color with a single, sudden rainfall. This happens in some places of barren desert a few times a year, and it can seem miraculous from one day to the next. The sudden emergence of bright flowers swaying in the breeze across a large expanse when a day earlier only scattered dry brush existed can be breathtaking. It is as though a Rembrandt or a Michelangelo with a remarkable set of oils at his disposal painted from heaven a stunning landscape while we blinked an eye. But is this phenomenon in the desert not a telling symptom of what can happen to a soul when rain and sunlight combine to soak the dry crevices of inner darkness in a life? The sudden bloom of happiness in a soul can be inexplicably profound. Yet there is a reason, which the prayerful soul should know well. God pours down rain on the dry sands of our soul at unexpected hours, usually after long delays of waiting, and the consequence is bright colors that have never been seen. The love of God for the desert is remarkable, including the desert of souls. The divine impulse to wait no longer and to pour himself in a gift of bright fecundity on a barren terrain can be striking. Yet it is real and repeated that God cannot hold back from manifesting his personal love for the souls of the desert who wait for him and his rains of love.

~

A paradox is present in every genuine spirituality. We possess an innate desire that cries out for the gift of God himself. The desire for God resides in our created nature. It is experienced even without grace, drawing us in the direction of infinite vistas. On the other hand, the satisfaction of this desire, even initially, is possible only with grace. Our human nature, in other words, is insufficient to satisfy a desire innate to our very nature. Only God can satiate this desire, and he can do so only if we turn to him in a direct and personal manner. As Saint Augustine remarks, we are restless until we rest in him. God has carved into us a need for himself that never ends in this life. But we find him only by a personal pursuit of him. We can ignore this restless urge and wander blindly, seeking the favors of a seductive world that proves to be incapable of satisfying the deepest longing of the soul. We can bury the infinite longing concealed within that desire and expend ourselves on wasteful and sinful pursuits. But if we acknowledge this restless agitation for certitude at the depth of our soul and pursue the God who is concealed inside it, this desire can become a silent longing that may in time overwhelm all other desires in life. This is what happened in the life of every saint.

~

The silencing of Zechariah, his descent into nine months of muteness after he asks for a sign from the angel Gabriel to confirm the promise that he and Elizabeth will have a child despite their advanced years, would seem a punishment for his lack of faith. He questions how he can know something that contradicts all reasonable expectation. He has already lived many years with the disappointment of childlessness; his question is understandable. By this time, now an older man, he has long surrendered his earlier hope of having a son or daughter. His petition for a child, once a fervent daily plea, has disappeared entirely from his prayer. When Zechariah in his priestly tone of voice demands a sign, the angel Gabriel rebukes him, and Zechariah's tongue is physically bound. Initially the thought of a punishment may have troubled Zechariah's soul, but this may not have been Zechariah's view in later life. At first, surely, he enters a state of muteness with regret for his lack of respect and docility to the angel sent from God himself. He should have known better. But within a short time, he may have realized a great favor had been extended to him in this enforced silence. The silencing of his own tongue may have led him to an exquisite appreciation for silence as a completely new experience. The wasteful distraction of speech became daily more apparent. A discipline of reticence even in his interior thoughts quickly developed that he may have continued to cultivate even after the recovery of his speech. He likely acquired a profound love for silent prayer while waiting for the birth of his son, so different from prayer recited simply for correct ritual observance, and it would remain with him. In those nine months he becomes a man open to the mystery of God, able to listen in prayer without his own voice interrupting the silence of God speaking to his soul. He becomes the man who as a father would influence a love for the desert of solitude and silence in the great contemplative soul of Saint John the Baptist. There is an important lesson here. Our mistakes are sometimes essential openings to the discovery of our greater truth in the eyes of God. So many fruits of the spiritual realm may have some link to a failure to perceive what God was asking initially.

~

"And he dwells more in secret, the more he dwells alone. . . . The Beloved dwells secretly with an embrace so much closer, more intimate and interior, the purer and more alone the soul is to everything other than God" (Saint John of the Cross).[5] A hidden layer of deeper truth in ourselves is perhaps what most attracts God to our soul when we seek him in a serious life of prayer. No effort of self-knowledge uncovers this truth. It hides as a secret truth that must be accepted in faith. And what is that truth hidden within us beyond our reach? We must accept in faith that God, with the tenderness of a father for a young child, pierces the inner depths of our soul and rests the gaze of his love there. In these deeper regions, the soul is most vulnerable and in need, and most alone, and precisely for that reason we are held in a tender embrace by divine love. If we acknowledge this divine embrace in the silence of prayer, the true mystery of our personal identity begins to be felt. It is an important realization, if we are seeking greater interiority of soul and a deeper love for God. Much suffering in life, much confusion, may thereby

[5] Saint John of the Cross, *The Living Flame of Love*, 4.14, in *The Collected Works of St. John of the Cross*, 713.

be avoided. It is a mistake on our part, by contrast, to think that the external events in life, a biography of sorts with its many pains and possible achievements, somehow reveals us. What we consider our identity may be largely a self-creation of dubious stability, shifting in contour and shape with the passage of time. Underneath this external image of self is in fact a naked vulnerability, a hunger within our soul, which is our deepest reality. The accumulated experiences of life that seem to form our identity deceive us in a certain way and keep us from realizing the bare hunger for God that burns within our soul. Yet this vulnerability to God, this hunger for God, is present always before the eyes of God. It begins to awaken as we pray more quietly and lose sight of ourselves more completely in prayer. If we are fortunate and committed in prayer, we may in certain moments of self-forgetfulness be given a mysterious taste of God's immense personal desire for our soul. This sacred embrace by God of our soul is only partially known at any time, but it is the core of our soul's truth. We should seek to know it as a gift that can only be received in faith. Yet this same divine hunger for our soul will be known with startling clarity when we cross the threshold at death into eternity. We need to seek this truth now in faith if we are to become fully alive spiritually in the present hour of our lives.

∼

The discovery of an indestructible reality within the core of our soul is an important experience of deeper prayer. We cross a threshold of truth in sensing the mystery of God's gaze on the immortal reality of our soul. The certainty that God turns his eyes uniquely upon our soul, a soul created by him and unlike any other, can be given to us as an undeniable truth in prayer. Just as we recognize our identity in the mirror, we may perceive the truth that God gazes on the reality of our soul as uniquely precious to him. At that point it is no longer a question of belief or hope that we will live after death. The immortality of our soul is grasped clearly enough as an indisputable truth. We sense with certainty that we are known across the threshold of eternity where all things exist outside the restrictions of passing time. But there is a further requirement for our soul after this discovery. Once we realize God's gaze on our immortal soul, we must allow ourselves to be abased, to be diminished, to become less. We are invincibly assured of God's gaze of love on us to the degree we descend into the mystery of our soul's nothingness. Our soul must choose an attraction for immolation that may seem at first contrary to knowing itself as indestructible. The indestructible core of the soul must allow a divine fire sent from God to burn away all semblance of an importance in ourselves. The indestructibility of the soul is fully realized only in passing a threshold of this internal immolation. We must offer our soul in union with the self-abasement of the crucified Christ of Calvary. Then we may begin to realize what it truly means to be uniquely immortal in soul.

~

Love for God can only be poorly understood from the experience of love for human persons. Love as a longing for another, as surrender to another, as a generous self-giving to another, are aspects of genuine love. There may be parallel realities whether love is for God or for a human person. But love for God is certainly different and enters a realm of mystery far beyond our capacity to realize what is happening. We cannot pierce inside the truth of God's reception of

love from our own lowly heart and soul. God draws us to
love him in a manner that keeps his response to our love enclosed always in a mystery beyond reach. We cannot know
what it means for God to be touched by love, to be tender
in his delight in us. We have no way of knowing his depth
of longing or his surrender to our own desire for him. We
are stopped short by a barrier of mystery when we want to
know whether God is moved by our words of longing for
him. Yet we do have perhaps a deeper inchoate sensitivity
at moments when he seems to react to a phrase or a burst
of desire from our heart. Those who go far in their love
for God seem to break down the sense of any separation between their heart and God. They come to believe with great
certitude that God is capable of being moved by a return of
love. The gaze of God on their soul from a vantage of timeless eternity does not keep them from a certainty that he
knows their longing of soul and has immediate responses to
this love that are personal and mysterious. Every deep love
of a soul for God is subject to irresolvable experiences of
paradox. We can be certain on some days, strangely, that his
heart has been touched by a desire for him we expressed
with love, even when we are convinced of having little but
the most meager quality of love.

~

To know ourselves as known by God is essential for our
love to deepen in prayer. Yet this knowledge is in one sense
impossible to conceive. It cannot be sought as a concrete understanding in prayer. We have no way of perceiving what
God sees in looking at us, and yet in prayer we can know at
times that his eyes are full of love. Saint John of the Cross
writes beautifully that for God to gaze is for him to love,

and for him to look is for him to love. It is this truth we
need to seek in prayer. Knowing ourselves in an examination
of conscience, though necessary as an exercise of humility,
cannot compare with an awareness of knowing ourselves in
silent prayer as looked at with love by God. A deep layer of
soul can rest in prayer with a certitude that God is exercising a divine act of love toward the depth of our soul in that
hour. This cannot be compared to the common declaration
that God loves us. In one sense, contemplation is to remain
in a great silent receptivity to God while under the gaze of
his act of divine love. Our silent prayer ought to seek a real,
personal, and mysterious certitude of being looked at by
God and known by God. In turn, our soul should long for
him in that same moment with our own blind gaze of love.
This awareness and this longing are enough in any hour of
prayer; nothing more is needed. Prayer at such times is to
be silently aware of an unseen depth in the inner recesses
of the soul where God concentrates his gaze of love upon
us and draws love from us.

～

It may seem that we pass many of our days in prayer searching to keep God close at hand. But let us remember he is the
God of mystery and therefore elusive in keeping companionship with us. Our experience of who God is in a single
day can be unstable and tenuous from one hour to the next,
fluctuating in contrary ways. All along he may be watching our reactions, even as his constant presence abides with
us. There are days, for instance, that catch fire in the early
darkness of the morning with a desire to offer all to God,
holding nothing back, but that by the same night end in a
weary discouragement that little has been done for him that

day. There can be restless nights of broken sleep, agitated in mind and memory, that by dawn bring a surprising depth of quiet before a tabernacle and the flickering sanctuary lamp. There can be a day when the mystery of Jesus hiding in the poor seems hardly concealed but that suddenly explodes later with the harsh voice of a poor man cursing God and all things holy. There can be a unique peace while praying the Angelus at noon before an image of Mary that is followed in the next half-hour by a woman's dark eyes on a New York subway staring with contempt at the Roman collar of one's priesthood. There are days of church bells tolling crisply at three o'clock as though united with Jesus' cry of thirst from the Cross that are succeeded later in prayer by his terrible silence in death. There are evenings of prayer with desires to know the clear path that lies ahead until a conviction arrives of trial and uncertain steps that must soon be walked. All these diverse experiences, even in a single day, affirm the need to lay one's life blindly before the mystery of God. It is impossible to reconcile the shifting contradictions of incompatible experiences—until we realize that they are all pieces in a single mosaic taking shape day by day. In the eyes of God, they form a single pattern, and he sees them all in one gaze. For much of life, we are at best only beginning to glimpse in love what we cannot see with a complete view.

~

The contemplative yearning to be released from self and to belong entirely to God is a cause of interior tension. God hiding within us is a great reality, but this indwelling presence of God nonetheless confronts our indomitable self-interest getting in the way. The indwelling presence of God within us does not make our human personality disappear. Rather, something else happens that demands patience on our part. As we grow in love and in a deeper surrender to God, he begins to make more quiet use of us outside of prayer. By this means we are helped to fade increasingly from our own view when we return to the silence of prayer. It seems that God does this in a quite calculated manner that can be said to resemble the employment of a servant by a master. In some households, there are only occasional needs for a servant. The remaining time a servant is simply on call, waiting and available. The impression for a prayerful soul, because it loves the beloved divine Master, can be that God makes use of our service haphazardly and unpredictably. He calls us to serve a task for himself and then discards us for a time. We would prefer to be needed all the time, to be useful in a continuous manner. The infrequency of being asked to provide a particular service can frustrate our soul. Yet in all this we learn over time that we belong no longer to self. Our life is at the beckoning and summons of God, and he is free to forsake our availability or to return suddenly with another request. We may long for the latter, but perhaps we learn to love more deeply in the time of being forgotten. These lessons in humility we take back into prayer, and they carve into us a quality of self-forgetfulness essential to prayer.

∼

If we look back, most of us must realize that we received quiet spiritual influences early in life that perhaps made their profound impact felt only much later. For years my father went to daily Mass while working in an office building in lower Manhattan. But what strikes me even more today when I look back at my youth is his monthly commitment as a member of the parish Nocturnal Adoration Society.

Once a month he would wake up in the middle of a Saturday night and spend an hour in prayer alone in the parish church before a monstrance and the Blessed Host. There must have been few members because he seemed always to be assigned to the early hours after midnight. At times I would hear from my bedroom his alarm clock and then the slow footsteps and the front door of the house open and close. The thought today of my father praying alone, like a monk in a darkened monastery chapel, is moving. It stirs my own desire to give myself in a dedicated manner to prayer. At his funeral, I gazed from the sanctuary as a priest into that same parish church and found myself after Holy Communion thinking with gratitude of him alone in an empty pew there on those many nights praying before our Lord. I had a great regret at that funeral Mass that I had never asked him as a young boy to take me with him on any one night.

~

To the extent that we seem to rely on the touch of God's hand toward us as a measure of his reality—whether it be that he reaches out his hand to us to extend a caress of love and approval or even slaps or pushes us away—we are making a mistake. The hand of God holds all things in an open infinite gesture of enclosed love in which the farthest limits of our world are like water cupped in the open palm of his hand. Our soul itself lies within that enclosure of his hand like a drop of fresh rain gazed upon in the sunlight by God himself. Everything in creation is within his immediate reach, nothing is distant, all things are a point of loving focus open to his eyes. His hand, when it encloses us, is security itself, and to rest within his grasp is a goal we should pursue without end during this short life. Once we give over everything to him, and accustom ourselves to this habit, we will see that all the events of our life remain within his care and mysterious protection.

15

THE DIVINE INVITATION: BECOMING A VICTIM OF GOD'S LOVE

It is not human activity alone which can help us, but Christ's passion: my true desire is to take part in it. From now on I accept the death that God has destined for me, in perfect union with his holy will. Accept, O Lord, my life and my death for the intentions of the Church, to your glory and your praise.[1]

—Saint Teresa Benedicta of the Cross

You do not save your soul as you might save a treasured possession. You save it as you lose a treasured possession: in surrendering it. We must save ourselves collectively, we must arrive together before the good Lord. What would he say if we arrived before him, came home to him, without the others?[2]

—Charles Péguy

If we want to have a love which will protect the souls from wounds, we must love something other than God.[3]

—Simone Weil

The prospect of a personal experience of immolation may be the secret invitation to all who aspire today to deeper

---

[1] Saint Teresa Benedicta of the Cross, quoted in Wednesday Audience, Pope John Paul II, May 3, 2000. www.vatican.va/content/john-paul-ii/en/audiences/2000/documents/hf_jp-ii_aud_20000503.html

[2] Charles Péguy, in Hans Urs von Balthasar, *The Glory of the Lord*, vol. III, 443.

[3] Simone Weil, *Gravity and Grace*, 112.

relations with God. This possibility is likely to be a serious offer from God to souls in our own time. The invitation demands a willingness to be crucified as a victim of love with Christ. That can seem intimidating until we ponder the true greatness of a full gift of love to our Lord. The appeal of love is experienced as we perceive the release from self it brings. This is true in human love, and more mysteriously it is true in our love for God. To love him is to lose ourselves; to gain him is to die to self as a predominant concern. Immolation is a daunting word and even can arouse a great fear until we begin to taste the delight of losing ourselves for a greater love. The real meaning of immolation—being burned for love of Jesus crucified—is to allow fire to inhabit our soul. This fire of divine love is what makes a soul a victim of his love. Perhaps it is not a difficult perception once it is seen, only difficult to maintain as the personal path to greater love. All that might be held back and kept for ourselves must be handed over to God, cast away, given away, at his disposal to be used. He stirs the fires of immolation so that we may belong no longer to ourselves, but to Jesus Christ crucified. In a very real sense, the crucified Lord at Calvary becomes mysteriously one with us by concealing himself more secretly within our lives. In a certitude that is inexplicable, we can know his presence at Calvary drawing us to disappear into the silence of self-offering he embraced in his hours on the Cross.

~

The possibility that Jesus asks some souls to offer themselves as victims of his love seems to be a quiet truth of the current day. This invitation differs in a distinct manner from the older notion of a victim soul of reparation. A victim soul in the older sense of the term offered a life in expiation for the sins of humanity. The acceptance of victimhood was to pay the debt, as it were, for the suffering inflicted upon our Savior. The response by God to the offering of the soul was the bestowal of trials, allowing a soul to make reparation for the terrible offense of sins against God. A victim soul enjoyed a privileged relationship with God, but at a serious cost, usually of physical hardship and various trials. Something quite different is at work in a soul becoming a victim, not of reparation, but of Christ's love. It is an expression that Jesus used explicitly with Saint Teresa of Calcutta. He told her in locutions at the time of her call to begin the congregation of the Missionaries of Charity that he wanted Sisters who would offer themselves as victims *of his love*. The phrase suggests that a soul in this act of offering would invite our Lord to pour out his love in excess, a love that will stretch the soul beyond its capacity to bear this love. The excess of love will bring both a suffering for the soul and a privileged intimacy with God. Divine love given in excess is a mystery seen concretely in Jesus' crucifixion at Calvary. And the unique manner by which God loves a soul in excess, making a soul the victim of his love, is to bring that soul into a share with his Passion. The soul becomes, as it were, victimized by divine love in undergoing its own passion of love for God. A holy vulnerability to God's love ensues, drawing a soul into the secrets of divine love wounded in the Passion of Christ. A mysterious entry into the wounds Jesus suffered at Calvary is then likely. The heart of Jesus will manifest to us the excess of his love treated by so many in the world with callous indifference. We will suffer this knowledge of his rejection in a manner beyond a capacity to restrain or limit this awareness. We will be a crucified victim of his love crucified. His wounds will become our soul's wounds, his rejection our soul's rejection, his giving of himself in love our soul's own need to pour itself out in love until we arrive at some form of a death by love.

∽

A soul becomes a victim of divine love inasmuch as the love of God becomes too great to bear. Divine love overwhelms the soul, burns the soul, inflames it with an unmanageable desire for self-giving, until, in the end, by giving all of itself to divine fire, it disappears and only ashes seem to remain. The notion is not a poetic conceit. It seems that God in our time is leading some souls to such an offering out of love for him. And how is this recognized, and what is the catalyst? These souls, already serious about God, moved by a desire to give all to God, come to a day when they desire nothing but to offer themselves in some unlimited and unreserved manner, not knowing at the time perhaps all the implications of what they are doing. They do not realize perhaps that they have been chosen for a form of immolation that will give great delight to God and be fruitful for souls. Yet, in fact, this desire for self-immolation has usually been hiding as a hunger in their heart for an extended time. They carry a desire within their soul, perhaps for years, a desire beyond their comprehension, and they are often unaware of its presence. Then, as this desire begins to reveal itself explicitly, they are taken captive by a sense of a fire stoking deep longings in their soul. At first, they think they have no choice but to live with this desire and bear the discomfort. In truth, the fire is a longing for God, but it has much deeper implications. This fire is a desire for a complete offering to God, for a pure gift of the soul to God. And God answers their hunger to love with his own gift of love in a way that cannot be controlled or held in check. In God's greater love for such a soul, he extends the gift of himself beyond the soul's capacity for receiving it. The gift of love from God seizes the soul and takes over, as it were. Indeed, it suffers this love as though it has become a victim of divine love, a victim to love's constant demands. Henceforth the soul cannot anticipate or prepare properly for the expressions of divine love. It suffers the Divine Presence as a kind of uncontrolled fire beyond its ability to contain or limit. Yet the immolation for a soul, the burning away of itself for God, is what it wants more than any other gift it might receive from God. Soon it recognizes that its soul has one purpose ultimately, which is to give itself sacrificially to God for the sake of souls. It wants nothing else but to complete this offering by becoming more united to the Passion of Jesus. The wounds of the heart of Jesus then draw it like a magnet. Indeed, the Passion of Jesus becomes unusually attractive to ponder. The soul wants to enter inside Jesus' wounds at Calvary and know them as its own. It has become a victim of his love, and it savors this state as a privileged condition of soul.

$\sim$

"I want souls to know that by the Vow of Victim they enter into a life of union with Me. . . . They must know that the Vow of Victim means: *to imitate My Eucharistic life.* I desire that there be some of them everywhere, in every state of life" (Jesus to Sister Mary of the Holy Trinity).[4] Those who are serious enough to pray that Jesus might live his life within them make a courageous request. They may find that he answers this prayer, not as they expect, not by favoring them

[4] Sister Mary of the Holy Trinity, *The Spiritual Legacy of Sister Mary of the Holy Trinity*, 341.

with a sense of special closeness, but rather by replicating some portion of his Passion in their lives. For most people, this is a small taste of his Passion; and never is it identical in two people, for the possibilities are endless. Yet there may be a common feature in the divine reply to this prayer for a deeper offering, which casts light on all that follows in a life. Jesus offered himself to a sacrificial immolation on the Cross at Calvary. Resurrected in heaven, he continues to make the same sacrificial offering in an unbloody manner at every Mass. Those who have the courage to pray that Jesus might live his life in them ought to allow themselves, through their union with him in each Mass, to become with him a sacrificial offering as well. We should recall at each Mass that he offers himself in sacrifice in a manner mysteriously close to the breathing of our soul: namely, that while dwelling within our soul during a Mass, he offers himself. Our soul can become aware that the mystery of his sacrificial act is taking place, not just on the altar by the words of the priest, but within us as well. As the sacrificial act of the Consecration takes place, he is drawing us in the depth of our soul to be offered with himself. There is a sacred invitation at each Mass to draw nearer to Jesus' self-immolation and to offer ourselves to a union with his Passion. Inviting our Lord at each Mass to live more deeply within us, we should expect his sacrificial offering at Calvary to descend upon our lives in noticeable ways. Perhaps then, we, too, are destined over time to become victims of his love, just as he is the sacrificial victim. By offering ourselves to his sacrificial love at each Mass, we will be offered in turn by his love as a sacrificial immolation united to his Passion. And this means that we will be fruitful in immeasurable ways for the salvation and sanctification of other souls.

~

Perhaps the only way that divine love carves real depth into souls is by piercing them with interior fire. The fire is a particular kind of suffering, a struggle in prayer of varying degrees. Wherever there is greater love for God in prayer, it is inevitable that he hides from souls. Indeed, it is their great longing for him that seems to hide him even more. If they did not love him with intensity, he would not be so hidden. Yet many souls pierced by this fire of God's concealment are unaware of what is taking place. They do not understand it, and they suffer from it. The condition is not so much a trial of faith, although it can be that, too, but a suffering of love itself. These are souls who have no doubt or uncertainty that our Lord is near in the silence of a tabernacle. Yet a barrier seems to keep him distant and apart, his face blocked from sight. There are days of prayer for them as though they are facing nothing but a blank wall, with no door that might open, no corridor to walk down and explore. A room behind that wall has become the divine place of hiding, and there seems to be no way to reach it. If a door suddenly came into view, they would hurl themselves through it. And sometimes this trial is not temporary, but long in duration. They may seem to themselves at a standstill for days and weeks on end, incapable of drawing notice from the Lord, with no way to be heard through the thickness of that terrible wall. Yet it is just as true that often these same souls depart from an hour of prayer with a longing to give themselves more fully to others and to live for the salvation of souls and a surprising energetic strength to do so. It is a clear sign of God listening tenderly to a soul that thought itself speechless, cut off from his closer presence.

~

There are consequences to our soul in becoming more vulnerable in our love for God. We may discover, for instance, that a deep love for God is possible only after an incapacity to love afflicts our soul for a lengthy time. The path to greater love for God may pass through an extended time of this inability to love, a seeming paralysis of the heart. Our desire to give to God can continue to express itself in acts, but our soul in its inner core may feel empty and without love. In that inner vacancy, our soul's vulnerability to being wounded for love intensifies. Unknown to itself, we are being prepared for a greater love. It seems there is a secret threshold of love that must be crossed precisely at the time we are suffering from an inability to love. And there is in fact a way to cross that threshold. A lifting of our eyes to the face of Jesus on the Cross at Calvary must necessarily occur in an hour of prayerful silence. In that lingering attention directed to his face at Calvary, in searching for the sight of his eyes, we may realize a deeper truth of the crucifixion. The gaze of his eyes from the Cross exposes a vulnerability in God himself, a distinct inability of Jesus on the cross to love in his humanity to an unlimited infinitude. His human suffering, as horrific as it is, cannot extend infinitely, and Jesus suffers from this inability to give himself in his suffering to an infinitude of love. When we turn our soul to a gaze of love upon the face of Christ at Calvary, and perceive this wound of our Lord in suffering the human limits of his love, we can be crushed beneath this holy awareness. He would have loved more, suffered more, were it possible in his human nature. It seems that our Lord has great compassion on a soul at this moment in the silence of prayer.

The painful awareness that our Lord poured out all, and then suffered from having nothing more to give, invariably constrains the human heart unable to love. The experience within our soul of an inability to love somehow unites secretly in that moment with the Lord's inability to love in his humanity to infinitude. Jesus may then draw a surge of desire from our soul to release itself into a fresh vulnerability to being wounded by love. This is not an impulse to a rekindling of love, but much more a new experience of the true nature of love. The desire to love our Lord henceforth must find the eyes of the crucified Lord in his isolation at Calvary. His look of vulnerability to being wounded is mysteriously tender in receiving a recognition of love. Our soul can know in that hour, almost miraculously, that its own emptiness of love has passed. The presence of love returns as the heart is shattered in an instant by the vision of this crucified man Jesus exposing the vulnerability of God being wounded by his love for each of us.

$\sim$

It is a striking thing to consider how often women who desire to love and be loved allow themselves to become victims of love, but to their sadness and harm. They give themselves body and soul to a man out of love, without the commitment of marriage, hoping for a permanence in love, and then, when the relationship fails, they find themselves used and painfully cast aside. They become, sadly, victims of their love for these men. They allow their vulnerability to love and their desire as a woman to be loved to lead them to illusions about love. Without commitment, with nothing more than a declaration of love, they take the risk that their gift of body and soul to a man will be reciprocated in a lasting

way. Yet so often the result is a grave wound to the heart
of a woman, who is scarred in her natural vulnerability as
a woman when she has given her love to a man and then
finds herself later cast off and rejected. When our Lord invites a soul to become a victim of his love, the vulnerability
of the soul to be wounded for love is utterly different. The
possibility that some experience of suffering will enter a life
is real. But the suffering will always unite a soul to Jesus in
a manner that would not occur without this offering to be
his victim of love. In this case there is no casting aside of
a lover, no callous parting, but rather a union of hearts in
a suffering that can only unite and never divide or distance
them. There is suffering, surely, in offering oneself to a willingness to suffer for greater love, but the suffering itself has
a power of attraction for a loving soul by bringing a soul's
love into a mysterious proximity with the heart of Jesus.
Perhaps the deeper discovery of our Lord will always mean
a passage through his heart to some interior experience of
the rejection he experiences from souls. Almost every soul
that has offered itself as a victim of his love seems to know
in time also a rejection from others. But it experiences as
well in this solitude a profound desire of the soul that embraces Jesus Christ crucified in his solitude on a cross at
Calvary. Perhaps many women who have known rejection
in their personal lives are ideal candidates in their pain of
solitude for a deeper union of love with our Lord himself
in his crucified isolation.

~

There is a further recognition for us to enter more deeply a
great love for God. Our experience of an incapacity to love
except in a meager way is an inescapable condition. Yet this

does not mean that a release cannot take place. First, we must face this painful frustration, and then we must turn as a beggar to our Lord. If we speak openly to him of our inability to love and beg for his love to fill our empty heart, he answers this prayer. To the degree we make this a prayer of real depth, he will not refuse such a request. It is precisely what he desires, that is, to give us his own love to live within us, replacing our dry coldness with his own fires of love. This request, however, must be the prayer of a beggar. We must be fully aware of our poverty in love before asking. And, in truth, there is another condition that ensures the fulfillment of this request. We ought to ask for the Passion of our Lord to penetrate our interior life more deeply. The interior wounds of our Lord, when they are freely requested by our soul, are always a catalyst to greater love in the core of the soul. The heart does not become a vessel of divine love except when the interior wounds of Jesus' heart unite with our soul's own interior desire. Perhaps no great love can be given to a soul that has not openly agreed to accept Christ's Passion more deeply into its interior life.

～

Saint Damien of Molokai became a victim of love in his dedication to his lepers. He suffered the consequence of loving his people too much. In fact, we do not know what occurred in the hour in which he contracted the disease of leprosy after living safely for eleven years among the lepers of Molokai. Yet God knows what happened: indeed, the possibility is that an act of loving too much, of loving incautiously, without a thought of himself, perhaps of holding a dying leper in his arms, embracing a leprous face to his own, soothing the soul struggling to cross the eternal

threshold, perhaps this is the hour that confirmed the long
excess of his love over many years. There is no great love
without a willingness at some point to risk all. Saint Teresa
of Avila once wrote: "Those who in fact risk all will find
that they have both lost all and gained all."[5] Damien would
surely nod in complete agreement with these words. He became a victim of his excess of love; he died much younger
at forty-eight years than a more careful approach to lepers
might have given him. But he would not, I think, opt with
a second chance to exercise anything but his impulsive love
for the lepers who had captured his heart and given him a life
of exceeding love far beyond anything he previously understood before arriving in Molokai. Those who find a depth of
immense love in this kind of sacrificial complete self-giving
perhaps laugh at the suggestion of seeking longevity in life.

~

Only those who are wounded by love become true victims
of love. But what does it mean to become wounded by love
in the deepest spiritual sense? We need to turn to the Virgin
Mary and ask her to share her experience at the foot of the
Cross. Not just her suffering at the sight of Jesus' tortures;
there is the horrible wound she received in watching a dying man—the other criminal on the other side of Jesus—
adamantly refusing repentance and losing his soul. It is a
terrible wound to pray for someone who nonetheless loses
his soul. This was likely the experience of Mary at Calvary.
She prayed for this "other" criminal at Calvary who reviled
her Son and joined in the taunting mockery of Jesus. She

[5] Saint Teresa of Avila, "The Book of Her Life," 16.7, in *The Collected
Works of St. Teresa of Avila*, vol. one, trans. Kieran Kavanaugh and Otilio
Rodriguez (Washington, D.C.: ICS Publications, 1987), 151.

may have turned her pity toward him in an extraordinary manner of prayer. She saw the desperation of a hardened heart who knew nothing in the moment of his dying pain but anger and bitterness. She had an exquisite empathy for the heart of a young man violent with frustrated guilt for a wasted life. And she prayed for him, but perhaps in this case without the power of intercession before the throne of God that she would later possess in history. God preferred that she become a victim of love, pierced in her heart at Calvary, which is what took place when this man expired unrepentant, cursing the Romans as he suffocated in agony, unable to lift himself to breathe with his broken legs helpless to aid him.

~

Those who are wounded in their soul in seeing someone die unrepentant may experience as a result a thirst for souls they would otherwise never know. Perhaps we must see a soul lost, or at least encounter this as a true possibility, an immediate and real likelihood in a concrete life, if we are to embrace the seriousness of a spiritual life lived for souls, even for unknown souls. Holiness is self-oblation for others, not just in service to human needs, but primarily for their eternal salvation. The deeper desire for such a life may require in some cases this tragic experience. Perhaps it comes only after we have been taken captive by desire for the salvation of a soul and then find ourselves thwarted, put off, finally expelled from a life. The thought that a soul may have been lost must almost attack us with an insurmountable regret that we did not do more to avert the eternal, irreversible tragedy. Even Mary, the mother of almost infinite compassion, may have suffered from a terrible realization at Calvary that a soul was lost because more prayers were needed. Her eyes were attentive to her Son's agony, and, perhaps understandably, she did not exercise a concerted effort of prayer for this "other" criminal at the Cross until after Jesus had died and she fully realized the danger. And by then, it was too late. She seems to have lived the centuries in heaven since that day seeking that this should not happen ever again.

~

In 1990, when I was in my first year as a priest, I remember a call to the rectory from a mother asking me to visit her son dying of AIDS. At that time there were no medications for AIDS, and young men who had abused drugs or lived gay sexual life-styles were dying swiftly and helplessly as though thrown into a pit of devilish punishments for sin. Already as a seminarian, I had seen many men die at Mother Teresa's first AIDS hospice in Greenwich Village. After receiving the call from the mother, I visited the South Bronx apartment expecting a quiet anointing. The mother answered the doorbell and took me to the door of a bedroom, which she opened slowly. Immediately upon seeing me, a priest in a Roman collar, standing next to his mother, the young man lying in his bed, about twenty-eight years old, leaned up on his elbow and began spewing foul curses in my direction. But quickly he turned the vulgarity upon his mother for bringing this contemptuous such and such into his bedroom without his permission. I raised my voice to say that he should not speak like that to his mother, but she pulled me away forcibly by the arm and closed the door. The venom of his shouts continued even from behind a closed door. The mother apologized as though she had been at fault, and then after a promise to pray for her son I had to leave. I tried to visit again without calling beforehand, but I was met at the door by the mother, embarrassed now, telling me that a visit was impossible and would not work. He died a few days later. The funeral was unlike any funeral I have experienced as a priest. No one there but a father and a mother in a front pew; no relatives, none of the former lovers, no one. The possibility of a soul renouncing the chance for salvation and choosing the destiny of eternal hell is not unreal. Perhaps it is more real than we envision. Priests may have more direct experience of this terrible truth, but many priests ignore or blind themselves to it. But others are never reconciled to the painful effects, and personally I would say I have never forgotten.

～

Perhaps we only know someone with a deeper love when we come to know that person in the wounds of the heart ordinarily kept private and hidden. This truth is essential for our relations with Mary, the mother at the foot at the Cross at Calvary. The wounds of her heart at Calvary extended beyond the terrible sight of her Son Jesus undergoing a Roman crucifixion. She suffocated inside her heart in watching him struggle to catch his breath after each brief word he spoke on the Cross. She had always loved his flowing words in their precise cadence, but now she suffered in witnessing the short expressions spoken with great internal effort from his heart unable to breathe. This pain was immense, but a more piercing wound awaited her. It is the wound we must enter ourselves for a greater love of her. When Jesus was near death on the Cross and asked Mary his mother to turn to John and said to her, "Woman, behold, your son!" (Jn 19:26), she most certainly did cast her eyes on John, and with great intuitive awareness accepted to be the mother of John, of the priesthood and religious life, to be the mother of the Church in history. She understood the command and embraced all its implication. While her eyes were on John and her soul was in a deep moment of prayer, Jesus pronounced his word: "I thirst" (Jn 19:28). The simple phrase must have shaken her, and when she turned back to Jesus, she was startled, because perhaps she saw that Jesus had been looking at the criminal on the other side, the man who had derided and taunted him throughout his crucifixion for his supposed greatness. When Mary saw Jesus' eyes turn from this man after pronouncing "I thirst", she was moved with understanding. She understood intuitively the divine thirst of Jesus for that soul, and for the countless number of souls that would follow in history who would taunt Jesus with their rejection of his mercy while undergoing their own painful hours of dying.

~

The piercing of the heart of Mary is an enormous mystery in the event of Calvary. We tend to pass over this truth. Jesus with a loud cry gave his last breath, but the two men on each side of Jesus were quite alive. A man could remain alive on a Roman cross for four or five days, and these men were nowhere near death. The Roman soldiers, in a brutal action of depraved torture, broke the legs of the one, then of the other, and they slowly suffocated, unable to breathe because they could not lift themselves on the cross. The Roman soldier came and thrust a lance into the side of Jesus, piercing his heart and causing blood and water to flow visibly from the open wound. The great wound is Mary's at that hour, as she is pierced in heart, which Simeon had predicted thirty-three years earlier in the temple in Jerusalem. "Behold, this child is set for the fall and rising of many in

Israel, and for a sign that is spoken against (and a sword will pierce through your own soul also), that thoughts out of many hearts may be revealed" (Lk 2:34–35). The wound to her pure motherly heart is to see a man go to his death unrepentant, cursing the Romans, bitter and unhuman in his hatred. This is the great wound we must come to know if we are to live a life of intense zeal for souls. The knowledge of souls being eternally lost, which the current world is so hesitant to consider, is the opening to a different love for Mary. She in turn unites us to her Son's thirst on the Cross for the salvation of souls most desperately in need. That awareness is essential today for any real holiness.

~

The Virgin Mother Mary in heaven may find herself gazing at times at the wounds of Jesus, not in distracted manner, not saddened by their presence in his hands as she observes the gestures of Jesus, but mesmerized by the feelings of uncontrollable love that these wounds seem to draw from the depths of her heart. We can assume that at Calvary, or prior to the crucifixion, she asked Jesus that she might enter fully into the suffering of his heart when he would suffer on the Cross. She did not want to stand apart, watching in compassion, offering only sympathy and a mother's closeness. She desired to share herself in the depths of his internal pain. Her own vulnerability to be crushed by pain combined with a desire not to withhold herself from pain. Perhaps she insisted, in a forceful motherly manner that would allow no refusal, in a mysterious communication with her Son, that she, as his mother, would not allow him to suffer apart from her. Her offering became for her an entry into the heart of Jesus as he went through his Passion. She witnessed his pain at the

loss of souls and embraced fully this same desolate awareness. A truth became consequential for her as a result, and
she wants to teach this to souls who desire to be close to
her. The crucial instruction is this: a desire to intercede for
souls becomes powerful only after the loss of souls becomes
real and devastating and pierces the heart and soul. A soul
united to Mary becomes one with her suffering for souls.
They are wounded together and united by these wounds
with Jesus on the cross. This quality of union describes in
effect a victim soul of love. A victim of love has the courage
to face the crushing truth of souls being lost and the pain
it causes to the hearts of Jesus and Mary. She became the
first victim soul by requesting a union with the immense
wound of Jesus at the loss of souls. For us to be fruitful in a
greater manner for souls, we must offer ourselves as a victim
soul united to her victimhood. Our heart must be crushed
by wounds of love that penetrate the heart mysteriously.
Unless we allow our heart to be shattered by the wounds
still afflicting the Lord's heart, and Mary's heart at Calvary,
we will never love him with a real sacrificial outpouring of
love. A love for Mary as the first victim of love can attract
us to make the same offering of love she made so fruitfully.

～

John the apostle may have gone to Calvary and the crucifixion not simply to remain close to Jesus out of his great
love for the Lord. He may have already enjoyed deep relations of love for the Virgin Mother of Jesus. He went to
Calvary to stay close to her in her hour of need. He is the
beloved disciple not only to Jesus, but because he is dear to
the heart of Mary, and Jesus loves what he sees of Mary's
special regard and affection for this young man. He goes to

Calvary to be a comfort to Mary in her hour of grave trial, and Jesus observes this in his gaze upon the two of them standing side by side. John consoles Jesus by being there and becoming the one person he can entrust to his mother upon his death as her adopted son and protector. But this closeness to Mary will also inevitably introduce John the young priest to the spiritual exigency of victimhood. If he is to share in the mystery of a depth of love that lives within his new mother, he must accept a new awareness. A discovery will come in time for him. Her silence in prayer after the death and Resurrection of Jesus will reveal slowly over time that Golgotha concealed vast implications still awaiting his spiritual response. She was aware of the choice of John as a contemplative soul and would wait perhaps for John to watch and examine her, sensing her inner wound at the loss of Jesus, but realizing in time that a greater wound pierced her heart and soul. John may be the first soul to learn from Mary how to be a victim of love for souls. He is the only apostle not to die a martyr, living to an old age. But he is the one apostle perhaps to discover what it is to live in oneness with Mary's victimhood for souls who reject the love of her Son. He learned from her to be a victim of love for those who risk the loss of their souls, and this offering of his life replaced the need in his case to die as a martyr.

16

LIVING THE MYSTERY: THE PROVIDENTIAL CLOSENESS OF GOD

I have the feeling that what is asked of *us* is to live in the whirlwind, without keeping back any of our substance, without keeping back anything for ourselves, neither rest nor friendships nor health nor leisure—to pray incessantly and that even without leisure—in fact to let ourselves pitch and toss in the waves of the divine will till the day when it will say: "*It is enough.*"[1]

—Raïssa Maritain

A man is religious to the very degree that he recognizes everywhere these reflections of the divine Face, that is, that he lives in a sacred atmosphere.[2]

—Henri de Lubac, S.J.

There will always be a Chair at the Sorbonne for the one who declares that the saints were fit for an insane asylum.[3]

—Charles Péguy

Perhaps we misconceive God in thinking he must observe consistent patterns in his relations with us. In fact, he is under no obligation to do so. No law in his nature requires

---

[1] Raïssa Maritain, *Raïssa's Journal* (Albany, N.Y.: Magi Books, 1974), 230.

[2] Henri de Lubac, S.J., *Theology in History*, 231.

[3] Charles Péguy, in Matthew W. Maguire, *Carnal Spirit: The Revolutions of Charles Péguy* (Philadelphia: University of Pennsylvania Press, 2019), 98.

him to act in accord with any set rule, as it were, except that
of divine love in all its mystery. Yet love in God is an infinitely open mystery capable of unusual surprises. The actual truth may be that God, because his love stretches into
unfathomable mystery, resists every prediction, every facile
anticipation, of what he will choose toward us, including
in the circumstances of history. Precisely because his love
has no limits or boundaries, his actions resist every attempt
to predict his plans. Look at any life that has gotten close
to him. God in these lives seems so often to prefer surprise
to predictability, unannounced interventions to clear indications of his next move. It is not in the divine interest
of love that any soul should foresee clearly what God will
do. Instead, the painful shock of events often forces us to
face him nakedly, which is precisely what God may desire if
we are to advance in faithful trust toward him. We cannot
clothe ourselves in an armor of preparedness for such occasions. The most vulnerable time for us is often the most
preferable hour for him. Indeed, he seems to wait for our
greatest hours of vulnerability to reveal his presence most
strikingly, perhaps when we are on the edge of collapse or
giving up. Our own defenselessness constrains us then to
face his mystery; otherwise, we may lose him, a free but
terrible option at such hours. The soul vulnerable to the
shock of his Divine Presence discovers on such a day an
entry into his divine reality that would otherwise be closed.
Perhaps the same truth for individual souls is at work in the
vulnerability of history to God's designs.

～

Despite endless variations in individual lives, souls of serious prayer display a common trait—an inward hunger for
God's hidden presence within their soul. This hunger has a

clear consequence even in the living out of mundane daily life. These souls are more directly in contact with the providential ways of God, more immediately aware of the quiet hints of his presence at work in a single day. Nonetheless, this remains essentially a hidden presence. God does not remove the cover of his concealment. The hiddenness enlarges the hunger of our soul, and God is pleased by that hunger. Contrary to expectation, no easy companionship with God occurs even in the most contemplative of souls, but rather a deepening conviction of the hiddenness of divine activity in which God seems always a step ahead of any direct view, never clearly in sight except as he is leaping ahead and disappearing. The souls of deeper prayer learn that if there are real encounters with God, they must be sought in the hiding places of divine poverty. Proximity to the hidden God offers no promise of any felt satisfaction awaiting our soul. His Divine Presence is never a possession to be enjoyed as a form of privilege. Perhaps a significant threshold is crossed in prayer when our soul perceives no defeat, no real frustration, in bearing the pain of inward emptiness and unsatisfied desire, but rather finds within the empty caverns of our soul a deeper longing for God than any experience we have previously known. In a yearning for God that is buried deeply inside our soul and is never satisfied, we touch the divine mystery in a way that stretches beyond any other experience of love.

～

"He has not left me alone, for I always do what is pleasing to him" (Jn 8:29). No prayerful soul can read these words of Jesus without a painful desire that one day they might become our own spontaneous cry to God. In fact, these prayerful souls know how often he does seem to leave them alone, sometimes for lengthy stretches of time in prayer.

They return each day in prayer to his silent presence, and yet there are long periods when an unseen barrier keeps them from seeing his face or listening to his voice. They await an instruction for a way to give him special delight on that day, but they are deaf and blind in the hour. The words from Saint John's Gospel that Jesus has not been left alone by his Father may almost draw pangs of envy from certain souls. These souls long precisely for the day in which he will not leave them alone. They offer themselves and ask for this favor, that he might be a companion in all things touching their lives. At the same time, they are perhaps too restless and anxious in wanting to know what might please him most. They are like all people consumed with love for a beloved, desiring to give delight. They want to exalt with love the one who is loved, in small or great ways. The trouble may be in thinking too much about how to accomplish this. It is impossible at times to know with certainty what is pleasing to him. At times we can only make tentative gestures hoping that our desire to love is known to him. Yet this desire most certainly is known to him and is pleasing to him. We may not know what he prefers in every action, but the shadows clouding our vision are not shadows for him. And perhaps he does not leave our soul alone, despite our anxious thought, because we are intent to pour out generosity in a gift of ourselves to others on that day. He may hide himself while observing our soul's unawareness of his gaze, but he is not blind himself.

$\sim$

When we anticipate our Lord's desires, catching hold of them before he makes a request, this is a sign of love. It may happen more easily when our desire to please him is strong in prayer, without knowing yet what he wants. Perhaps he will not leave us alone in a day when a desire to please him has filled our earlier prayer. Then it is more likely that we may perceive clear opportunities to give a delight to our Lord without his explicit request for a particular action. This does not imply the need for some mystical insight of the moment. It does suggest that love between God and a soul can be an exquisite dance in which at times our soul is led, and at other times we take the lead. The humility of God allows this surprising initiative of our soul in taking the lead in love. Our soul honors him by refusing to make passivity to his divine direction the sole compass of love. Love is far more than faithfulness to the obligation of divine commands. Rather, the measure of our love for God is a state of surrender within our soul when we have already given all and yet continue to offer ourselves as though there is more to offer. To belong all to God in this manner is to receive more often an anticipatory sense of what will give delight to God. The soul of greater love does not wait for an explicit clarity to arrive about what God wants. The desire to give delight to him becomes already an uncanny indicator of what does please him. And this takes place at times without effort, perhaps because God draws forth these recognitions in a way unknown to us.

~

To surrender ourselves in service to our Lord out of love for him is not a small thing. If we repeat a promise that we desire to give all, it is very likely that smaller promptings from God increasingly affect our life—small self-denials, small sacrifices in love, small acts of consideration for the other. We can easily ignore opportunities for pleasing him until we are giving ourselves more fully to him. The more united our soul is to God by a prayer of greater explicit offering, the more pronounced is the urge to give God the fullness of ourselves in the small offerings that fill a day. God seems to treasure the act of taking us into the greater humility of our nothingness by asking us to be faithful in love to smaller generosities. With God nothing is small when the offering at the heart of these actions reaches into a great depth of love in our soul.

~

Intense surrender in an hour of silent prayer will always extend its effects beyond that hour. Inevitably this is so, but there is a pattern to observe. After a deeper surrender to God in prayer, there remains a need to finish something still incomplete. Now that prayer is concluded, there are concrete actions of that day still unknown that await discovery. A sign of this is that we depart prayer with both dissatisfaction and a strong desire for God, as though our love for God is too confined and now needs stretching. Our soul longs for release, and it will find this release only in turning to sacrificial actions. These actions do not require dramatic heroism, but they do demand self-denying choices that will be costly to ourselves. Routine generosities will not do. What is striking is that sacrifices of this sort seem to become more available as we take prayer more seriously. In a day they approach us like visitors knocking at our door. This mysterious pattern clearly happens because God makes these opportunities possible. But let us remember: the sacrificial actions outside prayer are an overflow of the sacrificial act of surrender inside prayer. Our soul needs to experience this connection and to honor it. Jesus surely wants us to recognize that a surrender to himself in prayer will urge us to concrete sacrifice in action. The joining of these acts and spiritual impulses becomes a deeper entry into the mystery of his love.

~

"Terrible is the strength of the soul entirely subject to God's will" (Jacques Maritain).[4] Our own initiative of self-offering is crucial in this link between surrender in prayer and sacrifice in action. In both cases we want to give God more of ourselves. The best way to do so is always to offer ourselves to him. A surrender to God in prayer is only an initial act and yet of great importance. It ignites the flame and unleashes the hunger that persist outside prayer. The hunger for God simply takes on a new expression when we choose sacrificial actions. Now, with prayer concluded, the attraction can be strong for sacrificial actions that can be offered in love to God. We must be alert in leaving prayer to the possibility of actions of generosity, even small generosities. Otherwise, we will experience a heaviness and dissatisfaction in our later return to prayer that has nothing to do with a trial or purification in prayer itself. What has been left unfinished in prayer, as it were—the need to choose sacrificial actions outside prayer—must be a clear desire in departing prayer. Otherwise, without that resolute intent, we are likely to return to prayer with a task undone and suffer from this incompletion. The more that acts of surrender are sought in prayer, the more a sacrificial impulse is bound to animate the soul outside prayer. But we must run with that desire for sacrifice and put it into action in concrete ways.

~

Christianity displays a magnificent array of elevated concepts and images radiating the mysterious truth of divine revelation. But without a personal choice on our part to

[4] Jacques Maritain, *The Degrees of Knowledge*, trans. Gerald B. Phelan (New York: Charles Scribner's Sons, 1959), 365.

embrace the hard work of sacrificial tasks, the beauty of God's revelation in Jesus Christ can remain an abstraction that never finds a deeper home in our heart. Perhaps the most reliable evidence that the truth of divine revelation has quietly conquered our life is when we have become unfit for mere worldly living. And this always means that sacrificial living and a certain indifference to worldly comfort and pleasure has taken hold of our life. And this in turn never occurs except when prayer, even extended time spent in prayer when it is possible, has become an irrefusable attraction.

~

We cannot advance in the life of prayer unless a greater attention to God outside prayer becomes the prelude to actions in a day. An unfailing sign that our soul has found God more deeply in prayer is a growing impossibility to make choices in a day without some advertence to God. This condition may seem to imply a delay before acting, a need to turn to God for guidance and strength prior to particular actions. But the actual effect of deeper prayer is more subtle and mysterious than mere dependency on God. A new sense of Jesus' profound words—"apart from me you can do nothing" (Jn 15:5)—awakens. The words do not signify simply a powerlessness to act without him, or an inevitable failure to bear spiritual fruits without grace and his aid. They imply also that after a time we no longer live alone, but rather that his presence accompanies us at all hours. An undercurrent of desire for pleasing God increasingly burns inside our heart. We are led often to what will give delight to him without trying to be led. On some days, perhaps, it can all come rather easily, swiftly, without much thought. Without an effort on our part, his presence allows us to know almost instinctively what can touch his heart. It is as though an instinct for pleasing God is operating within our soul to cast a momentary light on what will delight him. The ease of all this has its source in a life of prayer. If wanting God above all else consumes all desire in the soul, this should not be so surprising. Nonetheless, the constancy of it requires alertness and often quick responses of generosity. For God wants our personal initiative to be exercised in pleasing him.

∼

The mystery of divine companionship may combine at times a gritty realism with circumstances of seeming chance. An encounter with a poor man on a city street speaking words that seem to answer a prayer that we have cried out that same morning—can it be that God steps out of hiding in a stranger's disguise, wanting to be known? I remember years ago, at an hour of uncertainty about a possible call to the priesthood, I was praying daily for an answer and for some sign. Then I passed an old man in dirty clothes sitting on a park bench in the Bronx near the Missionaries of Charity convent. He caught my eye, and then he reached out his worn, unclean hand, which I took in my own. After some words of conversation, as I turned from him, walking away, I heard his voice behind me—"keep going, don't look back." The words caught me and even stunned me. Can the voice of God be speaking through a man at such a moment? At this point in life, I have no doubt about that. In an unexpected instant, God's desire may flash in front of us, without further proof or confirmation, but leaving an uncanny sense of the Divine Presence. It is not God's manner to enclose himself in a permanent state of concealment;

rather, he lifts the veil briefly at certain unusual hours. And it may be a poor man and a brief remark that reveal God most eloquently. Let us not discount or dismiss this truth. It is what we must believe, if we aspire to know firsthand the mysterious nature of a God who is humble. Perhaps this conviction becomes more undeniable to the degree we become poor in spirit ourselves. Then, when we are in need in some deeper way, we may hear God hiding himself in the poor man in front of us.

~

At first glance, apparent contraries may seem to be irreconcilable, opposed in a manner that can never be resolved. The meaning of one truth seems to be the opposite of the other, in direct contrast to the other. Yet in the spiritual realm, this appearance of opposition tells only a partial story. Our encounter with the poor, for instance, may convey only a single side of what should be perceived as a double-edged reality. The poor man stands before us in all his sad ruin, perhaps even drunk in the hour, yet Jesus hides his Divine Presence of love for this soul standing in front of us beneath the features of his coarsened face. With deeper spiritual insight, the contradiction that remains beyond our capacity to reconcile—a poor man in need, and the presence of God in hiding and loving a soul—may not disappear at all. Rather, it may urge us to a deeper recognition. If we become more prayerful, a barrier that we naturally set up between these two realities—a real man and a hidden God—may more often break down. The poor man and the presence of Jesus lose their difference, and they become one in the moment, no longer incompatible with each other. The two realities are capable of mysteriously fusing in a united sacredness at a deeper layer of reality. This insight may cast an unmistakable sense of truth upon our vision of the poor that is often missed. Our blindness suddenly lifts, and we see sharply, differently, with an intuitive gaze. We pierce for a moment the actual complementarity of a poor man and Christ himself in a real encounter with a poor man. The surface view abruptly changes, and we know intuitively a union between God and a man. We are no longer blocked by the barrier of possible repugnance toward a poor person that was impeding our sight from the truth hiding in that encounter.

⁓

The small moment often contains within it the capacity for an immense gift. It is a principle of great importance in the spiritual life. The common tendency is to think the opposite and expect that significant spiritual opportunities must come wrapped in a veneer of importance or intensity. It is a worldly habit of judgment that often holds us back from deeper spiritual recognitions: the mistaken assumption that the poorer the appearance, the rougher the surface, the less likely to find a precious jewel. The mistake keeps us from perceiving hidden truths of beauty within people. Even more harmful, it impedes a gratitude to God for small gifts that is essential for a serious spiritual life. A gift from God is easily missed when we do not anticipate the chance to honor God in the small moment, the small person, the small event. Without a habit of attention in this manner, no sense of wonder will be ready to erupt spontaneously at the presence of unsought beauty appearing before our eyes. The beauty is often found in the unsolicited moment of a day, in the sudden sight of a poor man's ability to pierce our heart with compassion for him. This can happen regularly if we open our eyes to look with love at the lonely faces of solitary poor people. So often these same people grant a gift of their eyes when we allow ourselves to receive their look, instead of turning away. It is a gift from God himself that is received in that small moment.

~

No law of gravity exists in our relations with God. In fact, just the opposite seems to be the case. We are not thrown back to the ground after finishing a prayer that has gazed in loving adoration toward God. Rather, on some days, we seem to be lifted over a barrier by such prayer and granted an elevated perception of our Lord's presence when we conclude prayer. We should expect this different quality of vision, so that we may receive fully the fruits of prayer. Otherwise, our wounded nature will quickly pull us back down to the mundane agitations of an impatient life. Serious commitment to prayer has its consequences. A secret fire burns steadily at the depth of our soul when we are serious about prayer. It is this interior fire that overcomes any subjection to a law of spiritual gravity. There is no end to this fire extending its reach if we cultivate a deep longing for God. Deeper love for God operates precisely in an opposite manner to natural gravity. The force of love's gravity will draw us toward the depths of God himself hiding within our own being. And this form of gravity is experienced at times, paradoxically, as a plunge into depths that at the same elevates us toward unknown summits of longing where our Lord is encountered, despite the apparent contradiction in this phrase. The plunge into depths seems often to be indistinguishable from a leap upward into unlimited longings for God. Everything in this spiritual movement of grace is contrary to a law of natural gravity. The way of love is a pull downward into interior depths only to arrive at what can seem heights of intense longing in our contact with God.

~

Placing ourselves alone before God, naked and alone before his eyes, is perhaps not typically sought in prayer, despite what we think. And yet standing nakedly before God is an essential condition for realizing that an eternal destiny awaits us beyond this life. Without this perception, we evade the harder spiritual truths, never lifting the veil into what is most real in life. Priests at times encounter this neglect. It seems that many people, near the end of life, suffer a vague anxiety that some crucial search has been ignored and that it is now too late. This is not a question simply of having religious faith. Many people with faith have never known in life a sufficient desire for God that would take them to their knees in a lengthy cry of need for him. They have never allowed their nakedness of soul to be exposed openly before God. We should not wait for our deathbed to pray in such a manner. The risk of never longing for God during life is often to experience, in the solitude of that last period of days and months, the broken fragments of a lifetime of memories vying for attention at the confused end of a life. It is to risk suffering a harder death, even with faith. At any time in life, and especially at the end, if we are willing to pray in a bare, open need for God, he answers with his presence. God seems, indeed, quite adept at taking the smallest invitations of desire for himself and leading a soul to his open presence. I have seen it many times with people in the last months or weeks of their lives. Priests surely have this experience, that people who have prayed little in life, ignoring God, are often quite ready to be led like a child in prayer when they are soon to face God.

~

Even when God has been absent from a life, a desire for him remains in the soul. This desire for God cannot be destroyed, even by persistent sin or betrayal. At times it may light up again in a life and be recognized. It is said, for instance, that Fidel Castro requested the Sacrament of Anointing when he was dying. Conversions do occur, sometimes after a long taste of fatigue and disgust with the terrible loneliness of sin. The great danger, on the other hand, is that a coldness to God closes a soul in upon itself. If the natural desire for God in a soul is suffocated and finds no release, unnatural consequences show in due time. A deformation of the desire for God can take place so that the soul likely makes a god of itself and worships itself. The idolatrous hunger for pleasure, possessions, power, or egoism replaces God with the adoration of self-love. The natural desire to lean out in hunger to God has turned inward in a destructive withdrawal into self-hatred. The pain of every spiritually tragic life reflects a desperation to appease a hunger at the depth of our being. Often a terrible cost ensues in that effort, indeed, the only real tragedy in life. The hunger for God can be satisfied only by God himself.

~

Most ordinary people try their best to ignore the thought of death. Yet perhaps God uses this inevitable truth of human life to bring souls to an awareness of himself. In 1923, soon after the publication of his famous poem "The Wasteland," and four years before his baptism into the Church of England, T. S. Eliot, while on a visit to Verona with a decidedly atheistic Ezra Pound, confessed to him privately: "I am afraid of the life after death."[5] The morbid sound of this remark might provoke the thought that he was a man suffering from psychological strain and illness. In fact, it was likely a sign of spiritual life quickening. By that time, in his mid-thirties, Eliot had fully tasted the horrors of hell in his personal life and in an aberrant marriage; yet, even in doubt, this damaged man had an undeniable sense of the immortality of the soul. Would that we all might share his remark to the depths of our heart. The thought of the life after death is suppressed or forgotten in lives to their own peril. And, indeed, fear of what may come after death is a most salutary anxiety if a man is living in a manner that cannot but face a painful judgment. And for someone close to God, the thought of facing God one day is an arousing jolt to return to a spirit of greater self-giving. For Eliot, this painful time in 1923 was preliminary to his decisive conversion to the certitude of Christian belief within a few short years. It is striking in every life that eventually finds God how suffering the absence of God is so often a prelude to a leap of final conviction toward the mystery of God.

~

[5] Lyndall Gordon, *T. S. Eliot: An Imperfect Life* (New York: W. W. Norton, 1998), 210.

During the three years of his solitary life in a cave, as his love for souls intensified, it may be that the stars did shine increasingly brighter at night for Saint Benedict. Perhaps on one unusually clear night he looked at the vast spectrum of lights in the sky and, in gazing at the stars, he suddenly realized the countless number of souls that he would now take into his own soul and serve in his prayer and in his ascetical denials. The luster of the stars and the beauty of their configurations may have captivated him with the thought that Jesus contemplated these very same stars during his forty nights in the desert of Judea, preparing for his public life. Indeed, on that night filled with the beauty of countless stars, Benedict may have understood his own taste of spiritual darkness in a new light, seeing that it is a share in the suffering of Christ for *all* souls as Jesus hung in agony on the cross at Calvary. Every soul is beloved by God, and Benedict in his solitary state gazing at the night sky may have come to see this truth with a mystic's vision. If so, with courage, beneath a night sky filled with the immensity of stars, perhaps he offered himself for all souls alive at his moment in history in a very profound manner. Following Jesus to Calvary, he would be a servant and slave for the salvation of souls. To this day, he teaches generous souls that the great gift of self to our Father in heaven is to embrace this kind of slavery for souls. It would be striking if Jesus had such a thought, too, as he gazed at the sky in the Judean desert during his forty long nights. Jesus in his Passion became a lowly slave, a slave of love, in accepting to pour out himself in the tortures of the Passion for the most miserable of sinners. Surely an analogy is possible. Each star in the night sky is precious for its light just as the eternal life of even the most desperate sinner is dear to the Heart of God. And the most miserable sinner has been at times each of us. The saints, despite their misery and failings, lived a slavery for souls, like Jesus at Calvary, precisely by taking *all* souls within their heart. The saint is a slave of love, given up to an offering for *all* souls, who then fill the heart of a saint like the stars that encompass the night sky. Nothing in the night sky is out of place or forgotten. Likewise, no soul can be outside the desire of a saint. The great daily prayer of a saint may be that souls, especially among the dying, are touched by God's grace and cross a threshold of faith and repentance and by God's mercy attain their salvation.

~

We can never know how often a deathbed conversion occurs. Certainly, this possibility of conversion taking place in the last hours of life shows variations in historical eras, whether we live in a time of belief or in a time of greater indifference to God. It is not that God's mercy is different. But the inclination to seek God's mercy at the last moment may not be so strong in certain eras. Death may sweep men away without much thought in some periods of history more than in others. It may be a measure of the spiritual quality of the era in which we live how often souls are snatched away from eternal damnation because God intervenes with a gesture of grace at the last moment and the soul responds. On the other hand, there is a great need in an era when men and women do not give much attention to eternity to pray for the dying in a state of mortal sin who may receive then a grace to recognize God in that last hour of life. We live in such an era, and we should make such a prayer for the dying in need of grace a daily habit. The providential hand of God may indeed be desirous of touching many souls on their deathbed who had in our time the disadvantage of living at a time of unstable and tumultuous Catholic faith.

17

AN HOUR OF TESTING:
THE CALL TO SPIRITUAL INTENSITY

Error is like the foam on the waves, it eludes our grasp and keeps reappearing. The soul must not exhaust itself fighting against the foam. Its zeal must be purified and calmed and, by union with the divine Will, it must gather strength from the depths. And Christ, with all his merits and the merits of all the saints, will do his work deep down below the surface of the waters.[1]

—Raïssa Maritain

No one can anticipate the final testing, and it alone can reveal to us what really belongs to us and what does not. The extreme situation, in which a man is left only with his true possessions, has laws of its own.[2]

—Josef Pieper

Today it is not enough to be a saint; but we must have the saintliness demanded by the present moment, a new saintliness, itself also without precedent.[3]

—Simone Weil

What does it mean in the history of sanctity, in the real lives of saints, to become a friend of Christ? "No longer do

---

[1] Raïssa Maritain, *Raïssa's Journal* (Albany, N.Y.: Magi Books, 1974), 158.

[2] Josef Pieper, *Scholasticism: Personalities and Problems of Medieval Philosophy*, trans. Richard and Clara Winston (South Bend, Ind.: St. Augustine's Press, 2001), 34.

[3] Simone Weil, *Waiting for God*, trans. Emma Craufurd (New York: G. P. Putnam's Sons, 1951), 51.

I call you servants, . . . but I have called you friends" (Jn 15:15). He directs us in these words not simply to remain a loyal servant of his commands, restricting our spiritual ideal to faithfulness, but to extend ourselves beyond limits or boundaries. Quite literally, in small and great ways, we are to lay down our lives for him as the beloved friend of our soul. Martyrdom has always been the implication contained in these words, and we ought to return to this awareness today. The intensity of Christian persecution, to the point of suffering torture and death, has varied in different eras. The courage of the early Church, with so many anonymous martyrs among poor and simple people, is the touchstone of an ultimate friendship for Christ. But today, in a world that may grow more openly contemptuous of Christianity, martyrdom is lurking as a real possibility, at least in future decades. Our friendship with Christ may require a willingness to die for him, or else it has only a value of sentiment. A last era of the Church, when it does come, is very likely to face this test of martyrdom in various forms—loss of life, but deprivation also, as we may see already in some lives, of career, comforts, ease, and security. What was suffered in the early Church of the Roman Empire, when Christians were largely a powerless minority, may be repeated in the marginalized remnant who remain still faithful within the Church at a later date in this century. It will be a measure of our soul's love for Christ crucified that we perceive this test clearly and surrender ourselves heroically to Christ, as he lives his Passion again in that last period.

$\sim$

As time goes on, the need for greater interiority of soul will be a serious demand among Catholics. With the secular culture darkened by a hostility to truth, and the Church perhaps in her leadership demonstrating little moral courage, souls of God may have one of two options. In rare cases, they can choose some form of separation from society and a life of greater solitude and prayerful silence. The other possibility is to remain in the world, but while living in the world to embrace a commitment to prayer that would seem inappropriate and excessive in more ordinary times. The danger is that without one or the other option, good people will drift spiritually and be defenseless before the confusion that may internally afflict the Church. They will find themselves unsure and unguided, questioning what the Church seems now to permit, and in many cases may risk losing faith in the Church in her historical tradition as an authoritative teacher of truth. The only secure protection will be a dedicated approach to prayer. Those who give themselves to serious prayer may come to recognize, in a manner unique in history until that time, that Jesus Christ is living his Passion again within his own Church. Because of this realization, a deep interiority will carve itself into souls serious toward prayer. Amid the ecclesial turmoil, the spirit of prayer among a portion of souls will perhaps intensify in a manner unlike any time in history. A shared suffering for the Church will unite these souls of prayer in a hidden way. They will have an impact on one another, and they will know that they are mysteriously bonded in their devotion to perennial Catholic truths.

~

A type of metaphysical anguish may be already a subtle and concealed form of contemplative suffering today. The grave offense to the sacredness of truth in our time is quite real, yet perhaps often taking place unseen to the eyes of those who give themselves to serious prayer. But perhaps the contemplative souls need to awaken to the true state of the time we are living. Serious souls of prayer are seeking a God who is increasingly rejected in his truth and cast behind a barrier of indifference in society. The indifference to God is more than a lack of interest. There seems to be a spiritual conviction permeating a large segment of the world that the very idea of the Christian God no longer serves any purpose. In this view, it is best to keep the name of God buried in obscurity, locked away as though in an archive of dusty artifacts. For many, the reality of God is nothing but a myth of a bygone era, meaningless and no different from the gods of pagan invention. In effect, our all-holy God finds no admittance at the brass door of modernity. The repeated demand of the dominant voices of our time is to discard him from discussion. This disdain for God cannot be ignored, and the prayerful person must necessarily suffer it. The pursuit of God is never a private enterprise, cut off from the current day; it must suffer the spiritual wounds of a historical era. Modernity breathes an odor of unbelief, and no contemplative soul can evade the noxious encounter with the societal disparagement toward God. Indeed, the bitter taste in realizing this hostility to God in our own time is not unconnected to the inability of our soul at times to persevere in optimism. He is a wounded Lord in our day, just as the soul is wounded at times, and we have no recourse on some days but to draw near to the crucified Lord rejected increasingly in this era. He died in torture to save us, but also to teach us how to offer ourselves. The darkness that is intensifying is never without a burning light at its center. But let us awaken to the truth of the time in which we live.

∼

The private afflictions of contemplative souls may offer a clue to understanding the sufferings that may await the Church in the coming decades. These struggles of contemplative souls at times intensify as an extended trial of faith. A contemplative soul may plunge involuntarily for some time into a period of self-doubt and insecurity, at a loss to restrain and subdue its sense of internal darkness, no longer able to find a comfort in God. As trials of this sort continue, the silence of God may seem to repeat a single deafening word of his disappearance. With more time, the darkness may close in on a soul, bringing, in the most painful cases, even a conviction of a rejection by God. The survival of the soul, indeed, its elevation in sanctity by means of this trial, takes place for the sole reason that it continues to exercise intense certitude in faith and to love our Lord deeply. Even in blindness, a soul can hold fast to the dim shadows of divine love that hide within the core of the soul. An endurance through darkness by a cleaving personal love for Jesus crucified is always possible with grace, and indeed it is the path to great love for some souls. The Church herself may enter at some point in time into her own variation of the dark night of the soul. This trial will be a suffering felt acutely by those Catholics most faithful to the truths of Catholicism, truths that may find themselves under siege within the Church. There are times in history when a response of remarkable courage is needed, even from those not prepared for heroism. In periods of calamity there are always souls who leap far beyond their age of maturity to answer to a heroic destiny. Something like this must happen among souls if the Church undergoes her own trial of faith as the years continue in our era.

∽

The capacity of serious souls of prayer to assent firmly with unquestioning certainty to Catholic truths that are ignored or disparaged or undermined even within the Church will be a hidden form of protection of Catholic faith in the Church. Souls of deep prayer will uphold and secure the truth of Catholic faith inasmuch as they live a greater contemplative purity of faith in their prayer. Catholic revealed doctrine embraced as unassailably certain despite the agitation of dark confusions within the Church may become in future years a necessity as in no other time in history. This profound quality of pure faith in contemplative souls will safeguard the interior heart of the Church from the contradictions that may afflict it in a more public realm. It will be the most prayerful souls who exercise this mission of preservation in the Church of that time. Others will fight painful battles in the public arena of conflict within the Church. The souls of deeper prayer will be silently carrying them in their self-offering and prayer. Sometimes the public and private roles of service will coincide in the same priest, religious, or lay person. As in all periods of Church history, the great defenders of Catholic truth will be deeply prayerful souls.

∼

The contemplative souls in a last era of the Church will be servants of a holy preservation of the faith in a manner like the monastic scribes in the monasteries of the Dark Ages. In this case, they will not copy sacred texts and manuscripts for the sake of posterity, while witnessing the collapse of the Roman Empire and surrounded by barbarian corruption. Instead, contemplative souls of all types will exercise their souls in an exquisitely pure faith in the realities of divine revelation. The sacred truths of Catholic revelation will rise boldly in their certitudes and consume their contemplative pursuit of love for God. This submersion of contemplative lives in the truths of revelation will intensify as these sacred truths may seem to look on some days like scattered shards tossed about by the winds of cultural nihilism. The metaphysical touchstone of the contemplative life in that time will be the stark reality of God. All their contemplative effort will be to live in a love for the reality of God personally present in his infinite magnitude within the small nothingness of their creaturely life. The outside world may become metaphysically and spiritually barren. Spiritual truth may be ignored and discounted. But the contemplative souls in all walks of life will preserve the sacred truth of the creation and its subordination to God. They will preserve the reality of revelation itself, that we have a God who has revealed his own life in the great Man of Nazareth who was God in the flesh. They will be souls of great love for the holy Presence of our Lord in the Eucharist and for his Mother Mary.

∿

"The hiding place of the Word of God is . . . the bosom of the Father, that is, the divine essence, which is alien to every mortal eye and hidden from every human intellect" (Saint John of the Cross).[4] So proclaims Saint John of the Cross in beautiful words. Jesus as Son returns to the heart of the Father, not to withdraw or disappear, remaining apart from us, but so that we might seek him there and find him there. Our discovery of his hiding place is a moment to treasure in the life of prayer. We find his exalted humanity, still carrying

---

[4] Saint John of the Cross, *The Spiritual Canticle*, 1.3, in *The Collected Works of St. John of the Cross*, trans. Kieran Kavanaugh and Otilio Rodriguez (Washington, D.C: ICS Publications, 2017), 478.

the wounds of his Passion, hiding in the secrecy of the Father's expansive love. This love is overwhelming for those who enter inside it. It is a true hiding place, a place of rest, but also a place of great longing, a sharing in the thirst of Jesus on the Cross for souls. We find that the thirst of Jesus proclaimed on the Cross in the last moments of his life is an inconclusive cry. It was not finished with the sound of that cry, but rather extends itself into souls throughout history to the present day. The painful desire that Jesus pronounces to be known in his love for souls continues because souls of a deeper love will always thirst with his own thirst for the return of souls to his divine love. There is a hiding place of great mystery that we enter in surrendering our soul to this longing within our own soul for the salvation of souls. The hiding place is somewhere near the core of the heart of Jesus even as he lives exalted in the bosom of the Father at this very moment. We must desire to be one with his wound of love, one with his thirst and desire for souls.

~

In his arrest and trial, in standing before Caiaphas and the Jewish elders and the false witnesses, Jesus maintained the reserved silence he had earlier kept about the crucifixion that would take place. His refusal to defend himself and instead his choice to remain silent is striking to ponder. The silence of our Lord in these dark events was not a silence of resignation. It was a resolute silence toward all that is sacred in the divine plan. What is perhaps most sacred in Jesus' Passion is the secret depth of his suffering at Calvary. Jesus' Passion is the consummate example of a sacred silence on God's part, a reserve and discretion that may extend to the suffering of the Church in the decades of our era, the significance of which is not yet clear. The precise manner of testing that the Church will undergo still awaits the years to come and future events. If it is God's way of discretion not to reveal entirely what is to come, as happened in Jesus' life regarding a death by crucifixion, the reason may be to cast us blindly into events. The absence of comprehension will serve to conceal Jesus' Passion relived within his Church in that time. The trials of purification for faithful souls who live through that era will unite them in a mysterious way to the Passion of Jesus. It is possible that the saints already in heaven might encourage an essential insight for souls in that time. They might tell us that deep fissures of self-offering carve their way more effectively into us when the offering of our soul is made blindly, in a condition of incomprehension. In a time of ecclesial confusion and trial, the most fruitful offerings will be linked to a lack of knowledge of what is taking place in the Church. The possibility even of betrayal by some parties within the Church will not be known before it takes place. This suffering within the Church may display a remarkable resemblance to Jesus' silence about the manner of his execution by a Roman crucifixion. We will not know the manner of suffering and trial until it is upon us. We will have to live a silence of incomprehension, a silence of not knowing entirely what is being fulfilled in the plan of God.

$\sim$

In response to the moral aberrations of the time, the last era of the Church may witness a healthy resurgence of asceticism among serious souls and a desire to deny comfort and ease in life as a necessity if we desire to give ourselves fully to God. The recovery of the ascetical spirit in the Church will be a striking phenomenon, because it will occur precisely after a rather long period of relaxation in the Church regarding the practice of asceticism and of denial of physical comforts in life. Perhaps the Gospel account of Jesus in the desert will have a role to play in this development. The realization that ascetical living is no longer optional may be a sign precisely of being in a last era of the Church when that day does come. When we embrace more decisively a sense that it is indeed a short life and that significant indications point to the serious testing of this time in the Church, the choice for self-denial in comforts is clear. Many souls naturally will not find this an appealing approach to spiritual pursuit. But it may happen that the connection of our own time with Jesus' period in the desert suddenly is understood more vividly. The desert time for Jesus was a confrontation with the devil, perhaps for all the forty days. The realization of the need to choose a greater mortification and poverty in our physical life of available comfort, denying our personal life in painful ways, may spread contagiously among souls as we perceive the time in which we live.

~

The asceticism Jesus lived in the desert is meant to become, at least in disposition, the asceticism of the souls that love him. The dynamic of self-denial is not for the sake of self-creation to a more exalted spiritual state. The emptying of self in asceticism is to unite ourselves with the desert experience of Jesus. But what was that experience? Jesus laid himself open and vulnerable to the devil in the desert by entering a complete solitude and silence and by denying himself in a radical manner the comfort of physical satisfactions. We can follow this path, not by extreme ascetical practices, but by emptying ourselves in a voluntary discipline of our daily life-style, entering thereby into a confrontation with the devil in which we choose in emptiness to give our all to God. Asceticism has no reason other than to turn all our desire completely to God. The last period of the Church is very likely going to re-discover this lost value. It will be a definite sign of hidden fruitfulness in the Church. Never does the Church die in her fruitfulness. In fact, she may intensify in her rigors and fruitfulness, at least in a segment of loving souls, precisely when all seems to be collapsing around her. In that last period, the great fruitfulness of the Church may come in part from a disparagement of comforts and even a decisive habitual practice of hard self-denials in order to bring wavering souls to God in that final era of the Church.

~

We are told that Jesus was led by the Spirit into the desert to be tempted by the devil, and for forty days the devil did tempt him. These forty days of deprivation, without any food, perhaps never in one place for long, barefoot on rocky terrain, alone and silent in the harsh confines of the Judean desert, enduring the heat of days and the desert cold of night, without a single physical comfort, are a great mystery in his life. The mystery is buried inside the secrecy of the interior life of Jesus in that time. It is possible that Jesus lived these days pondering at times the Passion he would endure at the end of his public years. There in the desert it is very possible that he already took upon his human soul the sins of humanity in anticipation of bearing all the sins of history upon his human soul in his crucifixion. Indeed, this desert solitude of forty days was a long persevering taste of the desolate isolation he would experience in Gethsemane. In the forty days, he fought off the same demonic temptation that returned to him in the garden and afflicted him throughout his Passion. Already in the desert, prior to his public life, the devil may have tempted him to stare openly at human betrayal and to admit the futility of his divine desire for souls. The evil one may have whispered repeatedly of the wastefulness of the love he would pour out for lost souls who will reject him. And another inner reality of significance may have been at work in the inner life of Jesus. It is possible that he sanctified the ascetical life of a deprivation from comfort for all of history. He embraced and drew into his own inner life the great strength that comes from denying self in asceticism for the sake of spiritual fruitfulness. He became one himself with the power of grace that flourishes when solitary prayer and personal sacrifice are undertaken in serious ways. He blessed and sanctified the ascetical life as an indispensable weapon needed to defeat the devil. And many souls in history, even to our own time, have embraced this truth. He is one in the desert with all the ascetics of the centuries who offer themselves in love. He is one with the souls of our own time who are ascetical in their offering for the souls currently in great need.

~

"If any one thirst, let him come to me and drink" (Jn 7:37). We are to drink from Jesus himself. These words deepen in meaning when we ponder what happened after Jesus suffered his crucifixion. The heart of Jesus at Calvary was pierced by a lance after his death and poured out blood and water. Jesus had already died bodily when the lance was thrust into his heart. But the Divine Presence of the Son of God remained united to the body of Christ in death. If we are thirsty for God, we must drink from the wound inflicted upon the body of Jesus as he hung on the Cross in death. That wound is an entryway into a sacred mystery of the heart of God. The lance pierced to the depth of his human heart, and the blood and water flowed out from the deeper recesses of his heart. If in our thirst for God, we follow the path of the blood, we will seek to enter the inner recesses of the Heart of God. The blood is a divine invitation to us to enter the wounds of love in God. We are to drink from him in a real manner, entering the wound in his divine heart. We are to enter the secrecy of his heart and drink from his blood poured out for souls. The blood and water that flowed from his heart in death, once received into our own heart and soul, are to become in the depth of our soul a great thirst for souls. This truth will come alive more than ever in a last era of the Church.

～

The flow of blood and water from the heart of Jesus in death completes his cry of thirst released in the last moments of his suffering on the Cross. He cries out his thirst for souls, dies shortly after, and then he pours out blood and water in death after this piercing by the Roman soldier. It is all a single word and gesture. The two events are joined together, the wound casting light on the lingering echo of his cry of thirst. In this cry from his heart and this piercing of his heart, he expresses in a union of word and gesture his infinite desire for souls. We are invited to drink of the same desire for souls. But let us be aware that it entails a painful union with his infinite divine thirst, far beyond our capacity to endure. This drinking from the wound of his heart after his death, while hearing at the same time the lingering sound of his cry of thirst, is nonetheless a spiritual necessity.

It is an essential path to the reception of his gift of the Holy Spirit, who teaches us to thirst for souls. An intense longing for souls is a preeminent gift of the Holy Spirit, a lesson repeated throughout history, the lesson of the great resurging wave of divine desire for souls shared with souls who love the crucified Lord. The cry of thirst from Jesus on the Cross so near his death can be heard echoing in history as a divine appeal to us to live for souls. Likewise, the piercing of his heart can be gazed upon as a divine appeal to know his wound of love whenever a soul is lost. We need to receive this divine thirst for souls and the divine wound at the loss of souls and make this thirst and this wound our own. One thing is certain in a love for the Passion of Christ. The soul who receives the eyes of Jesus on the Cross will be drawn to suffer for him in a thirst for souls. By gazing on him, we drink of the divine desire that souls come to the heart of Jesus. We enter the wounds of his heart, and we desire to pour balm on these wounds by bringing souls to him. We begin to live the thirst for souls, to the extent we become holy, that Jesus himself suffered on the Cross at Calvary.

~

"Out of his heart shall flow rivers of living water" (Jn 7:38). These are the next words of Jesus after inviting those who are thirsty to come to him, and again they can inflame depths of desire within us. The flowing waters of a river of desire is a telling image. These waters pour forth from the soul that is filled with the Holy Spirit. Jesus used the same phrase of living water with the Samaritan woman. "If you knew the gift of God, and who it is that is saying to you, 'Give me a drink,' you would have asked him and he would have given you living water" (Jn 4:10). The living water is an image of God's intimate action within a life. Our soul is to carry the living presence of God within it, to be permeated with his presence, and to overflow with his secret action at work within us. It is striking to consider that Jesus did not speak of the Holy Spirit as a placid, tranquil lake, without a stir or movement on its surface, but rather invoked the power of a river of living water. A river is moving, never stationary or static, always seeking a destination. "The water that I shall give him will become in him a spring of water welling up to eternal life" (Jn 4:14). The soul is to receive this powerful, living presence of the Holy Spirit in its interior core and allow itself to be compelled and moved by God's desire. Never does the reception of the Holy Spirit lead simply to rest and comfort for the soul. The soul is galvanized to seek for the good of souls whenever the hand of God touches it and will flow out in a search for souls without God. The living waters of the Holy Spirit given to a soul are to overflow from that soul and bring other souls to a taste of God and his real presence.

∼

The image of fire is another clear evocation of the Holy Spirit and an important truth for a last era of the Church. Jesus was speaking of the Holy Spirit when he said: "I came to cast fire upon the earth; and would that it were already kindled!" (Lk 12:49). God intends that the fire of the Holy Spirit should make burnt offerings of us. That is the primary reality in the gift of the Holy Spirit to a soul. But we should understand clearly what is to happen in time. The thought that we are to be on fire in a sensible manner, emotionally

elevated by the Spirit's presence in our soul, is perhaps an excessive expectation. The fire of the Holy Spirit surely does
burn away dross and purifies us in an exquisite flame of
conquering love upon our soul. The fire in this case flows
like a liquid heat into the core of our soul. Not emotion,
but a realm of deeper "soul desire" is awakened as the Holy
Spirit penetrates us. Our soul is invited to release itself to
a divine action within it. We cannot know how God exercises his mystery of divine movement within us, but we
can have a certitude that he is present and working. The
reality is truly a work of fire. The soul is burned but does
not succumb to the pain. It burns, but it is not diminished.
It undergoes the effect of fire and its destruction, and yet it
remains able to emit flames outside itself of love to others.
The fires of the Holy Spirit are best assimilated when our
soul is willing to become whatever God desires, small or
great, hidden or known, a soul of concealed sanctity or a
servant of his purposes in a more public manner. The souls
of the holy ones are filled in all cases with this fire. They
often lead lives that are completely incongruous and out of
place with the ways of the world, and that is a sign of God's
predilection for them. They live by a fire within them and
can find no home in the surroundings in which they live.
The fire within them has become their home. This is their
ultimate truth and their spiritual greatness. We are bound
to see this truth as the years continue, and yet it will also
be a truth concealed by the preference of God for hiding
his presence.

～

The immolation of Mary, as depicted in the Gospels, cul-
minates at the foot of the Cross. But it does not end there.

As Mother of the Church, she unites herself to the immolation of her children throughout history. She guides them, takes them by the hand, leads them forward to become one with the Eucharistic immolation of Jesus offered in daily Masses. She is the Mother of all the souls in history who offer themselves as victims of her Son's love. These are Eucharistic souls, souls who love our Lord in his hidden presence in the tabernacle and in the Mass and spend themselves in offering for others through their sacrificial lives. These souls are dear to Mary. Through them she recovers her presence at the foot of the Cross repeatedly throughout history, hearing again Jesus' request that she become the Mother again of the children who endure the darkness of Calvary in the current day. Her own desire for immolation becomes inseparable from the hidden souls who offer themselves in immolation to her Son for the sake of souls. She will watch with a very special love in a last epoch of the Church as holy souls are joined to the crucifixion of her Son. If her Son's Bride, the Church, is torn at any time by internal suffering, she will stand, as she did at Calvary, one in heart with her Son. The same strength she gave to Jesus she will extend to her children who faithfully cling to her and remain committed in love to her crucified Son.

∽

The presence of Mary in a last era of the Church will likely be a return to a hidden presence, as has been her motherly presence for most of history. In this manner she will live the concealment she exercised in the last week of Jesus' earthly life. She will likely no longer be seen in apparitions, yet she will be mysteriously and powerfully at work. She will gather the lowly and the humble in the Church into a recognition of the time at hand. The whisper of this Mother will be quietly heard by prayerful souls, without publicity or drama, that the time has come, and this message in prayer will be received with a deepening certitude. A remnant in the Church of the pure and lowly will embrace this word- less message in silent prayer as a bestowal of clarity on the troubling questions of the time. The sight of turmoil in the Church, the danger of some unseen rupture at the center, will not frighten or disturb souls united to her. It will be understood that they, her lowly ones, must occupy a place of pure surrender in the heart of the Body of Christ which is the Church. The Church, despite turbulence and signs of apostasy in some areas, will remain faithful to a promise of union with the crucified Body of her Son in this rem- nant of the lowly. The words of the Magnificat will ring now in prophetic fulfillment as the lowly are lifted up with the Mother who gathers them to her maternal immaculate heart.

～

The presence of John the apostle, the contemplative soul at Calvary, is clearly in the plan of God, and not just to have one of the Twelve as an eyewitness to the hours of the cru- cifixion. The presence of John standing next to Mary allows Jesus to command the exchange between Mary and John— " 'Woman, behold, your son!' Then he said to the disci- ple, 'Behold, your mother!' " (Jn 19:26-27). And Mary un- doubtedly understands the deep significance and pronounces again a *fiat* of surrender to the divine request. She is the vir- gin Mother once again as these words of Jesus near his death place the Church of many sons and daughters under Mary's maternal care for the rest of history. But a prophecy may also be concealed in these words, which was recognized by Mary. For she knows, in these last minutes of her Son's suffering at Calvary, that in offering her complete "yes" at the Annunciation thirty-three years earlier—"Behold, I am the handmaid of the Lord; let it be to me according to your word" (Lk 1:38)—she was saying "yes" to the death of her Son and, indeed, to the terrible suffering she was now enduring. The command by Jesus to Mary to behold your son may have come with the realization that she could not say "yes" to this request, taking this child, the Church, to her maternal heart, without the promise of the same pattern repeating itself. Her "yes" in Nazareth at the Annunciation was already by reason of her complete surrender to the plan of God a full consent to the crucifixion at Golgotha. And now, with Jesus dying before her eyes at this late hour of the crucifixion, Mary must have realized in gazing at John that the Church herself would follow the pattern of her Son's life and eventually be crucified in her own Passion. She cannot look up at her Son nailed to the Cross without seeing as well the other son John, that is, the Church herself, nailed to a cross of climactic historical events in the Church's last era. The Passion of Christ will repeat itself mysteriously in those days in the life of the Church, and the Mother of God will stand beneath that cross on which the Church is nailed. She will gather those who are her own children into her maternal protection and offer them together with her Son's oblation at Calvary. The Masses in that last era offered by holy priests will often be joined to a profound recognition of this immolation of holiness within the Church. Mary herself will be the intercessor for that special grace.

In the present state of the world Christianity must become a heroic Christianity. . . . It will consist, *above all*, in resisting with courage, in the face of the world and perhaps against one's own self, the lures and seductions of a false ideal, and in proudly maintaining, in their paradoxical intransigence, the Christian values which are threatened and derided. Maintaining them with humble pride.[5]

—Henri de Lubac, S.J.

[5] Henri de Lubac, *The Drama of Atheist Humanism*, trans. Edith M. Riley and Anne Englund Nash (San Francisco: Ignatius Press, 1995), 129.